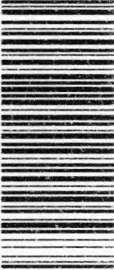

CW01465759

FLY,
WILD
SWANS

Also by Jung Chang

Big Sister, Little Sister, Red Sister: Three Women at
the Heart of Twentieth-Century China

Empress Dowager Cixi: The Concubine
Who Launched Modern China

Mao: The Unknown Story *(with Jon Halliday)*

Wild Swans: Three Daughters of China

FLY, WILD SWANS

My Mother, Myself and China

JUNG CHANG

WILLIAM
COLLINS

WILLIAM COLLINS

An imprint of HarperCollins*Publishers*
1 London Bridge Street
London SE1 9GF

WilliamCollinsBooks.com

HarperCollins*Publishers*
Macken House
39/40 Mayor Street Upper
Dublin 1, D01 C9W8

First published in Great Britain in 2025 by William Collins

1

A catalogue record for this book is available from the British Library

HB ISBN 978-0-00-866106-9
TPB ISBN 978-0-00-866107-6

Set in Janson Text LT Pro by Six Red Marbles UK, Thetford, Norfolk

Printed and bound in Great Britain by CPI Group (UK) Ltd, Croydon

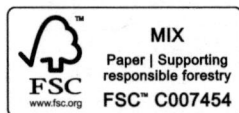

To my mother
whose deathbed I am unable to visit

CONTENTS

A FEW KEY DATES

Manchu dynasty (the Great Qing)	1644–1911
Republic of China declared	1912
The Kuomintang under Chiang Kai-shek rules China	1928–1949
War against Japanese invasion	1937–1945
Kuomintang–Communist civil war	1945–1949
Communist China founded under Mao	1949
The Great Famine	1958–1961
The Cultural Revolution	1966–1976
Mao dies	1976
Deng Xiaoping's reforms start	1978
Xi Jinping takes over	2012
Xi becomes the supreme leader for life	2018

RUSSIA

KAZAKHSTAN

MONGOLIA

XINJIANG

GANSU

QINGHAI

NINGXIA

Jiuzhai Valley (Jiuzhaigou)

SHA

Golden Sand River

Minjiang River

Deyang

SICHUAN

TIBET

Himalayas

NEPAL

Chengdu

Chongqing

Luding Bridge

Dadu River

Yibin

BHUTAN

Xichang

Red River

INDIA

Miyi

Tucheng

BANGLADESH

Panzhihua

GUIZHOU

YUNNAN

Kunming

GUA

MYANMAR

VIETNAM

Mekong River

LAOS

Yangon

THAILAND

Bangkok

China

| 0 | | 300 miles |
| 0 | | 400 km |

PROLOGUE

This book is about my mother and myself – and inevitably also about my grandmother and my father. Our stories are dramatic partly because they have been taking place in China in the last hundred and twenty or so years, when the country has been turned upside down many times by tempestuous changes. But equally importantly, my parents and my grandmother were extraordinary people who swam against the tide, and so ran into bigger waves. Born into such a family, I was thrown into an eventful life.

Many years ago I told our stories in *Wild Swans: Three Daughters of China*. The book begins with my grandmother's birth in 1909 – and her foot-binding as an infant – when China was under the last emperor, moves through Mao Zedong's rule (1949–76), especially its last decade, the horrendous Cultural Revolution during which my parents were subjected to painful ordeals, and finishes in 1978 when Deng Xiaoping officially ended the Mao era and started the 'reforms' – and I, at that propitious juncture, became one of the first Chinese to leave Communist China for the West.

The year 1978 was a watershed moment. Since then nearly another half a century has gone by, and China has risen from a decrepit and isolated state to a global power, challenger to the United States' number-one position. In those decades, although I have been living in London, my life has been entwined with my native land. My mother lives there, so I visited her almost every year, until recently when the political climate made this impossible. I travelled around the country to research my books, including *Wild Swans*, a biography of Mao (co-authored with my husband Jon Halliday), and that of Empress Dowager Cixi (1835–1908), the last great imperial ruler who brought medieval China into the modern age. Most of those researches were conducted while my books were (and are) banned. My experiences dealing with the regime in those years were rich and revealing.

China is now at another watershed moment: Chairman Xi Jinping worships Mao and seeks to build a Maoist state with capitalist features. This new Xi era is greatly affecting the lives of my mother and me. I felt the time had come to write a follow-up to *Wild Swans*, to pick up where I left off and bring the story of my family – along with that of China – up to date.

My father and my grandmother died tragically in the Cultural Revolution, which I wrote about in *Wild Swans*. They have stayed in my mind and so are often recalled in this book. In fact, the past has never been far away in my subsequent life. It has shaped me, and moulded present-day China, and what's more, it promises to herald the future.

I have called this book *Fly, Wild Swans* as a tribute to my mother, whose deathbed I am unable to visit. She has given me wings so I can take to the sky and be free. It is so much thanks to her that today I live freely and write freely.

1

Childhood in Mao's China

(1952–66)

'You are a good Communist, but a rotten husband!' my mother said tearfully, her hands cradling her round stomach that was bursting out of her shirt made of locally produced rough cotton. Underneath her hand and inside her stomach, I was kicking and stretching, ready to pop out. It was March 1952, over two years after the Communist Party had seized China from the Kuomintang (the Nationalist Party) in late 1949. Both my parents were Communists, my mother fairly new to the Party and my father a veteran. In fact, he was the governor of the region where they were, Yibin, which was a prefecture of southwest China's Sichuan province and covered over five thousand square miles.

My father was born in 1921 in the region's capital, also called Yibin, a two-thousand-year-old hill city nestled against green, misty, tea-growing mountains. At its feet, two rivers, the crystal-clear Minjiang and the soil-laden Golden Sand, join up to form China's longest river, the Yangtze.

Being born by the side of the great river up the hill in an ancient city may sound romantic, but it was the source of my mother's bitter feelings towards my father. Doctors had pronounced that my birth would be exceedingly difficult with a high probability of a haemorrhage and that I could die during delivery and drag my mother to the other world with me. They had advised that she be transferred to a hospital in a larger city, where there were proper facilities and specialist obstetricians. And yet my father had refused to accept their advice.

To be transferred from Yibin to a bigger city was neither routine nor easy, but it was not impossible. As the governor, my father could say the word and my mother would be moved to the best hospital in the region. He declined to give the order. He said he could not authorise special treatment for his wife, as the Communists had vowed to end nepotism.

My father had joined the Communist underground in Yibin in 1938, when he was seventeen, while working as an assistant in a bookshop. He had lived through hunger and injustice and was easily persuaded by the left-wing books he read that the Communists would be better than the Kuomintang. In particular, my father took their pledge to eliminate corruption, which to him was the root of all the evils of the old China, most seriously, and since becoming governor had gone out of his way to deny 'favours' to his own family: his mother, sisters, brothers and relatives. One of his cousins, Big Uncle, had asked for a recommendation for a job in the box office of a local cinema. My father told him to go through the official channels. An older brother working for a tea-broker – Yibin is one of China's major tea-producing areas – was put up for promotion as a manager. It fell on my father to clear the promotion, and he vetoed it, arguing that his brother was not capable enough and that he would not have been put forward if he had not been the governor's brother. My father's whole family was incensed; my mother exploded: 'You don't have to help him, but you don't have to block him either!' His brother never spoke to him again.

My mother was devastated by my father's refusal to move her to a properly equipped hospital. At first she thought that he did not care whether she, or their baby, lived or died. Gradually she persuaded herself that my father had had no choice. If he had ordered her to be transferred, people in Yibin would have said the Communists were no different from all the old governments and were only in power to benefit their families. But her mood was only transformed into one of joy when, surrounded by nervous doctors, I miraculously came out of her body a healthy baby, weighing over ten pounds, with her unharmed.

My mother believed in the Party, too. Ten years my father's junior, she had already been a member of the Communist underground before she was sixteen. Her city, Jinzhou, was in Manchuria in northeast China, 1,500 miles from Yibin. It had been under Japanese occupation until 1945 when Japan surrendered at the end of the Second World War. The Kuomintang government under Chiang Kai-shek took over, but my mother quickly became disenchanted with it, after its intelligence agents killed her school friends, one for bringing into the city a pamphlet written by Mao. After her then boyfriend was arrested and tortured, she sought out the Communist underground. Among the things she did for them was to smuggle military information out of Jinzhou to Mao's army in the outskirts. At the time Mao was wrestling with Chiang Kai-shek for control of China.

My father was in the besieging army, and heard a lot about my mother, '*that extraordinary seventeen-year-old girl*'. He imagined her to be like a fire-breathing dragon, and was pleasantly surprised when they finally met after the Communists seized Jinzhou in 1948 and my mother came to report to him. In front of him, in a simple, faded blue gown, was a tall, slender and graceful young woman, pretty and soft-spoken. In his world, crude manners and loud shouting epitomised being 'revolutionary', and my mother appeared like a breath of fresh air. My father noticed that though she was gentle, she was never meek; she gave firm commands without raising her voice, and talked in a clear and precise way, never rambling. My father was bowled over. My mother was very taken with him, too. Although he did not have a soldierly bearing, thin in his baggy green army uniform and shorter than her, my mother was immediately attracted by his unusually big, dreamy eyes, and thought he looked like a poet. They fell in love, married, and marched with the Communist army from Manchuria south to Yibin, where, while my father was the governor, my mother became the head of the city's Youth League.

My mother was popular with the young people she worked with – and much loved by my father's large, extended family. On the day she was introduced to his mother, tradition demanded she perform a kowtow to her mother-in-law. My father said kowtowing was a degrading custom which the Communists were committed to abolishing, and he would not kowtow to anyone. My mother said she would, telling him that doing so would make the Communists look more human. She wanted to please her mother-in-law, and she also had a flair for performance. After she went down on her knees and put her head on the floor three times, everybody laughed in delight. My mother then went on a kowtow spree, and followed my father's unmarried sister, Aunt Junying, into the family's large and beautiful back garden to do dozens of kowtows to the trees and shrubs. The women in my father's family were devout Buddhists, and believed that all plants were alive with souls and would appreciate gestures of friendship. Although she had not been raised as a Buddhist, my mother was delighted by this ritual. She had grown up in the pharmacy of her stepfather, Dr Xia, a renowned practitioner of Chinese medicine, which was largely plant-based. She became acquainted with all kinds of plants, and believed in their healing powers. They were like family treasures to her. Chatting about them fondly and knowledgeably with my father's nature-loving family, my mother won their hearts at the first meeting.

So when I was born, all the adults in the family wanted me to be like my mother, and gave me the name Er-hong – 'Second Wild Swan' – as my mother's name, Xia De-hong, contains the character for 'wild swan', *hong*. This character evokes the image of a large, beautiful and strong bird that flies long distances across the sky over great mountains and rivers. My father loved the image associated with the character, and addressed my mother in his letters to her: 'My beloved Wild Swan'.

My mother knew my father loved her. A year after I was born, when she was in hospital again giving birth to my brother Jin-ming, her boss and friend, a Mrs Ting (Zhang Xiting), a woman with a willowy figure and flirtatious repartee, tried to seduce my father, and he rebuffed her in no uncertain terms. He knew that Mrs Ting was determined and could try again, but more worryingly that she was a vindictive person who would go to extraordinary lengths to persecute people who crossed her, with the help of her husband, who was the head of personnel in Yibin. Terrified that she might harm my mother, who worked under her, my father took the earliest available train to Chengdu, capital of Sichuan, and, after a day's travelling north, he went straight to the governor of the province and asked to be given another job. He did not mention Mrs Ting, but cited the difficulties of working in his hometown with too many relatives. He then waited in Chengdu, and sent my mother telegrams urging her to leave as soon as possible. This was why I, at the age of one, moved to Chengdu in June 1953, when my brother Jinming was a month old, and my mother's traditionally mandatory period of postnatal convalescence was over. She took me and my elder sister, Xiaohong, leaving Jinming behind with my father's family as he was considered too young to travel.

Chengdu, the capital of several ancient kingdoms, became my home for the next twenty-five years. It sits on a fertile plain which, thanks to a great irrigation system constructed around 256 BC, is known throughout China as the Land of Abundance (*Tian-fu-zhi-guo*). The city was rich in culture and for centuries had been a hub of activity for several religious beliefs: Daoism, Buddhism and Confucianism. In the numerous courtyards that lined its alleyways, hibiscus trees with large pink flowers thrived in the temperate climate and made Chengdu the City of Hibiscus. In the centre of town stood the old palace, shaped like the Forbidden City in Beijing, its magnificent gate tower similar to Tiananmen Gate. It was often called Little Beijing. Marco Polo had been here in the thirteenth century and written about its prosperity – and its silk production. Chengdu is known as the City of Silk, and the river that flows across it is the Silk River, *Jinjiang*, in whose many meandering tributaries people used to wash the weaving instruments. Making silk was a way of life – even I took part when I was a child. One of my early memories was of gathering armfuls of mulberry leaves, feeling their fluffy underside, and feeding them to silkworms in large flat baskets several times a day. I watched the baby caterpillars eating hungrily, growing fat quickly, and before long from each of their plump little mouths a barely visible thread starting to emerge and spin round the caterpillar itself – until in no time a cocoon was formed. A long, fine silk fibre would be extracted from inside the cocoon and wound onto a hand reel. I remember trying to pull a thread, only to see it break in my clumsy fingers.

Chengdu was also famous for its cuisine. It had numerous

restaurants, many with distinctive specialities and fanciful names. As a child I was mesmerised by those names but rarely went to any. Communist officials were strongly discouraged from visiting restaurants, which the Party identified with a hedonistic lifestyle. This was no small sacrifice for my mother who loved food, and hankered after the dishes that she, from Manchuria, had never tasted.

My father was made the deputy director of a major department in the Sichuan Provincial Party Committee, the Department of Public Affairs, which managed education, health, sports, publications and art institutions of the province (Sichuan was the size of France with sixty million people). My mother became the director of the Department of Public Affairs in the Eastern District of Chengdu, looking after similar things but on a lower level. We moved into 'the compound', a large enclosure that incorporated several former streets and included the Second World War US Army club. Most top officials worked and lived there, with their families. There were guards at the gate, gardeners to maintain the grounds, excellent chefs and a fleet of cars with drivers.

My mother was not entitled to a car and rode to work every day by bicycle. Except for Sundays, she and my father were seldom at home before we children went to bed. We were effectively brought up by my maternal grandma, Yang Yufang, who had come from Manchuria to live with us. Then in her forties, she looked very different from my mother. While my mother wore a sort of Communist uniform for female officials at the time, the so-called 'Lenin jacket', which was double-breasted and tucked in at the waist – a foreign style – my grandma was always clothed in a traditional cotton top with knot buttons on the side, all of which she made herself. She made her own cotton shoes, too, for her 'bound feet', which looked very small, narrow and pointed, and on which she hobbled rather than walked like my mother. She would frown from time to time as she steadied herself while walking, but her eyes, very bright, always seemed to be smiling.

My grandma made our family life tranquil and loving. She forbade my parents from telling us off at mealtime ('No criticisms when they are eating. They won't be able to digest their food properly'), and made sure that if my parents had an argument, it was never in front of us. I can only recall one row between my parents, one evening when I was about nine. I did not know what it was about, but heard my father shouting and my mother challenging him vehemently in her customary soft voice, yet uncharacteristically in tears. I felt so frightened that I closed the mosquito net over my bed to try to hide myself. But the net was too flimsy, and I burst out, not crying but bizarre, intense nervous giggling. 'Er-hong is *laughing*!' cried my father as he stomped past my bed, looking flabbergasted, and I think that may have put an end to their row, as my mother raced over and folded her arms around me. Throughout my childhood, I felt nothing but love from my parents, who never uttered a harsh word to me. Even their rare criticisms were carefully worded and delicately delivered, as if I were an adult whose feelings they must not hurt.

I went to school when I was six in 1958. I walked, always with friends, twenty minutes there, and twenty minutes back for lunch; and did the same in the afternoon. The route was mostly alleyways, and on the narrow pavements cabbages and other leaves were laid out to dry for making preserved vegetables (which I loved). The stretch I liked most was along the Imperial Canal, a two-thousand-metre moat surrounding the old palace. Although the palace was largely gone by the time I started school, some ruins remained, and the moat was intact, its green water fresh and clear next to willows and camphor trees on the banks.

*

My parents' faith in their Party was shattered during the Great Famine between 1958 and 1961, when some forty million people died of starvation. Though they did not know the full scale of the famine or the cause of the catastrophe, they knew enough to realise that it was man-made and the responsibility of their Party. Unlike in the past when they had found reasons to excuse the Party, this time the Party was unforgivable. I remember my father once said to me out of the blue – which I now think was him talking to himself – 'Why did we make revolution in the first place? We made revolution because people were starving. We wanted to give people a full stomach.' I was startled by the agitation in his voice and on his face. Later I learned that he wrote a letter to Mao to voice his views, which was the only thing one could do to influence policy; but he was persuaded to withdraw the letter by the provincial governor, who was a friend, and who reminded him of the likely disastrous consequences for his family. A sense of guilt weighed on my father – on him more than on my mother because he identified more closely with the Party, whereas she had had reservations and kept a psychological distance.

My mother's disillusionment had come almost as soon as Mao's army entered her city and she encountered the real Party, an organisation so different from her own group of partisans. She was astonished to realise that the wonderful things she had dreamed of – equality, kind treatment of women, and comradely warmth – were not there. The biggest shock came when, aged eighteen, she left Jinzhou to travel with my father to his hometown Yibin over a thousand miles to the south. As a senior official, my father was assigned a jeep; but my mother, without a high rank, had to walk. My father would not give her a lift because that would be deemed 'nepotism', and my mother – both of them, for that matter – would be reprimanded if she got into his car. One night, after a whole day of trudging and carrying her bedroll, feeling utterly exhausted and sick all the time, she burst into tears while trying to sleep on the ground of a temple where her group were packed close together. My father was lying next to her, and he hurriedly cupped her mouth with his hand, whispering that she must not let people hear her cry. But some did and complained to the group leader, who told her off the next day, saying that she had behaved like 'a precious lady from the exploiting classes', and was 'disgraceful to cry after walking a few steps'. Of course, no one, not even my mother herself, knew that she was pregnant. Soon afterwards she suffered a miscarriage and lost her first child.

She nearly died and contemplated leaving the Party to study medicine, her ambition before she got married. My father was so alarmed that he begged her almost in panic not to quit, telling her it would be treated as desertion and dealt with accordingly. From his reaction, my mother realised that once you joined the Party, there was no exit (a crucial fact that kept the Party going). She stayed on, persuading herself to accept the Party's point of view, but she was never as wholeheartedly committed as my father.

As their devotion to the Party waned, my parents stopped working so hard and spent most evenings at home. They checked their children's homework and took turns to give us extra tuition. My mother taught us maths, and my father coached us in Chinese language and literature. On those evenings my siblings and I were allowed into my father's study, lined from floor to ceiling with thick hardbacks and thread-bound Chinese classics. We had to wash our hands before we touched his books and were told never to turn the pages near the binding as it could tear the leaves.

Apart from academic excellence, what my parents wanted most from us was to grow up with moral principles. While my sister and I both had names with my mother as a model – my sister's name, Xiaohong, meant 'to be like' Mother – each of my brothers was given a name that represented our parents' aspirations. The character Zhi, meaning 'upright', was given to Jinming; Pu, 'genuine', to Xiaohei; and Fang, 'incorruptible', to Xiaofang. My father's own name, Chang Shou-yu, reflected his dedication to those ideals. His original name had been quite different. When he joined the Communists, he took a nom de guerre, Wang Yu, with 'Yu' meaning 'foolish', because people who adopted those principles were often regarded as being 'foolish'. (Wang was the surname.) When he returned to Yibin, he reverted to his real surname, Chang, but called himself Shou-yu, meaning 'Keep being a man who is considered foolish'.

I entered middle school in 1964 at the age of twelve. My school, the Number Four Middle School, was the best in Chengdu. It had been founded in 141 BC and was the oldest government-funded school in China. Housed in an old Confucian temple, it had a grand front gate that boasted sweeping roofs, stately red pillars and high thresholds of solid thick wood, to make the entrance more ceremonious. At the centre of the campus stood the grand temple itself. Although the statue of Confucius inside had been removed when the Communists took power, replaced by half a dozen ping-pong tables, it still had a grandeur, with massive wooden interior columns, two giant bronze incense burners down a flight of stone stairs, along with a pair of towering stone slabs engraved with Confucius' teachings. As the approach to the temple, there had been a big empty square designed to create a sense of reverence. Now it contained the sports field and a two-storey classroom building, behind which was a large garden. A small canal ran across it, under three arched sandstone bridges decorated with carved miniature animals on top of the balustrades. I particularly loved the small wooded hill at the back of the campus, where, in biology lessons, we learned about the leaves and flowers. I was so riveted that I wanted to become a horticulturist – a plant hunter even, to discover new species.

In summer 1966, when I was fourteen, my life was turned upside down when Mao launched the Cultural Revolution. Like other children, I had grown up to regard Mao as God. There was a song we all learned to sing: 'Father is close, Mother is close, but neither is as close as Chairman Mao.' If we wanted to pledge what we said was true, we would declare: 'I swear to Chairman Mao!' So, when he called on young people to be Red Guards, his taskforce for the Cultural Revolution, it went without saying that we should do as Mao told us to. A Red Guard group was formed in my school, and it ordered every-one to stay on the campus to 'make Revolution'. But I shied away from militant actions that the revolution demanded, and kept claiming illness to try to stay away from school. I was crit-icised for having too much 'warm-feelingsism', and was not allowed to join the Red Guards.

The school I loved had changed into a terrifying place ever since Mao stood on Tiananmen Gate and told the young people to 'be violent', and to 'smash all things old'. The Con-fucian temple was wrecked, and a crowd gathered to pull down the giant stone slabs. Boys urinated in the bronze incense burn-ers, which they had toppled. They went around campus waving iron bars and hammers to knock off the heads of the small stat-ues. Gardens were trampled and battered. I heard that our elderly gardener – with whom I had chatted, as I had been fascinated by what he was doing – had been accused of being a 'class enemy', beaten up, and died. I cannot describe how frightened and repulsed I was. And there were more atrocities. One day all pupils were ordered to gather on the sports field to attend a 'denunciation rally', at which I saw a dozen or so of the school's best teachers being hauled onto the platform. My

English language teacher, an elderly man with courteous manners, was one of them; like the others, his head and upper body were forcefully pushed down, and his arms ferociously twisted behind his back into the so-called 'jet plane' position. On another day I was forced to watch my philosophy teacher being attacked in a classroom and made to beg for mercy by boys from my form because she had previously told them off dismissively in her lessons. One evening I was swept onto a truck to go on a 'house raid' after two female chiefs of a 'neighbourhood committee' had denounced a woman who they said was hiding a portrait of Chiang Kai-shek. In the house, I heard the woman's blood-curdling screams as she was stripped half-naked and lashed by a pupil I knew with the brass buckle of a leather belt, the standard weapon of the Red Guards. On yet another evening, I caught sight of a vague figure falling out of an upstairs window. The Red Guards had divided the pupils into categories based on their family backgrounds. Those from the 'good' families were the 'Reds', and those from the 'bad' families were the 'Blacks'. The 'Reds' were licensed to torment the 'Blacks'. That evening a seventeen-year-old girl who had been classified as a 'Black', and had had her hair half shaven leaving grotesque bald patches, threw herself out of a window. That night in the dormitory, the moment I closed my eyes I saw a human form smeared with blood. The next day I asked the Red Guards of my class for sick leave and went home. I desperately wished I would never have to set foot in the school again.

2

My Brave Parents in the
Cultural Revolution

(1966–78)

Home was no longer a refuge from the end of August 1966, when my father was taken into custody. That month atrocities like those in my school swept across China; in many places teachers were beaten to death. My father finally decided to speak up.

His sense of guilt at not voicing his opposition during the Great Famine had never left him, and now all the horrible things taking place were the last straw. He wrote to Mao asking him to stop the violence that was wrecking so many lives. My mother had tried to talk him out of writing, arguing that it was at best pointless and at worst suicidal. My father said that it was the only thing he could do. My mother said, 'You don't care about yourself. You have no concern for your wife. I accept that. But what about our children? . . . Do you want our children to become "Blacks"?' My father replied, 'I love my family. But I must do something this time.'

He asked my mother to divorce him and tell their children to disown him.

I was at home when my father was taken away, on the orders of the Sichuan Party bosses. My mother asked where he was being taken and was told that the Party had said 'No one is to know.' I walked with Father to the side gate of the compound, holding his hand. The long path was lined with grim-looking junior Party officials. My heart throbbed violently and seemed to be jumping out of my mouth. I felt my father's hand twitching in agitation and stroked it with my other hand. Outside the gate, he was conducted into a waiting car and driven away.

As soon as Mother and I returned to our apartment, she hurriedly packed a few things to go to Beijing to appeal for Father's release. I asked to go with her to the railway station. She agreed but did not explain anything, telling me that at fourteen I was too young to understand. I stayed with her overnight waiting for the train that would leave at dawn. Later she told me that she had wanted me to bear witness in case something happened to her, and I could also keep Grandma informed.

In Beijing my mother went to a 'grievance office'. Chinese rulers throughout history had set up this type of offices for the population to lodge serious complaints, and the Communists continued the tradition. As my father was a senior official, and my mother was one of the very few spouses with the courage to go to Beijing to appeal, she was received by Vice-Premier Tao Zhu, who was one of the Party leaders at the time, before he was purged for his own opposition to the Cultural Revolution. Tao Zhu ordered the Sichuan Party to release my father.

Although I knew that disaster was befalling my family, I did not think of rejecting the Cultural Revolution. Despite my loathing for the horrors in my school, I never thought of refusing to join the Red Guards. Those were Mao's orders, and to follow them was not open to question, just like to eat or to breathe. Such was the power of the brainwashing. So when I was told that all pupils who had not been admitted into the Red Guards could now be enrolled en masse on National Day, 1 October 1966, I returned to school and put on the red armband. By now the Red Guards had become a looser organisation, and virtually all my urban contemporaries were calling themselves Red Guards.

My membership lasted two weeks, till mid-October, when five girlfriends and I left Chengdu to go on a pilgrimage to Beijing to see Mao. My mother, having succeeded in getting my father freed, had returned home and was with Father. My family seemed to be all right, and I felt I could leave, as the pilgrimages might end soon.

Since August the regime had been encouraging young people to come to Beijing to be received by Mao – in a bid to stir up more frenzy for Mao's deification. Food, accommodation and transport by train were all provided free of charge for the millions of travelling young people, involving colossal administrative work that was managed by Premier Zhou Enlai. Mao made eight public appearances on Tiananmen Square. On the day of our turn – Mao's last show – the Great Helmsman stood in an open car driven along Chang'an Avenue across Tiananmen Square, passing by us and a million other youngsters who lined the avenue. (We had been informed about the review only the day before, after which we were not allowed out of the premises; and, as another safety precaution for Mao, we had all searched each other just before the rally for potential weapons, including keys.) When Mao's car approached, the crowds jumped up and down blocking my view, so I only caught a glimpse of his back. For a moment I thought I should feel devastated, as we had been indoctrinated to regard seeing Mao as the purpose of our lives. But fanaticism was not in my nature, and the consciously worked-up despair vanished the next instant. After travelling for two months in extreme discomfort – packed trains, blocked toilets, hunger and cold, itchiness from lice and inflamed knees from rheumatism – I longed to get home, and have a bath.

I returned to Chengdu in December 1966 and from then on had no more to do with the Red Guards or my school. With the arrival of the new year, violence and atrocities accelerated. Mao, having used the young Red Guards to create immense terror across the country, now turned to his real targets and began to purge Party officials who he believed had stopped following him. Those officials were termed 'Capitalist-roaders'. People from all walks of life were becoming Red Guards: workers, teachers, doctors, small officials . . . All subordinates were told to punish their bosses, as well as other designated victims. Brutal denunciation meetings became an everyday sight throughout the country.

My father was subjected to many such meetings at which he was beaten up repeatedly. He suffered more than most because he was not just accused of being a Capitalist-roader; he was condemned for having written to Mao to protest against the Cultural Revolution. He also defied the thugs who organised the meetings. At one, all the victims were ordered to kneel and kowtow and pledge loyalty to a huge portrait of Mao at the back of the platform. While the others did as they were told, my father refused. Thugs yelled at him, kicked his knees and yanked his hair to try to make him fall on his knees, but as soon as they let go, he fought to stand straight. Once during a fierce struggle, he cried out, 'What kind of cultural revolution is this? There is nothing "cultural" about it. There is only savagery!' 'I am absolutely against it – even if it is led by Chairman Mao!' Those were blasphemous words and brought my father more torture. Several of his ribs were broken and one eye was temporarily blinded.

My mother was also branded a Capitalist-roader, but because she had been a popular boss, always trying to help and protect people working under her, they more or less left her alone. She suffered instead at the hands of my father's persecutors, who demanded that she denounce him. She refused, and was put through scores of denunciation meetings, at one of which she was made to kneel on broken glass – I remember helping my grandma pick out fragments of glass from her knees. My grandma made padded knee bands for her, as well as a waist band, to cushion her from the punches and kicks of the thugs who liked to aim for vulnerable parts of her body.

Children in condemned families were told to denounce their parents, and I knew children who changed their surnames to demonstrate that they were disowning their fathers. Some even joined in the beatings of their parents. But my family grew closer. As a child, witnessing my parents' suffering and bravery, I loved and admired them intensely, and devoted myself to looking after them.

In March 1967, my father had a surprise visit from two old colleagues from Yibin: Mrs Ting, who had tried to seduce him years before, and her husband. It was to flee them that my family had left Yibin for Chengdu. Since our departure, the Tings' victimisation of their foes had grown to such a mind-boggling degree (once she sent a bodyguard to prison, accusing him of trying to rape her, when in fact he had rejected her advances) that many risked their lives to write and denounce them to the pre-Cultural Revolution provincial authorities. An investigation found them guilty of gross abuse of power, and they were sacked and expelled from the Party in the early 1960s. Now, with Mao purging the old Party officials and looking for replacements, he cleared the Tings and made them the bosses of Sichuan.

The Tings were forming their team and wanted my father to work with them, so had come to our apartment to make their offer, telling him that if he collaborated all the incriminating things he had said and written would be forgotten. My father refused them point-blank, and, according to the Tings, threw them out. It was right after they left that he wrote his second letter to Mao, which ended with these words: 'I fear the worst for our Party and our country if people like [the Tings] are given power over the lives of tens of millions of people.'

Before he sent the letter by mail, knowing it would be intercepted, Mother had asked him, 'What's the use? How could you possibly imagine Chairman Mao would listen to you?' Father had replied: 'I must do it even if just for my conscience.' He was arrested on the Tings' orders.

For the second time since the beginning of the Cultural Revolution, my mother was at Chengdu railway station, waiting for a train to take her to Beijing to try to get her husband freed. She decided that the only person who could help her was Premier Zhou Enlai, who had the reputation of being both authoritative and moderate. But how to get to see Zhou? She sat on the bench of the waiting area racking her brains when her eyes were drawn to a big banner under which stood about two hundred Red Guard students. They belonged to a group called 'Red Chengdu', and were going to Beijing to petition Premier Zhou against the Tings.

At that time the Red Guards had split into factions and were fighting against each other. In Sichuan the different groups had gathered under two camps each commanding millions of followers: 'Red Chengdu', which was more moderate, and another more brutal group that called themselves '26 August'. The Tings backed '26 August', and tried to suppress 'Red Chengdu' by violence. 'Red Chengdu' was sending this delegation to present its case to Premier Zhou, who was receiving Red Guard groups from all over China round the clock to sort out such problems.

My mother, who was very good at striking up a conversation, approached the students and told them she was also going to Beijing to appeal against the Tings, who had arrested my father because he had refused to work with them. The students became interested: my parents had been colleagues of the Tings and could potentially supply information to help topple them. My mother even managed to persuade them to let her go to their meeting with Zhou Enlai. The journey took two days and a night. While the students slept, my mother drafted a petition in her head to give to Zhou at the meeting. She wrote it down when they arrived in Beijing. At nine the next evening, she went with the group to the Great Hall of the People on the west side of Tiananmen Square. When she heard Zhou asking in conclusion, 'Anything else?', she stood up from the back row: 'Premier, I have something to say.' She gave her name and position and my father's name and position, and said, 'My husband has been arrested as an "active counterrevolutionary". I am here to seek justice for him.' As my father had a high rank, Zhou looked intently at her and said, 'The students can go. I'll talk to you.' My mother had anticipated this offer and had decided not to take it up. She replied, 'Premier, I would like the students to stay and be my witnesses.' And she handed her written petition to the student in front, who passed it on to Zhou. When Zhou asked her to speak, my mother spoke succinctly for a few minutes. She mentioned my father's (second) letter to Mao, but avoided giving the exact contents, saying only: 'My husband held some seriously erroneous views . . .', before stressing that he had acted in accordance with the charter of the Communist Party, which permitted its members to write to the top leader, however wrong their views might be. She could tell that Zhou understood her problem, that she could not spell out my father's words in front of the Red Guards. Zhou whispered to an aide sitting behind him and the aide handed him some sheets of paper with the letterhead of the State Council, which Zhou headed. He wrote a little stiffly – his right arm had been broken years before when he fell from a horse. After he finished, the aide read out what he had written:

' "One: As a Communist Party member, Chang Shou-yu is entitled to write to the Party leadership. No matter what serious mistakes the letter contains, it may not be used to accuse him of being a counterrevolutionary. Two: As Deputy Director of the Department of Public Affairs of Sichuan Province, Chang Shou-yu has to submit himself to investigation and criticism by the people. Three: Any final verdict on Chang Shou-yu must wait till the end of the Cultural Revolution. Zhou Enlai." '

My mother's spirits were hugely lifted as she heard point number one, because this could get my father out of prison – even though point number two meant he would still be subjected to denunciation meetings, and point number three left open what sort of 'verdict' he would get later. She turned to the two students next to her, and saw that they were thrilled for her. Yan and Yong, two Red Guards in love, stayed friends of my family.

Back in Chengdu, my mother showed the note to an old friend who had thrown in his lot with the Tings. For old time's sake, he did my mother a big favour by securing my father's release without taking away Zhou's note, which my mother desperately wanted to keep for possible use in the future. She did not tell her children about the note, nor my father – as he had come home with a severe mental breakdown.

The prison authorities had told my father that he was being sent home to be under the watchful eye of his wife, who had renounced him and was now his prison warden. Confused and furious, one day my father struck my mother – for the first and only time in their lives – causing her left ear to be badly damaged and almost deaf. The Tings refused to allow him psychiatric treatment. It was Yan and Yong, and through them

'Red Chengdu', that got my father treated. The dominant Red Guard group at Sichuan Medical College belonged to the camp of 'Red Chengdu'. My father was admitted to its psychiatric clinic and recovered. When I visited him there and saw him well again, I was so happy that I burst into tears, and rushed to a bathroom to have a good cry. He, and my entire family, were immensely grateful to the students. But my father politely, yet firmly, declined their request to collaborate to bring down the Tings: it was not the right procedure for him.

Meanwhile, my mother gave the note from Zhou to my grandma for safe keeping. My grandma folded the thin piece of paper into a small roll and tucked it into the cotton upper of one of the padded winter shoes she had made for herself.

Life for my parents in 1967 and 1968 consisted of end-less denunciation meetings and periodic detentions. Over those long and dark days, I ruminated about the society I was living in. On the night of my sixteenth birthday, in 1968, I wrote my first poem to express my feelings, and was polishing it when I heard the door banging. Some Red Guards had come to raid our flat. My poem could bring disaster to my family and myself, and I rushed to the bathroom to tear it up and flush it down the toilet. Afterwards, hearing my grandma sobbing in the next room, I thought to myself: We are told that socialist China is paradise on earth. If this is paradise, what then is hell? At the time I did not blame Mao. His deification had blocked any contemplation about him. It would take many long and dark years for Mao's responsibility to dawn on me, and for me finally to say to myself: 'Of course it is Mao who is ultimately responsible for all the deaths and suffering!'

One thing that turned me viscerally against the regime was that nearly all books were condemned as 'poisonous weeds' and bonfires were lit across China to consume them. Mao had declared: 'The more books you read, the more stupid you become.' Red Guards carted them off in house raids and burned them. Some books survived, as they found their way to the black market. My teenage brother Jinming frequented a black market in Chengdu and built up an impressive collection of foreign and Chinese classics, which he hid ingeniously in different places, including under an abandoned water tower in the compound. I was able to read them in those bookless years and to emerge from the cultural desert with my brain still functioning.

At home, my main responsibility was helping my grandma look after my youngest brother Xiaofang, who was five in 1967. I went everywhere holding his hand, so all my friends knew him well. My friends and I hung out a lot – we had time: there was no proper schooling in the whole of China for some ten years.

In 1968, Mao's new set-up, the Sichuan Revolutionary Committee headed by the Tings, was officially installed, and my family, along with the purged old administration, were thrown out of the compound. We were given some rooms in a house in Meteorite Street, so named because a meteorite had once fallen there. The house-moving had been left to my grandma and us five children as my parents were in detention and no one was designated to assist us. It was our friends who helped with the move; without them we would not have had any beds to sleep in.

From the beginning of 1969, my family scattered. My parents, my sister, my brother Jinming and I were sent out of Chengdu one after another to distant and different parts of Sichuan. My parents were trucked to separate quasi-labour camps on the eastern edge of the Himalayas, about four days' journey to the south from Chengdu. Euphemistically termed 'cadres' schools', those camps treated the inmates slightly better, with a little more freedom and a little less back-breaking labour than the Gulag-style labour camps. But life was harsh, especially for people like my parents who were deemed enemies. They were given the hardest jobs to do and had no Sundays off. While my father in his camp in Miyi County had to endure frequent denunciation meetings in the evenings after a whole day's exhausting work, my mother in hers in Xichang County was forced to stand for the lunch break with her head bowed, facing the other inmates, in sessions called 'field-side denunciation' and 'never forget hate'. This practice was stopped only after my mother protested to her immediate boss that she could not carry on working without resting her legs, and the boss was not totally unreasonable and saw her point.

My father's camp was particularly pitiless because it was under the control of the Sichuan Revolutionary Committee with the Tings as the chiefs. Many victims killed themselves, mostly through drowning in the roaring river that ran across the camp, the 'Tranquillity' (*An-ning-he*). The inmates said the echoes of the river in the dead of night sounded like the sobbing of ghosts. The stories made me very anxious about my father, especially as he had already suffered a mental breakdown and could end his own life if his mind suddenly snapped. I was determined to go and visit him as soon as possible, to make him feel that he was loved and life was worth living. My mother was under less pressure than my father, but I knew that beneath her strong exterior she needed me, too.

There was no public transport to their camps. But there were trucks going nearby. China was building a major industrial centre, to be named Panzhihua, in that remote region, and convoys of trucks were transporting goods from Chengdu, passing by Xichang and Miyi. I could get a lift to the nearest spot on the road and walk the rest of the way – to my mother's camp for half an hour, and to my father's about two hours. I searched hard and found a kind driver who was the relative of a friend, and so could be trusted. He allowed me to sit on the back of his truck as the cabin was reserved for the relief driver.

At night we all stayed in small, dirty hotels, them with other truck drivers, and me in a large room with other female travellers. In this way, having been bounced about on the back of the truck for days, I 'gate-crashed' my parents' camps.

I never sent telegrams beforehand for fear the camps might refuse my visit. I reckoned that if I, then seventeen years old, just turned up, it would be difficult for the authorities to turn me away: the camps were in the middle of nowhere in deep mountains with no transport and no hotels, only howling wolves. So, after I had landed on them, the camps were compelled to give me a bed in a room for women and allow me to stay until the truck driver finished his rounds after some days and came by again to pick me up where he had dropped me off. I was treated with some warmth in my mother's camp, as everyone missed their children. But in my father's, the women in my room as well as most others looked through me with silent coldness. Although it was extremely unpleasant, I cared only that my visits, along with those of my siblings, made a life-and-death difference to our father.

In more than two years, I spent a lot of time on the road, and was hardly in the villages I was allocated. The first one was in the same region as my parents' camps, with pathless high mountains standing between us. It was in a county called Ningnan, four days' journey by truck from Chengdu, after which a day's trudge in the mountainous forests. Mao's plan for me and my contemporaries was for us to be peasants for life wherever he placed us. Subconsciously, I did not like his plan and struggled to change my lot, by getting out and moving to another village in Deyang County, close to Chengdu.

In late 1971, a political earthquake shook the country. Mao fell out with his deputy, army chief Marshal Lin Biao, who had ensured that the army backed Mao in the Cultural Revolution and had dispatched army officers to replace purged officials. Lin tried to flee China but died in a plane crash in Mongolia. He left a deep shadow that haunted Mao. Lin's son, an air force officer nicknamed 'Tiger', who had helped his father control the air force and had fled and died with his parents, had hatched a plot to assassinate Mao. Mao could no longer trust Lin's men who were running the country and so was forced to reinstate purged officials.

Like millions of others, my mother was rehabilitated. She was released from her camp and reassigned to her old department, where she had been the director. It now had no fewer than seven directors. The Cultural Revolution created countless victims, but also quite a lot of beneficiaries. My mother did not go back to work. She did not want to work for the Cultural Revolution. My father was not rehabilitated because he had opposed Mao, and the Party was yet to produce a verdict on him. But Lin Biao's downfall improved his life in the camp. Sensing that the Cultural Revolution was going to be reversed, people started to greet him with the occasional smile, and he was asked to sit down at meetings, which had never happened before. He was told to denounce Mrs Lin Biao, Ye Qun, and to 'expose her misdeeds in Yan'an', where they had been friends in their youth. My father said he had nothing to say. Eventually, he was released from the camp when it was about to be shut down.

The economy was recovering and factories were recruiting. A small machinery factory of several hundred people which used to come under my mother's Eastern District took me on. A few months before my twentieth birthday in 1972, I left my village in Deyang and was assigned to be a steelworker and then an electrician. I was no good at mechanical things and received five electric shocks in a month.

Before long I found myself falling in love with a fellow

electrician named Day, who was good-looking and played several musical instruments. I was smitten by the poems he wrote to me. One early spring day, after we had finished a maintenance job, we leaned against a haystack in the fields on the edge of the factory, enjoying the first glorious sunshine of the year. I longed to be in his arms, and he made to bend over to kiss me. But he stopped when he was close, with a heartbreakingly sad expression that distorted his face. An insurmountable barrier lay between us: Day's father had been a Kuomintang officer, and had been in a labour camp. He was doomed as a 'Black', and any family he would have would be 'Blacks'. Having witnessed the ghastly treatment of those people, I was scared. In fact, the whole factory was gossiping about our relationship, with the consensus that I should not be 'dragged into misfortune' and Day should 'stop courting' me. We both pulled back from committing ourselves. The Cultural Revolution had poisoned everything, including love.

Eventually I got over Day with the help of one incredible piece of news that overshadowed all my other thoughts: after having been closed for six years, universities were beginning to reopen to take in an extremely small number of students. I yearned to go. Mao ordered that unlike before the Cultural Revolution, students must now be selected from among 'workers, peasants, and soldiers' – but this suited me fine as I had worked as a peasant and was now a factory worker. I put in an application, and the factory held meetings in all the workshops to select one candidate. Most voted for me. They knew I had been working hard to prepare for university. The electricians' quarter had two rooms, and while the others had chatted and played cards in-between jobs in the outer room, I had stayed in the inner one poring over pre-Cultural Revolution school textbooks that I had taken a great deal of trouble to find: Chinese, maths, physics, chemistry, biology and English.

With other nominated candidates all over China, in 1973 I sat for exams, which were in fact rudimentary, and I passed with distinction. For the English oral, my mark was the highest in Chengdu.

Mao was annoyed that exams were making a comeback, as he had condemned them as 'bourgeois dictatorship'. The exams I had taken were declared void. But the Great Leader provided no credible alternatives for selection as university places were few and the numbers of applicants were huge. The only way to get a place was, inevitably, through pulling strings.

I was actually in a better position than most. The directors of the Sichuan Enrolment Committee were old colleagues of my father's. I knew he would love me to have a university education, and begged him to go and talk to them, to make sure that I would not be pushed out. My father did not want to do this. 'It would not be fair to people with no strings,' he said. 'What would our country become if things had to be done this way?' I started to argue with him, but sobbed uncontrollably and could not continue. Father looked in agony and got up to go with me. He walked slowly, with the help of a stick, stopping every now and then, battling with his mind as well as his legs. His health had been wrecked by the years of ordeal; his blood pressure was shockingly high, and he had had a few minor strokes. He was barely in his fifties and yet looked a hundred to me. My heart ached so much that when he turned to me and entreated, 'Daughter, would you forgive me? I really find it very difficult to do this . . .', I just said, 'Of course.'

It was my mother who helped me overcome the hurdle – like all other hurdles in my life. She went to see the directors – not to ask for a favour, but to show them my exam results as well as my factory's nomination letter. And the directors agreed that it was only fair for me to go to university. In October 1973, I entered the Foreign Languages Department of Sichuan University to study English.

I did not have a good time in the university, though. Most of my teachers, politically qualified to teach, had never spoken to an English-speaking person. The old textbooks had been discarded. In the new teaching material, Lesson One was the mandatory 'Long live Chairman Mao!'. Lesson Two, 'Greetings', was the literal translation of the then greetings between the Chinese: 'Where are you going? Have you eaten?' (*Shang-na-qu? Chi-fan-le-ma?*). That was the English salutation I learned.

Unlike my village or my factory, the university was a much more tightly controlled place, where Maoist politics ceaselessly intruded into my life. Every class had 'student officials', and above them 'political supervisors', to all of whom I had to make 'thought reports' frequently. Before each session, I would wander around the campus for a long time suppressing my dread. Among the endless criticisms against me was that I was 'white and expert', a ridiculous term which unfathomably equated being good at one's profession with being politically unreliable.

In 1975, the Party gave my father a verdict. It said he was not exactly a counterrevolutionary but that he had committed 'grave political errors' by having opposed Mao's policies. That year my sister Xiaohong's husband, whom my family and friends affectionately called 'Specs' (he wore glasses), was up for promotion in his factory. There had to be a 'political investigation' to check his family background, and the personnel officers of the factory came to my father's department. Specs' promotion was ruled out. Specs did not mention it to my parents for fear of upsetting them, but a friend told my mother. My father overheard their conversation. He was a man who hardly ever shed a tear, yet this time he cried to my mother, 'What have I done for even my son-in-law to be dragged down like this? What do I have to do to save you?' Despite taking large doses of tranquillisers, he was unable to sleep for days. My father died of heart failure on 9 April, at the age of fifty-four.

My mother wept day after day as she had never done before. She had lived with a difficult husband for nearly three decades, and had countless times felt bitter towards him for putting his principles above the interests of his family and herself. But she admired his character, and never stopped loving him. The grief triggered a high fever and my mother was forced to take to her bed. There she told herself that she must pull herself out of her sorrow and seize this moment of Father's death to try to get his damning verdict changed, as what had happened to Specs could happen to all her children. For me, who was studying English, I would never be allowed to have any contact with a foreigner. My father's death had roused great sympathy from his old colleagues and friends. My mother appealed to them from her sick bed, asking them to help her get a new verdict for him, telling them she was putting the future of her children in their hands. She even threatened the authorities that if she did not get a decent verdict, she would denounce them at the memorial service they were putting on. (The Party was committed to giving memorial services for senior officials at their deaths.) In the end, the authorities modified the verdict. But nobody dared to clear someone who had criticised Mao.

Eighteen months after my father's death, Mao died, on 9 September 1976. The news was officially announced through the ubiquitous loudspeakers that had become a part of the Chinese landscape. I heard it on the university campus. It was a sunless grey day in Chengdu, and we waited as a loudspeaker made scratching noises tuning up. After a while the Party secretary of the department walked to the front of the assembly, and, with a tragic look on her face, said in a low, halting voice as if to choke back tears: 'Our Great Leader Chairman Mao, His Venerable Reverence [*ta-lao-ren-jia*] has . . .' Suddenly we all realised that Mao was dead.

Before she finished, and before mournful music started, to be followed by a broadcaster's slow, solemn voice, hysterical weeping broke out all round me. Everyone appeared heartbroken. The woman in front, one of the 'student officials' of my class, was sniffling loudly, clutching a handkerchief. But I was dry-eyed. Tears just would not come. Perhaps I had used them up at my father's death, and before that the death of my beloved grandma, also brought about by the Cultural Revolution. Their deaths and those of so many others, and all the suffering, had long destroyed Mao's God-like status in my head.

My tearless face was dangerous, and I frantically searched for a place to hide it. The shoulder of the crying student official in front seemed to be a good spot, and I pressed my forehead on it, heaving appropriately to give the impression that I, too, was grief-stricken.

A couple of days later, I was home and saw Mother. Neither of us mentioned the death of Mao, as if it were a non-event. I had never told my parents my thoughts about Mao. I did not want to worry them or put them in a position of having to tell me their own thoughts. My parents had never talked to us children about Mao, either. Few parents in China dared to say anything that could be construed as offensive to the Great Helmsman.

Now, sitting across the kitchen table, my mother told me that she had just reported back for work at her department; she felt that at the age of forty-five, she had some energy and would like to put it to use. I asked her what made her want to go to work, as she still had that inexplicable fever following my father's death. My mother flashed me a smile, which, so rare from her in those years, suddenly made me want to cry. She said, in the softest voice but delivering the weightiest message: 'A new era is about to begin.'

Indeed, despite the mass wailing orgies all over the country, the mood of the nation was unmistakably against continuing Mao's policies. Less than a month after his death, on 6 October, Mme Mao, Jiang Qing, was arrested, together with the other members of the Gang of Four, Mao's closest assistants. (They were later tried, in 1980, and imprisoned. Also tried and imprisoned were the Tings in Sichuan.) The demise of the Gang of Four was soon made public officially and a mammoth rally to mark the event was held in Tiananmen Square. As the fall of the Gang of Four could be celebrated, people felt able to show spontaneous rejoicing. When I went out to buy drinks to celebrate with my family and friends, I found that shops had run out of liquor: there were so many parties.

I laughed as I had not done for years. And I waited, impatiently, for the coming of what Mother called the 'new era'.

With Mao's death, the Cultural Revolution that had lasted ten long years ended. It had created a hundred million victims even by official accounts. Mao's number-one enemy, President Liu Shaoqi, who had fallen foul of Mao because he had managed to stop Mao's policies that had caused the Great Famine, had died a painful death in incarceration. Enemy number two, Deng Xiaoping, also purged for disagreeing with Mao, launched a comeback, and China began to change. Deng made many speeches, and each of them sent my spirits soaring. Mass political victimisation would stop, and improving people's living standards was to be the Party's top concern – a common-sense policy that had been condemned by Mao, who had decreed never-ending 'class struggle'. Books that had disappeared for over a decade reappeared in bookshops, and people queued sometimes for forty-eight hours to buy them. When I graduated from Sichuan University at the beginning of 1977, I was picked to work there as an assistant lecturer on account of my academic merit, even though I was not a Party member and was regarded as politically unreliable – not to mention that my father had not been fully rehabilitated.

Deng restarted proper education in China after more than ten years, and ordered that university entrance must be based on academic exams. In 1978, for the first time since the Communists seized power, scholarships for going abroad were to be awarded on the basis of a national examination, which would be held simultaneously in three cities, Beijing, Shanghai and Xi'an, the ancient capital where the terracotta army was later excavated. After a qualifying exam in my department, in which I came top, I went to Xi'an, a day and a night's train journey north, for the national exam, for which sealed exam papers were flown in from Beijing. Outside the windows of the examination hall, showers of white willow flowers were sweeping across the city, dancing with my heart as I raced through the papers. I was awarded a 'distinction'.

Immediately, my mother, who had been trying to get my father a clean, positive verdict, stepped up her campaign. She knew that even though I was qualified academically for the scholarship, any words like 'political errors' in his verdict would still prevent me from stepping across the Chinese border. She lobbied the new provincial leaders, now headed by Zhao Ziyang, a great reformer. In Beijing another liberal leader, Hu Yaobang, oversaw rehabilitations of the tens of millions of political victims. Mao's spell was losing its grip of terror on the country. To enable the new authorities to have more confidence to produce the most positive verdict, my mother decided to hand over the note from Zhou Enlai, as it showed that he was sympathetic. Now, eleven years after Zhou wrote the note to her, my mother unstitched the padded cotton shoe in which my grandma had hidden it, and gave the note to the authorities. Soon afterwards a senior official turned up at our Meteorite Street home bearing a flimsy piece of paper. It was the Party's new verdict on my father. It said that he had been 'a good Communist'. This marked his full official rehabilitation, three years after his death. It was only then that I was permitted to study in Britain.

I flew out of China on a clear autumn night in September 1978.

3
_____

Out of the Cage

(1978–79)

With thirteen other Chinese students, one doubling as the political supervisor, I landed in London on 13 September 1978. I was twenty-six years old, and had come from a country that had been completely isolated from the outside world. I had only seen one Western film since early childhood, *The Sound of Music*, in Beijing, when a friend had given me an incredibly sought after ticket and I had ridden a borrowed bicycle for what felt like hours in a strong wind to a highly privileged place to watch in the open air. I had only read a few contemporary Western books in Chinese, published around the time of President Richard Nixon's historic visit in 1972 – including the US president's *Six Crises*, with the anti-Communist bits edited out. Even those books were only allowed to be read by authorised personnel, but a friend of my family discreetly lent them to me.

Although I had been studying English at Sichuan University for three years, the only foreigners I had met were some sailors in 1975, when I was twenty-three. My fellow students and I were dispatched to the Port of Zhanjiang, the former French colony Fort Bayard, on China's tropical south coast, to practise English with them. For us it was a once-in-a-lifetime opportunity. After travelling by train for two days, we waited eagerly in the International Sailors' Club, grabbing the sailors as soon as they entered. We had no idea what must be on their minds, especially as we only talked political slogans. One day a classmate rushed around with a piece of paper: a sailor had indicated he needed something urgently, and he had written, in capital letters, 'TOILET'. We had never been taught that word, after two years of learning. (I knew the word because I had been studying by myself some pre-Cultural Revolution textbooks, which had cost me much time and energy to find.)

Setting foot in London was like landing on Mars. I had no idea what the West was really like. In my childhood, the images of a little girl dying of hunger and cold on Christmas Eve in *The Little Match Girl* by Hans Christian Andersen, and a famished boy holding out an empty bowl, his big sad eyes begging for food, in *Oliver Twist* by Charles Dickens (translated into Chinese as *Orphan in the Capital of Fog*), had left indelible impressions. Although I had grown sceptical about the stories the regime had fed me, I had no mental picture of the West. I was bursting with curiosity and itched to go out and explore. As I wrote in my diary and letters home, I wanted to see everything, to understand everything, and to find out whether people here belonged to a different species, incomprehensible to me.

My excitement was dealt a heavy blow when, the day after our arrival, an embassy official came to our hostel and in an all-day talk stressed the *she-wai-ji-lù* – 'rules regarding contact with foreigners'. We were told never to step out of the hostel without permission, and even with permission at least two people must go together. And if those two people were related, a third person was required. Inside the building, the curtains on the windows facing the street had to be closed even in day-time. My bedroom, which I shared with one other, was unfortunately in that position. Feeling suffocated and yearning for a bit of real London, even the famed English rain, I lifted a corner of the curtain to peep out whenever I was on my own.

The hostel was like a dormitory in China. Everywhere in the corridors were spittoons, their white enamel yellowing from cigarette butts and phlegm. A strong smell of stir-fried food lingered in the air, the grease having seeped into the uphol-stery. The chef, who was from Sichuan and very nice, was too used to the smell to open the windows and let it out. Still, the food was delicious.

Two days later, when I was going crazy, an announcement came allowing us to go out. So off we went as a group to Hyde Park. When the magnificent oaks and chestnuts over the lush lawns came into view, I was ecstatic and longed to throw myself on the ground to embrace the grass. In my early teens, Mao had denounced cultivating flowers and grass as 'feudal' and 'bourgeois', and we were ordered to remove the grass from the lawns of our school. I had to suppress my misery and berate myself for having 'incorrect' sentiments. Although by the time I left China horticulture was no longer treated as an enemy of the state, there were still virtually no house plants, and gardens and parks were brutalised wastelands. Hyde Park became my favourite place in London.

The embassy organised sightseeing trips for us. Marx's tomb was obviously a must. Oxford Street, a famous shopping area, was a need-to-see – although we bought nothing. Our monthly pocket money, ten Chinese yuan, came to the princely sum of three pounds and eight pence. When we visited Blenheim Palace because Churchill was born there, we found ourselves unable to afford the entry tickets and so just wandered around outside.

I enjoyed those tours but felt no exhilaration. The group was a bubble, insulating me from the outside world, which remained remote and unknowable.

Moving as a group, we were quite a sight in the London streets: we all wore the same uniform-like blue jackets and baggy trousers, the so-called 'Mao suits', made for us in Beijing shortly before we left China, in a store which specialised in kitting out people going abroad.

The shop tailor was elderly with an efficient professional demeanour. When my turn came to be measured, I asked somewhat timidly, almost in a whisper, 'Are we *all* going to have the same clothes?' The tailor gave me a quizzical look but said nothing. When we returned to the counter where he wrote down my measurements, he took out from underneath a colour supplement from the *New York Times*, and it seemed to be about fashion. This was the first time I set eyes on this paper, although I had heard of it. There was no space for 'fashion' in Chinese newspapers, not even the one and only women's magazine that had existed before the Cultural Revolution, *Chinese Women*. To be interested in clothes was deemed sinful.

The tailor flipped through the supplement under the counter, stopping at a page of models in coats. Without a word he pointed at one, and I nodded. This happened in a split second. When the new clothes came, I flung open the wrappings and saw in one glance that my coat was different from the others. The standard coats were all cut in the same style, and all in charcoal black. But mine had a slightly different cut and its colour had a shade of grey in the black, a colour I had never seen. When I put it on, I felt instantly stylish. And I did not have to fear criticism, as the differences were so subtle that they would be hard to pinpoint.

*

The weather was still warm enough to wear only the Mao suit when my group moved into a boarding house near Ealing College of Higher Education, today the University of West London, where a course had been designed for us. We studied Western politics, society and customs, and read Shakespeare, Henry James and D.H. Lawrence. We were taken to the National Theatre to see *Look Back in Anger* by John Osborne, and to a cricket pitch to watch a match. We visited a wide variety of places, from Ealing Town Hall to the Leyland lorry factory. I devoured the recommended reading list. The beauty of Dylan Thomas especially touched me.

Every day we walked from our comfortable boarding house to college in small groups and came back together. After dinner we did homework and watched television, mostly old movies like *Anna Karenina* and *Wuthering Heights*. My fellow Chinese, with whom I was on friendly terms, focused diligently on their studies. I, too, worked hard and often went to bed after midnight.

But I was restless. The outside world was right there beckoning, yet it was beyond my reach. I felt like a bird in a cage, flapping its wings against the door and trying vainly to break out. 'Have a good time: that's what I must do!' I had written in my diary on my first day in London. But I did not even know what 'a good time' meant. One evening I heard that there was a spectacularly lit up funfair not too far from us, and I wanted to go and have a look. I had never seen one, as China had no such thing. At the dinner table, I proposed going, but none of my group was interested, perhaps a funfair was seen as a waste of time. Chinese culture disapproves of frivolity and worships hard work. Desperately wanting to get out, I pleaded, to no avail, and was miserable. At the long table were students from other parts of the world. A young man from Hong Kong, tall, wiry, with an interested smile behind his glasses, watched with bemused incredulity, before walking over and gallantly offering to go with me. It was now my turn to say an unreasonable no to his kind suggestion, much though I wanted to accept. I could not explain that I was not allowed to be accompanied by anyone outside my group, or to tell him that this was the reason why I was turning him down.

Luckily, there was no restriction on talking to others in the college. I was able to get to know people from other countries, as I was an enthusiastic partygoer. At one party a melancholy looking Russian student played the guitar and sang 'Yesterday' by the Beatles. I listened transfixed. This was my first experience of the Beatles, who had been derided in China as the epitome of Western decadence. To my delight, no one in my group objected to the music, and one even seemed familiar with the tune, which came as a most pleasant surprise. He might have been from a city such as Beijing or Shanghai, which had better access to the outside world than Chengdu.

One evening the French and German students threw a fancy dress party. My group went, somewhat ill at ease partly because we only had the Mao suits to wear. I lamented in my diary that everyone else had on colourful costumes except us, who looked solemn and stiff in our outfits. Today I think that perhaps we were the best and most suitably dressed, as nothing could be more fanciful than the Mao suits for the international students. When the thrilling music spurred more and more people onto the floor, I danced disco for the first time and was having wild fun – more so as I noticed that my fellow Mao-suiters were dancing as well, with wide grins on their faces.

The Mao suits brought some awkward questions. A young English female student asked whether a Chinese girl would be 'shot' if she didn't wear the 'Communist uniform' – to which we answered, truthfully, No; but we could not convince her why then we didn't ever seem to change clothes.

We did change, one day, after we watched a townhall debate. The British general election was coming – which Margaret Thatcher would win – and as British politics was very much a subject for our studies, we went along and listened to the debate earnestly. But my memory of the event was overshadowed by a subsequent chance discovery – a 'jumble sale' in a church that we passed on our way home. We had had no idea what it was, and just went in to have a look as the church hall seemed buzzing with activity. We were astonished to find that the clothes there cost only 5 to 20 pence apiece, and so we loaded up. In the next year or so, my wardrobe consisted largely of dresses from that jumble sale, and a student complimented me for 'always wearing beautiful vintage'.

My curiosity about people from different countries nearly landed me in big trouble. I went to a party given by the newly arrived Vietnamese students, and soon after I walked in, while I was still standing by the door, a girl from my group darted over from the corridor and hissed into my ear, 'Don't you know we are fighting a war against the Vietnamese? How come you are here talking to them?!' I wanted to retort, 'I am not a representative of the government', but thought better of it and followed her out. I did know China was at war with Vietnam, only could not see why that should matter to me. If I had stayed longer, and been reported to the embassy, at best I would have got a hefty dressing down, and at worst it would not bear thinking about.

Soon I made 'my biggest discovery', as I wrote home and to friends: that foreigners were not aliens; they were the same human beings as the Chinese. Once I knew I was able to understand them and be understood, I could not wait to lose myself in London's crowds. This involved breaking many rules, including visiting a pub. We had been specifically warned not to go into a 'pub', whose Chinese translation, *jiu-ba*, in those days suggested somewhere indecent, with naked women gyrating. The ban roused my keenest curiosity, so one day I sneaked out of the college and dashed across the street into a pub. At first everything was a blur as I was too nervous. Then I calmed down and saw there was nothing sensational, no drunkards throwing bottles, no dark corners where couples were fondling each other, and certainly no naked women. Only some elderly men sitting quietly, with pints of beer in front of them. I was rather disappointed. Still, for some time after it stopped being taboo, going to a pub remained the most glamorous thing for me to do.

The biggest rule to break was the ban on going out without a fellow Chinese chaperone. I wanted to be alone because only then could I really experience new things. In the college I received many invitations, but always had to say, 'Can I bring a friend . . .', which usually put people off and brought an end to the outing. An English girl once invited me for a weekend with her family in the country. I had to decline the invitation when she said, 'We only have one bed in our guest room.'

One day a member of the staff at the college, with whom I chatted often, invited me to go to Greenwich in southeast London, where the meridian line divided the hemispheres of West and East. When I mentioned 'bringing a friend', he misunderstood and said in a wounded tone, 'You are safe with me.' I was embarrassed, but was bound by our rules not to tell the real reason. I hated the compulsory lying and was very keen to go, and so when my group was next in the embassy, where we checked in regularly, I pleaded with the education counsellor to give me permission. Otherwise, I implored, this Englishman would think we suspected his motives, which would be 'damaging to Anglo-Chinese friendship and the reputation of our motherland'. At the end of this tosh the counsellor nodded, not without hesitation. That outing, I believe, was the first time that a Chinese under the supervision of the embassy went out alone, not on an official mission, but for pleasure.

The counsellor dared to give me this ground-breaking permission because China was dramatically changing. In December 1978, a milestone Party congress took place in Beijing: Deng Xiaoping was now unquestionably the paramount leader, and the Chinese Communist Party (CCP) formally dumped the core of Maoism, committing itself to opening the door of China and a degree of liberalisation. The post-Mao reforms officially began. Deng decreed that China must make friends with the West, which he saw as the only way to pull the country out of abject poverty, and indeed ensure China's survival. He went to the US for a high-profile state visit, soon after China established diplomatic relations with America on 1 January 1979. That the West was now a friend and not an enemy was a seismic shift that laid the foundation for the great post-Mao reforms. Control over us was immediately relaxed: the weekly obligatory 'political studies' sessions became more like an occasion to chat, and we had less and less to do with the embassy – even spending Chinese New Year with our own foreign friends.

I was elated by the news from China, although I was also aware that a twenty-eight-year-old man, Wei Jingsheng, had put up a poster on a wall in Beijing calling for democracy and was consequently imprisoned. Wei had pointed out that without democracy our springtime would not last. He had far sight. But at the time I was too busy taking advantage of the immediate changes, and was preoccupied with devising schemes to go out on my own. When the course required us to research an essay about the history of an object, I decided to write about 'gas cookers', although I had little interest in cooking or anything to do with machines. I had seen cookers during a group visit to the Science Museum, and had registered that the museum was a stone's throw from Hyde Park – and central London. Writing the paper involved research in the museum, which provided me with a legitimate excuse to travel to the places I longed to see – alone, as no one else in my group wanted to accompany me.

So for days I had the perfect reason to be wandering about London freely, indulging my craving to lie on the (by now very cold) ground of Hyde Park and staring at the sky through the crowns of the trees. Of course I took copious notes in the Science Museum, but I was also taken to tea in Piccadilly at Fortnum & Mason, which I was told was London's equivalent of 'the most famous teahouse in China'; and I was introduced to McDonald's hamburgers, which did not live up to my expect-ation of American cuisine. While I was in raptures exploring the city, my nerves were on high alert, watching out for pos-sible informers. Many a Chinese-looking person who wore clothes remotely resembling a Mao suit scared me into hiding my face.

One day a friend from college invited me to the cinema. My heart tightened when I accepted. This was not just because to go to a cinema with a foreign male was one step closer to the absolutely impermissible, but also because cinemas had a pain-ful association for me. My mother had been detained in a famous one in Chengdu, and I had often gone there hoping to catch sight of her. Sometimes she and other detainees were taken out to another place to eat when the canteen at the cinema was closed. At the beginning of 1969, just before he was sent to the camp in the mountains, my father was released from detention to prepare for the journey. I took him to the gate of the cinema several days running, in the hope of seeing Mother. We waited from before sunrise till lunchtime, walking up and down, stamping our feet on the frost-covered pavement to keep warm. Eventually one grey, foggy dawn, we saw her, in a line of a dozen or so silent and gloomy-looking men and women, each carrying a bowl and a pair of chopsticks and wearing a white armband with sinister black characters such as 'ox devil, snake demon'. My mother looked up to see whether I was there, and her gaze met my father's. They locked eyes until the guard shouted at my mother to lower her head. My father stood there long after her back had ceased to be visible.

The past had a habit of appearing before my mind's eye when I was about to have a good time. But rather than spoiling it, it enhanced my pleasure. The ornate auditorium, the dark-red velvet curtains, the thick-pile carpet – they might be the ordinary decoration for a cinema, but to me they were the height of luxury. And it was with a sense of bliss that I dipped into a bag of popcorn my friend had given me and settled into the amply stuffed chair to watch the film.

Perhaps it was that night that I returned to Ealing very late, the underground train pulling into my station after midnight. At the entrance the political supervisor was waiting. I said, 'I am sorry', dreading a stern questioning. But he only replied, 'It's late. We were worried about your safety.' He had real concern written on his face and he didn't ask me where I had been. I waited with my heart in my mouth for the next few days expecting bad news from the embassy. Nothing came. The control over our lives was indeed loosening, to my jubilation.

That summer, the one-year course at Ealing ended. The embassy told us that we could look for summer jobs ourselves, even from high street 'job centres', until scholarships from British universities were issued. We now had the freedom to find our own jobs rather than being assigned them, which thrilled me. As few openings were offered to more than one person, we were 'forced', as it were, to be out and about on our own. I no longer needed to feel like a criminal on the run when I went out alone.

Our new freedom mirrored a major emancipation in China: people there were now also able to choose jobs. Until then they had all been allocated by the government with scant consideration of individual wishes. That system had made millions of people miserable, especially when couples were posted to different parts of the country, officially given only twelve days a year to be together. The freedom to choose one's work was a key break from totalitarianism, and unleashed incalculable talent and initiative without which the Chinese economy would not have taken off. For years my mother had loathed the old practice as she had had so many people coming to ask her for help to transfer jobs, especially couples who wanted to be in the same city so they could have a family life. Now she worked unflaggingly to facilitate all such transfers.

During that exhilarating year, my correspondence with her was short, with few details. We were used to writing this way. When I was in China and we were separated, mostly because she was in detention or in the camp, it was only wise to write just a few essential lines to let each other know that we were all right. Anything more could invite trouble. When I was abroad, we expected our letters to be read by censors, at least randomly, as all cross-border correspondence was. (A Belgian friend studying in Beijing told me that once she had found in a letter to her an extra page professing passionate love, which was intended for someone else – clearly an error by some careless censor.) I gave my mother only brief sketches of my life and told her none of my adventures.

A good friend of mine working as a clerk in a government office wanted to take over a small factory to turn it round. My mother, who knew his abilities, moved heaven and earth to enable the transfer. When he came to thank her, they talked about me. My mother told him that my letters were few and far between, but that she understood because I was too busy. My friend said he had heard that a student who had gone to an American university had just returned to China with a nervous breakdown: he had buried himself in his studies and hardly knew what America looked like. My mother said with a proud, meaningful smile, 'Can you imagine our Er-hong shutting herself in a room working herself sick in a *new* world?' I was struck by how well my mother knew me. It made me so happy that she was pleased that I was busy enjoying my wonderland in the West.

4

Finding My Freedom

(1979–82)

With the new freedom of choice, in 1979 I applied to the University of York in the north of England to study for a master's degree in linguistics. My application was accepted, and I was awarded a scholarship. I was lucky: until then foreign scholarships had all been routed through the Chinese government, which allocated them to individuals. I had heard a lot about York: its medieval centre, its Gothic Minster and the carpet of white and yellow daffodils on the banks of the city walls – all of which I was eager to see. Before the autumn term started, I found a job working as the interpreter for the very first orchestra from Communist China to come to Britain to tour various summer music festivals. It was an ensemble of traditional Chinese music and part of the Central Conservatory of Beijing. The young musicians were charming, and their leader, Kun, was an uncommonly open-minded and tolerant Party boss, whose genuine friendly demeanour was in sharp contrast with the old forbidding look of Chinese diplomats in public.

At the Edinburgh Festival one day, a member of the group reported to him that several players had skipped a concert of classical music to stay in their hotel room watching a horror movie on TV. The informer suggested they should be given a severe reprimand and banned from watching unauthorised television programmes. Kun shook his head and said, 'They are young and let them have some fun. They can listen to classical music back home, but they won't be able to watch those movies.' He then said something that clearly discouraged informing.

The orchestra performed at the Durham Oriental Music Festival, which drew musicologists from around the world, all having high expectations for some 'authentic ancient Chinese music' promised by the programme. After the performance there was a discussion. A professor from America went on stage and played a tune from some Hollywood film on the piano, commenting with a puzzled look that a piece he had just heard, described as being two thousand years old, sounded very similar to the tune from the film. No one from the orchestra could respond. Few Chinese knew anything about the history of Chinese music. Our music lessons in schools never taught it. I myself knew practically nothing. Afterwards some people from the orchestra gathered round Kun and in the quintessential Mao-era style regarding foreigners, indignantly urged him to 'protest' against the 'deliberate provocation of the vicious American'. Kun gently calmed them down, saying that it was 'an academic discussion' and there was no need to get worked up; in any case, he said, the piece played was a modern arrangement of an ancient tune that had only fragments left, and in the future we should be more precise in providing descriptions. He explained to the American musicologist, who in the conversation emerged as someone who knew a lot about Chinese music, having studied it with great affection. Through Kun I saw hope in China really becoming friends with the West.

One morning I got up early and took a walk in the area where we were staying. The summer dew hung from tree leaves like sparkling pearls poised to drop in the morning sun. I spotted a little church tucked away by a honeysuckle hedge, its door framed by a clematis with large purple flowers. As I stepped on a stone path to try to get to it I saw a couple locked in a passionate kiss on a bench near the door. The girl was a musician and the man a young Hong Konger accompanying the orchestra. I turned and fled as fast and as quietly as I could, anxious they should not see me and be startled. I was delighted that the musician was so bold – and was happy because I had just started a love affair myself.

During the Cultural Revolution just a few years back, having a love affair was deemed an unspeakable sin. I had witnessed a denunciation meeting at which a woman who had had affairs was put on the stage with a plaque hanging from her neck condemning her as *po-xie*: 'worn-out shoes'. 'Sex' was a dirty word, and even sexual love was unmentionable. When a Vietnamese army song-and-dance troupe visited China, a love song in its repertoire was described as being 'about the comradely affection between two comrades'. In the couple of films we were permitted to watch – from Albania, China's only ally in the Cultural Revolution, when even North Korea was considered too soft on the imperialists – all scenes of kissing and touching were cut out. When I had boyfriends, we sat talking with a little distance between us, refraining from touching each other. The most I ventured was to steal a few chaste kisses on a riverbank. So the last freedom I was determined to taste in Britain was sexual liberation.

I began a relationship with Frank, a gentle and relaxed Englishman whom I met that summer. He loved oriental musical instruments and had once driven his battered car all the way to India to learn to play the sitar from a master. A bear of a man, dressed carelessly and never with a tie, he seemed to take everything in his stride with an otherworldly air about him. One of the escorts of the orchestra, an English woman and friend, noticed that I was spending a lot of time with him and warned me one day that he belonged to a 'lower class'. She was even openly snooty to him. He just shrugged and said to me mildly when I tried to apologise for her, 'Oh she is just insecure.' This was how I learned the word that so perceptively described a psychological phenomenon. Indeed, Frank was contented to be a drop-out and happy to make a living by doing odd jobs from driving mini-cabs to decorating houses – which might have been one of his attractions as I had been 'responsible' all my life.

I liked Frank's take on many things, and tried out on him some ideas about sex which I had learned in China. He laughed, amused and appalled at the same time. I had been led to believe that for a woman sex was her sacrifice for the man she loved; and to this Frank commented with mirth: 'That's rubbish! Women enjoy sex as much as men do; in fact, I've heard women say they enjoy sex more than men.' A girlfriend of mine in China had once told me in great confidence that if a girl lost her virginity before marriage, she could save herself by having a small operation to have her hymen sewn back on. 'What?' Frank bellowed. 'Are you living in the Middle Ages? I thought China was a country of progressives!' And he gave me an exaggerated horrified grimace.

I fell in love – not the romantic kind that was born out of sexual restraint which I had felt in China, but a powerfully physical one. After the orchestra left for China and before the

York term started, I had three weeks in London, which I spent with Frank. Fear shadowed me. From China I had brought a cautionary tale, which I believed: anyone who had a foreign lover would be carted off back to China, drugged and in a jute sack. When Frank drove past streets remotely near the Chinese embassy, I slid down the seat so nobody could see me from the outside. I bought make-up and daubed my eyelids bright green and my lips dark purple, telling myself that I was unrecognisable. It was the first time I used make-up.

Then I went to York, and I missed Frank terribly, to the extent that I could not think straight. I checked my pigeonhole several times a day hoping to see a letter from him, and restlessly counted the days to the next weekend when I could be in London with him. The weekends were not enough. I needed all my willpower to carry on with my studies. For many months I hardly wrote to my mother, sending instead only occasional cards for seasonal greetings.

My mother sensed that I was unusually deeply involved with a man. She had always been most relaxed about my relationships with men and never asked questions, implicitly trusting my judgement. In fact, she had total faith in my ability to handle myself. This time, it seems she felt the need to give me advice, in case I made a decision that I would regret when it was too late. She wrote and told me in uncommonly serious language that I must never, ever, get into a situation like that of Nora – the main character in the nineteenth-century Norwegian playwright Henrik Ibsen's play *A Doll's House*.

That play was famous in China in the 1930s and 1940s, when my mother was growing up, and it had made a deep impression on her – as on other feminists of her day. Nora represented the kind of life many of them were likely to get into: to be a wife who had no identity of her own and was completely dependent on her husband – and was miserable. The message for them was to fight for women's financial independence. Thanks to my mother, I was familiar with the name of Nora when I was a child.

My mother had become a feminist after seeing what had happened to my grandma, who at the age of fifteen, in 1924, had been given by her father to a warlord general to be his concubine. My grandfather, General Xue Zhiheng, was then the police chief of Beijing under a republican government. China had become a republic after the emperor abdicated in 1912. In that marriage, my grandma led a life of luxury with a large house, many servants and fistfuls of jewels. But she was the plaything of a man and was desperate to get out of that life. When my mother was a child, my grandma often hugged her and said, 'Remember: never rely on a man. Rely only on yourself.' When my mother was fifteen, in 1946, she rejected marriage proposals from rich suitors, and enrolled in a teacher training college that offered free tuition and board. She wanted to be able to support herself in the future as a schoolteacher, which was one of the few jobs open to women in those days.

Now that I was in the West where there were rich men around and material temptations – unlike in China where no man could be described as 'rich' – my mother was anxious that I should not enter a relationship that would result in me becoming a man's accessory. Normally she would know that I would never let such a thing happen to myself, but my abnormal behaviour in the past months caused her to fear that I might have lost my head and could make a wrong choice.

I had never mentioned Frank to my mother, and she was only giving me a general warning, reminding me that I must put my independence first. The timing of her advice was uncanny: it was at the very moment when I did lose my head, for the only time in my life. I had rashly decided to abandon my studies to go and live in London with Frank, who was

neither rich nor privy to my decision. I had gone to my supervisor and head of department, Professor Bob Le Page, and
asked to 'drop out of the course'. I said I found it difficult, with
many concepts new to me, and I did not think I could complete
an MA in one year.

Professor Le Page replied that he was most surprised to hear
me say this, as I was doing well and there was no reason what-
soever for me to quit. He looked at me with concern and said,
'Don't throw away all that you have achieved.' His words hit
me hard. I agreed to carry on. But a sense of discontentedness
tormented me.

My mother's letter finally pulled me out of my muddled
thinking and feelings. I saw that I had acted like a self-indulgent
idiot. I had wanted to discard lightly the opportunity for an
academic degree, an opportunity that was only available to a
handful of the most fortunate in the whole of China. I would
have let down my family and all those who believed in me and
helped me get this far, had Professor Le Page accepted my
request. Above all, this qualification was one crucial step in
securing my independence, and I was unforgivably whimsical
to have wanted to give it up just like that.

I reflected on my passion, and found that what I had felt was
not love in the full sense of the word. Searching my heart, I did
not really love Frank, as when I asked myself if I wanted to
spend the rest of my life with him, the answer was no. It had
been an infatuation, even if a wonderful one. We were too
different – academic excellence or worldly achievements meant
nothing to him, for instance. I ended the relationship, but
remained fond of this unusual man.

My mother, it seems, was like my guardian angel half a globe
away, looking out for me. Having helped me gain freedom, she
was now ensuring that I safeguarded that freedom well.

*

In spring 1980, my equilibrium was restored, and I was able to take in fully the beauty of York, which I had neglected when I was in the grip of my obsession. I noticed with a thrill the rainbows that appeared at the fountain on the campus in the sunshine. Suddenly the meadows were bursting with golden buttercups, their petals wide open. I bought a second-hand bicycle and rode round outside York, one night struggling to get back with a flat tyre, the paths lit only by moonlight. I joined various student societies, and with them watched great movies, went on hiking expeditions and served in a 'soup kitchen'. I was learning a little French, for my thesis and for my long dreamed-of trip to Paris, where I planned to be an au pair, in the coming summer holiday.

I worked cheerfully, with enthusiasm, finding the linguistics theories that had once bored me rather absorbing. After I had 'satisfactorily passed the Graduate Qualifying Examination', Professor Le Page recommended extending my scholarship to allow me to study for an M.Phil; and in March the following year, the university further upgraded me to reading for a doctorate.

Words cannot adequately express my gratitude to Professor Le Page. I shall never forget his kindness, his reassuring manner and his wisdom. I remember especially when I went to tell him about my proposal for a thesis. I rattled on about various linguistics theories, expressing my opinions. He listened and when I finished asked, 'Could you show me your thesis?' I was puzzled and said, 'But I haven't started it yet!' He replied, 'But you have all the conclusions.' That single remark, so simply delivered, untied a knot that had fastened on my brain by a totalitarian 'education' in China. There, I had been taught to make assertions according to the Party line, rather than drawing conclusions from evidence. In fact, people in China are still warned off searching for facts. Keep an open mind, look for and follow the evidence – this fundamental way of thinking would be my compass in my future as a writer of history.

On New Year's Eve, 1980, I went to a small party in London, where I met Yu Chun Yee, a Singaporean pianist and professor of the piano at the Royal College of Music. Courteous and amusing, he told me about his experience in Beijing where he had just been. He took his Chinese roots seriously, and had wanted to settle in China. One day his guide, a young woman, asked if she could have a bath in his hotel room. Yee thought this was a veiled way of proposing sex and was shocked. I told him the guide did genuinely intend just to have a bath, as most Chinese did not have baths at home and public baths were scarce. He was appalled, but we also had a lot of laughs together as we swapped stories.

Shortly afterwards, Yee came to York to see me. He made 1981 a joyous year for me. He expressed his love with old-world charm, surprising me with gorgeous jewellery and flying over a huge box of fresh orchids from Singapore when he was there. I felt much loved – and was learning a lot from him. We spent almost every evening in London going to concerts and afterwards, at dinner, he talked to me about the music and the musicians I had just listened to. The China days when militant tunes blasted day and night making my heart jump with pre-monition seemed far away, almost fading into memory. I was happy and relaxed.

Many weekends Yee drove five hours to York, and while there he taught me how to drive. I was clumsy at the wheel, which was a permanent source of laughter. When I took the driving test, the examiner chided me for not looking in the rearview mirror. I was nonplussed and asked, 'But why do I need to watch what's behind me? They are nothing to do with me. I am driving forward.' He failed me.

After passing my test second time around, I drove us

everywhere, somewhat precariously. When I proposed driving on the Continent for the summer vacation, Yee said with mischievous seriousness, 'Okay, but we must agree that you only drive when I am *not* tired; if I am, I drive.' In the south of France, I waded into the sea and with Yee's help started swimming. I had never been able to swim when I was in China despite the school lessons in a small river. Over there we had been told to imagine that if we did not swim across the river, we would be captured by pursuing American soldiers and tortured. Fear had given me cramps and I had been terrified of swimming – until now, in the Mediterranean.

I was working hard while playing hard, which was my ideal way to live. Fear gradually loosened its grip on me. Throughout those years in York, the Chinese embassy made hardly any contact. Each time my scholarship was extended, which meant I would stay on another year, I dutifully wrote, and the embassy acknowledged my letter. Otherwise I was left alone and enjoyed complete freedom. I barely thought of China.

In April 1982, Yee and I decided to get married. He was going to play a concert in Singapore in August and wanted to introduce me to his mother as his wife. With this decision, China forcefully re-entered my mind and I was confronted with the prospect of breaking another rule – this time a big one: that the Chinese were not allowed to marry foreigners. Yee was in fact ethnically Chinese; but he was Singaporean, and so a 'foreigner'. Just a few months before, in September 1981, a Chinese artist, Li Shuang, had been arrested in Beijing because she was engaged to a French diplomat. Chinese police went to great lengths to lure her out of the diplomatic compound, foreign territory where she was staying for protection, and pounced on her as soon as she stepped on Chinese soil.

The Frenchman was expelled from China, and she was sentenced to two years of 'education through labour', her 'crime' being 'damaging the dignity of the Motherland'.

The cautionary tale I had brought from China came back to haunt me, that anyone who had a foreign lover would be drugged and carted off back to China in a jute sack. Of course I had become sceptical about the story after the freedom of the past few years, but another danger – being branded a 'defector' if I did not return to live in 'the Motherland' after marriage – was very real and equally if not more frightening. Ever since I was a child, it had been drilled into my head that to leave China without permission was high treason and would bring the harshest punishment. Even if the regime could do nothing about me as I was outside its territory, it might well harm my family. I thought of my youngest brother, Xiaofang, who was a student of French at the Sichuan Foreign Languages Institute, located in Chongqing, the mountainous Second World War capital some two hundred miles to the east of Chengdu. With a sister as a 'defector', even though he had a flair for languages, he would never be allowed even to go near a foreigner, let alone go abroad. I could not bear bringing disaster to my family. When Yee said, 'You are in Britain. What can they do to you?' and suggested simply going ahead and marrying, I told him I could not do that. I wanted to proceed in such a way that the authorities would have no excuse to slam the accusation on me. I wanted to marry – and not be accused of committing any crime. I was also hoping that China would soon lift the ban on marrying foreigners or choosing to live abroad. After all, I had broken so many rules since I came to Britain only to see the rules themselves abolished in the end by the reformist government.

The practice in China at the time for people who wanted to get married was that they must first apply to their 'work unit' (*dan-wei*) for permission. Every person belonged to a unit, whose Party boss held power over their personal life. As the Chinese embassy had been a sort of boss of mine while I was in Britain, I wrote to it and humbly requested 'permission', cursing all the while the system that obliged me to do this.

The embassy turned out not to be my work unit, which, to my surprise, was the Foreign Language Department of Sichuan University, where I had last been before leaving China. Although I had stopped working there years before and had had no contact with it, its Party Committee was still my boss. And it lost no time in writing to give me orders. This old boss of mine had given me some of the most unpleasant times through petty, nasty accusations while I was studying, then working, there. Now it said no to my request to marry, and ordered me to return to the department immediately to start work, enclosing a list of jobs it had assigned me. It seemed it expected me to drop everything, my marriage and my doctorate, which was not yet finished, to rush back and do as I was told.

The letter brought back the old sensation of being owned by a work unit that had control over my life. Filled with anger, I tore up the letter, and dearly wished to drop all the pieces into the dustbin. But thinking of my family in China, I put the torn parts back together, and forced myself to pick up the pen to reply and argue my case.

Yee also wrote to stress that my marriage would only benefit the university and the country. First, he offered to repay the Chinese government scholarship that had supported my first year's studies in London. Second, we could both do some teaching in China for free (Yee had been invited to do so). Third, I could supply the department with language teaching materials from Britain. And fourth, perhaps the most valuable: the University of York had authorised me to recommend

teachers from Sichuan University to receive the same scholarship it had awarded me.

The Party bosses rejected all of our offers categorically and
demanded my return at once, without marriage. It was clear
that far from having the interest of 'the Motherland' at heart,
as they claimed, they cared only about putting me back into
the cage and holding on to the key. Their reply enraged me.
Still, I decided to keep a cordial relationship with them, and
with the embassy, from which a new counsellor now wrote an
officious letter telling me to go and pick up the letters from
Sichuan. (I sent my letters through international post, but the
Sichuan department insisted on sending theirs through the
embassy.) I politely declined, pleading a frantically busy schedule writing my doctoral thesis, asking him to forward the
letters by post.

All this time, I remained unmarried. And I could see there
was a scheme to get me back to China before the marriage took
place. Once I was there, they could easily keep me. From
Sichuan came demands: 'Please come back and discuss with
your elderly mother [she was only fifty] before making such an
important decision like marriage.' The embassy offered plane
tickets – *return*, presumably to make me think I could get out
again. I thanked them all and said I could not leave Britain as I
was at the last stage of my thesis, which was true. I planned to
deliver it to Professor Le Page in June.

I wrote to my mother in Chengdu at the same time I
informed the embassy. Her job then was the deputy head of the
People's Congress of the Eastern District of Chengdu, an
organisation that mainly dealt with grassroots day-to-day
issues. I told my mother about Yee for the first time, mention-
ing that he was a pianist. I knew she would be pleased for me to

marry an artist. I kept my letter brief, to disassociate her from any consequences of my action.

By the time my letter arrived, my mother had already learned about my plan to marry. She had come home one day to Meteorite Street to find her flat crowded with waiting officials. They were the Party bosses from my work unit, the bosses' bosses from the Higher Education Bureau of Sichuan, as well as all the other work units to do with foreign affairs in the province. From that moment on, daily visitors descended on her and bombarded her from morning till dusk with 'persuasion', centring on one thing: tell your daughter to return to China at once, or else . . .

Putting pressure on the family was a standard weapon of the Party to get its way. And many families buckled under the weight. But my mother, who had withstood superhuman pressure under far worse circumstances, was unfazed. She dealt with the 'persuasion' adroitly. She wanted me to marry the man I chose, and to live in Britain, but she did not want a head-on clash with the Party. Rather than refusing the authorities' demands outright, she circumvented the marriage issue, saying only that I must get my doctoral degree first before returning to China, an argument no one could dispute. Her main concern was that because I loved my family and would do anything not to hurt them, I might be 'persuaded' into jumping on a plane. She put me off the idea by writing to tell me emphatically that she would not see me until I had my PhD in my hands. And she both wrote to and made an astronomically expensive international call to the embassy to decline the plane tickets: 'Our Motherland needs money and please absolutely do not waste it on Jung Chang.'

My mother was anxious that there might be too much pressure on me, so she implored the embassy to let her, 'an old Communist', solve the problem for the Party, and 'Please do not pressurise my daughter who needs to concentrate on finishing her doctoral thesis.' She even tried to get me to make a statement that I left all decisions to her, hoping to divert the pressure onto her. I could see that she was also trying to take the responsibility for my decision not to return to China to live, so I would not be condemned as a 'defector'. My mother's efforts to protect me moved me deeply. I of course refused to let her bear the responsibility, and my mother fought me in our transcontinental correspondence, which now consisted of passionate long letters. April, May and June 1982 – in those months my mother wrote almost one letter a day, so anxious was she that I not make a wrong move and ruin myself. As she told me, she had never been in such emotional turmoil since my father's death in 1975.

My siblings were anxious for me, too. They wrote to say that I must under no circumstances think of them when making decisions, assuring me that they were quite capable of dealing with their own situations. My return, they warned, would not help them; it could even ruin them as well as me. Knowing their letters would be read by censors, and fearful that her other children might get into trouble, my mother ordered them in the strongest language not to write to me, and told me to stop corresponding with them.

One brother, Xiaohei, then a teacher of 'Marxist Theories' at an air force college in east China, ignored my mother and continued to write, saying explicitly 'Don't come back!'. He was anxious that his letters might reach me too late, and so sent telegrams repeating those words. In one letter, he wrote: 'You are out of the cage now. Don't get back in. Fly away, fly to the sky!' (He was an aspiring writer.) All his correspondence landed on the desk of the political commissar of his college, who summoned Xiaohei for a serious warning. The commissar was a kind man and had himself been on the receiving end of persecution, so rather than dishing out some ruinous punishment on Xiaohei, he just told him to stop writing.

With my family so strongly and reassuringly behind me, I decided to marry as soon as my thesis was finished and accepted by Professor Le Page – in that order because I wanted to show my mother that I was not a 'Nora' and was putting my independence first. My doctorate would also be my present to my family, as I knew it would mean a great deal to them. I worked hard in York, while enjoying its loveliest season, with daffodils in full bloom and the drooping branches of weeping willows long enough to touch the wildflowers on the meadows. Yee came to see me at weekends, while no one from the embassy bothered me. I was able to finish the thesis in June as planned, and delivered it to Professor Le Page, who accepted it. After that I left York and moved to London. Yee and I were married at a register office in London on 28 June 1982.

The next day I wrote to inform the Party bosses at Sichuan University, offering to help with its language teaching. Then I went with Yee to the Chinese embassy, to give them the news and show goodwill.

This was the first time I stepped on Chinese soil since I had gone to York and begun a free life nearly three years before. As we crossed the threshold of the eighteenth-century house in central London, where according to all the cautionary tales I could be detained, my legs went weak. Holding my hand, Yee could feel I was trembling. Later he told me he had never seen me so frightened. We squeezed each other's hands. I looked up the stairs, and recalled a story I had heard during my first year in London. A female student was said to have stayed in one of the rooms, before she was 'sent back to China' for having 'fallen in love with a foreigner'. At the time I had wondered what it meant by being 'sent back', how exactly that worked, and if she went back voluntarily, which seemed to be the case, how come she would do that. Now I knew. The pressure was too heavy and the fear of being branded a 'defector' too acute – and she did not have a mother and family like mine to support her.

The official at the embassy received my news of marriage in a non-committal manner. But he did not condemn me and was polite. It was after I came out of the building with this encouraging sign that I telephoned my mother and told her about my marriage and the embassy's reaction. She was so pleased that she went straight to her desk and wrote a poem. Poetry was traditionally a most important way to express one's feelings, especially very strong emotions. Like a love letter, a Chinese poem could use words which it might be embarrassing to say verbally.

Soon afterwards my mother was again overjoyed when I received my doctorate in linguistics that autumn and became the first person from Communist China to obtain a doctorate from a British university.

Some Party bosses from Sichuan University kept up lobbying to have me branded a 'defector'. But China was changing, and they found little support from other officials and ordinary people. My mother received sympathy and congratulations for my marriage from friends, neighbours, colleagues and even people she did not know. The tide of liberalisation was irresistible. I was once again full of optimism, and as 1983 began I started to plan my long-yearned-for trip back to Chengdu to see my mother and my family for the first time since 1978.

5

An Emotional Reunion

(1983)

In August 1983, Beijing lifted the ban on Chinese marrying foreigners. My mother, who had been telling me not to come back for fear that I might be kept from leaving, was assuaged, and Yee and I headed for Chengdu in September. Before we left England, my mother asked me to let as many people as possible know that I was only paying her a short visit and would be back in London soon. I was puzzled by this strange fuss. Only later did I realise that it was to pre-empt the scenario of the authorities refusing to let me leave while telling the outside world that I had voluntarily returned to stay. Having been in the Party for decades, my mother was always prepared for the worst. She would only relax after I had stayed with her for three weeks and then left Chengdu safely.

The Party was not the only force to make her anxious. One piece of malicious gossip deeply unsettled her. When Yee and I were about to leave London, she wrote and told me to ask Yee to dye his hair, which was greying as he was forty-five years old. There was a rumour circulating in Chengdu among people who knew about my marriage that I had married 'an old man', with the innuendo that I might be his 'concubine'. The malicious suggestion, so outlandish, did not bother me, and I was surprised that my mother should care so much and make such a demand. It was so unlike her. Yee did not want to dye his hair, nor did I want him to. So we did nothing. But I was distressed for being so confrontational with my mother. Just before we left our hotel for the airport in Guangzhou, where we had stayed for a couple of days to change planes, my distress became acute and I looked at Yee enquiringly. He nodded, and I hastily brushed some black ink on his hair to cover the grey. On the flight, which was about three hours, when he leaned back, the ink stained the white cover on the headrest, and he sat up straight to avoid touching it. Seeing him being so uncomfortable, I felt very upset.

My mother, together with some of my siblings and friends, was waiting at the foot of the plane to meet us. Chengdu airport at the time was only a strip of airfield, built during China's war against Japan for the Flying Tigers, American pilots who were helping China. Before she hugged me, whom she had not seen for five years, my mother went straight to Yee and apologised for making him dye his hair. She said she had acted on impulse and had made a mistake. Those were her first words to us. When we got home, Yee rinsed off the ink.

Years later, when my mother was telling me about my grandma's life, I suddenly understood why she had acted in that uncharacteristically panicky way. The innuendo had touched a raw nerve.

My grandmother suffered most of her life for having been a concubine, even though she had had no choice when her father married her, then fifteen years old, to General Xue. When the general, my grandfather, died in 1933, she fell in love with a

Manchu doctor of traditional medicine, Dr Xia, and they wanted to get married with her as his proper wife, not a concubine. The doctor was a widower, and the children in his extended family were against the marriage, telling him that marrying a former concubine as a proper wife would bring shame to the Xia family. When Dr Xia insisted, his eldest son furiously shot himself in an attempt to make him change his mind. The son did not intend to kill himself, but he died from an infection. After Dr Xia and my grandma went ahead and married, living in his household was hell. My mother, aged four, was bullied relentlessly and nearly died when she was pushed down a dry well in the garden. Feeling guilty for the death of his son, Dr Xia gave away his possessions to his children and left his (and my grandma's) hometown, Yixian, to move to another city, Jinzhou, to start a new life with just my grandma and my mother at the advanced age of sixty-six. Most of his children refused to see him for the rest of his life. This family tragedy was a permanent source of anguish for my grandma, and as a child my mother could feel her mother's intense pain. One of the reasons why she was drawn to the Communists was because they promised to abolish concubinage. They did, but she was then dismayed to find that her bosses in the Women's Association also despised her mother and wouldn't even sit with her mother at her wedding to my father. All that humiliation and anger rushed back when my mother heard the rumour with the innuendo against me, and all she could think about was how to protect me from being hurt when I was in Chengdu.

My mother embraced me at the airport with a lot more emotion than when she had said goodbye to me five years before as I was leaving for Britain. Then her hug had been brief and almost casual, as if my going to the other end of the world was just another phase in our lives. To see me flying away had been for her unclouded joy. But now she greeted our reunion with apprehension as well as happiness, fearing that I might be walking back into a cage and the door might be shut. She told me later that her heart was beating fast when she had her arms around me, and she held me tight as if to prevent me from being taken away.

Still, her exultation far outweighed her trepidation, and I noticed that her face was radiant, smoother now in her early fifties than in her much younger days. When I kissed her on the cheeks, her skin felt beautifully soft – completely different from a kiss I remembered well, when she was in the camp; then her face had felt like dried tree bark.

She had organised a minibus to bring us all home. There were no taxis, and passengers had to find their own transport. Home was now in a newly built, typically nondescript 1980s block of flats, in unadorned cement with no aesthetics to speak of. The buildings had been constructed in a hurry to accommodate the vastly increased population since the beginning of the Cultural Revolution in 1966, during which virtually no new housing had been built. They were hotly fought over, as numerous families of three generations were living in just one room. My mother had been allocated hers because the house in Meteorite Street, in which we had had a few rooms, was to be pulled down to make room for more apartments.

The new home was small. But my mother could at least lead an easier life, as it was kitted out with modern comforts such as a bathroom with a shower and a toilet. There was natural gas for cooking instead of the dirty and labour-intensive beehive coal stove which she had been using at Meteorite Street. She had bought some electric appliances – a water heater, a fridge and a washing machine – all of which I had never seen in China.

She had to be careful about how much gas or electricity she used, though: only officials of Grade 13 and above were entitled to meters with large capacities, and my mother was Grade 15. Her unexalted grade was the result of my father's anti-corruption zeal in 1953, when the civil service ranking system had been introduced, and my father, the governor and in charge of vetting the rankings proposed by government offices in Yibin, demoted my mother by two grades, with the reason that her department had set her grade too high because she was the governor's wife. Both my mother and her department were furious, but there was nothing they could do.

My mother was immensely excited about my return, and had spent days cleaning the flat with my siblings, who were all back. Chengdu was unbelievably dusty because of all the building work. She had rushed round to find things she thought Yee and I might need, including a newly available Western-style mattress, as the Chinese were using wooden planks which she was worried would be uncomfortable for Yee. The moment I came in the door and admired her embroidered net curtain, she jumped onto a chair to try to take it down and give it to me. I was so touched by her excitement that while stopping her I embraced her with tears welling up.

She tried hard to make Yee feel welcome. On learning that he loved playing bridge, she invited good players to make up a four. She wanted Yee to taste all the dishes of Chengdu, famed as a gourmet city, and hired at great expense a renowned chef. I had never eaten so well, even though her small flat was filled with greasy smoke all day long. I did not regret it too much when the chef resigned after a few days, pleading exhaustion, as our family was large, and friends and acquaintances kept dropping by to congratulate me on my marriage, whom we naturally invited to stay for meals.

After that my sister volunteered to be the cook, and the rest of us chipped in. The atmosphere in my family was particularly loving and cheerful on that visit: I was at last back and safe after the scare surrounding my marriage the year before, when my family had been threatened that if I went ahead I would only be able to return in disgrace. My siblings all had good news in their lives to report as well. My sister Xiaohong, an administrator in the Chengdu College of Chinese Medicine, together with her husband 'Specs', had just been allotted a mud-brick room of twenty-two square metres, plus a three-square-metre kitchen – a huge deal, as to have a place to live, and to cook, dominated everyone's mind. Their room was considered large, and was given as special treatment by the factory where he was working, with the reason that they had 'overseas relations' who might come for a visit; otherwise they would have only been entitled to a room of fifteen or sixteen square metres. Jinming, the oldest of my three younger brothers, who had supplied me with dozens of books during the Cultural Revolution, had been awarded a master's degree in physics at a university in north China two months before. Xiaohei, the brother who had supposedly been teaching Marxist theories at an air force college but had instead urged his sister to seek capitalist freedom in the West and got into serious trouble as a result, had left the air force and was now a journalist. Xiaofang, the youngest of us, had just graduated from the Sichuan Foreign Languages Institute.

For the first time in ages, my mother had all her children with her, three with recently obtained academic qualifications, valued especially highly by the Chinese in those days. While she was very proud of us, we were all grateful to her as we knew that none of us could have achieved what we had without her immense efforts.

We laughed together as never before, and even danced to a tape recorder in my mother's tiny sitting room. My brothers talked about their could-be girlfriends, and everyone offered suggestions. People could express their love much more openly now, and lovers had begun to embrace and kiss in public when dusk descended. I had brought home jeans and bras, which thrilled my siblings and our friends. While jeans were deemed a bit embarrassing for people over thirty, bras were coveted by every woman, even though they did not always fit perfectly. Chinese bras were uncomfortable and crude-looking, and they spoiled a woman's shape rather than enhancing it. Gone were the Mao suits for the young. Xiaofang, now twenty-one, sported a Western-style jacket and flared trousers, matched with long flowy hair, a 'look' that young men had picked up from a 1977 American film *Man from Atlantis*, which was all the rage in China.

We went out together. Every now and then I felt sad when I saw ugly blocks of flats had replaced virtually all the graceful old houses, run-down though those had been. But I was mostly in high spirits because the city looked like a place that, having been battered by a cruel winter, was embracing the first signs of spring. In a street corner market, I saw something I had missed for some twenty years – peasants selling cut flowers. In the old days they had laid the flowers in bamboo baskets carried on shoulder-poles; now they tied them onto the bars of bicycles. Restaurants with bright plaques were doing brisk business; so were teahouses, for which Chengdu had been famous but which had been summarily shut down in 1966. A friend of mine had just opened one of the city's first Western-style 'cafés', where we ate cakes with chopsticks.

I visited my former middle school, where I had witnessed so much destruction and brutality. The scars from the past were visible everywhere, not least the Confucian temple, which was in a state of collapse. In front of it, by the sports field where denunciation meetings had been held, I bumped into an old

teacher, who immediately recognised me even after some fifteen years and called out: 'Isn't this Chang Er-hong?' It was my
teacher of Chinese language and literature, who had been
partly responsible for me changing my name from 'Er-hong' to
'Jung' when I was twelve. At the time we were being taught to
keep China 'red', and one day this teacher told his class: 'If you
don't follow the Party closely, our country will change colour,
from bright red to faded red . . . then to capitalist black.' It so
happened that the Sichuan expression for 'faded red' had the
same pronunciation (*er-hong*) as my name. My classmates giggled. That evening I begged my father to give me another
name. He suggested an ideogram that expressed his desire for
me to write good prose at a young age. But I told him I wanted
'something with a military ring to it'. Mao had just called on
the whole nation to 'learn from the People's Liberation Army',
and many of my contemporaries were changing their names to
'Wang the Army' or 'Li the Soldier'. Somewhat reluctantly, my
father gave me my new name, Jung, meaning 'martial affairs'.
It was an arcane word evoking the image of battles fought by
knights in shining armour with tasselled spears on galloping
horses. Although I wish I could still call myself Second Wild
Swan, I am Martial Affairs.

Across the road from my mother's flat was the Party
headquarters of Sichuan, 'the compound', where we used to
live before the Cultural Revolution. Inside the gate, guarded
twenty-four hours a day, I had lived a cocooned life as a child,
quite used to a (by Chinese standards) luxurious apartment,
and had taken privilege and hierarchy so much for granted that
when I first arrived in London, I thought England was won-
derfully 'classless'. (My views have of course changed over the
years, not least through my association with 'lower-class'

Frank.) The compound had been the site of brutal denunciation meetings against my father and other victims. I took one
look at the gate from a window and looked away.

The street outside the compound was unusually smart for
Chengdu as it was asphalted and lined with big French plane
trees. One day my siblings and I walked beside the long wall of
the compound and turned into a mud street with shabby mud-
floor dwellings on the other side. The houses had no windows,
and the inhabitants had to leave the doors open to let in light
and air, or to sit on the narrow pavement when the weather was
fine. Standing outside one of them we looked up towards the
compound. The balcony of our old third-floor flat still looked
grand from where we stood. When we were children, our
father had forbidden us to play there because, he said, us having
fun would be an affront to the people in poor living conditions
across the street.

Father was very much present in our family reunion,
although he had been dead for eight years. My siblings and I
reminisced about his courage and integrity. The fact that he
had felt forced not to put our interests first did not stop us
from loving him. In Mother's flat so many things reminded us
of him. Talking to my mother while she was lying down, I could
not help recalling one afternoon shortly before his death in
1975, when I brought him tea to this bed. He opened his eyes
and out of the blue started talking about Big Uncle, the cousin
of his from Yibin who in the early 1950s had asked him for a
recommendation for a (poorly paid) job as a ticket seller in a
cinema. Father had turned him down, telling him to go through
official channels. Big Uncle was so hurt that he never saw my
father again. From his bed, Father told me in a pained voice
that Big Uncle had needed a job because in the Communist
'land reform', he had lost the small plot of land that had provided him with some rent for a living. Father said, 'I have been

thinking about Big Uncle. I was so heartless not to have taken pity on him who after all had had his livelihood taken away by us [the Communists]. When I was a boy, he had in fact given me the money so I could travel to Yan'an [Mao's headquarters]. What sort of man did I become? I did not have the basic human feeling of gratitude . . .' Father's voice faltered. He asked me to send some money to Big Uncle. I knew Father meant the money to be his apology.

In the last few years of his life, Father often felt remorse. I heard him reproach himself when I was staying with him in his camp in the mountains. He talked most about my mother, saying that he had hurt her many times, but she had always forgiven him. He recited to me poems he had written for her expressing his sense of guilt and love. One day a letter came from Mother with the news that she had been diagnosed with a disease called scleroderma, hardening of the skin that could spread to the internal organs, and that doctors had given her three or four years to live. As soon as my father read the letter, he went to ask the camp authorities for permission to go and see her. When they refused, he burst out crying, howling and sobbing, in front of a whole courtyard of people, many of whom used to be thugs who had manhandled him at denunciation meetings and knew him as a 'man of iron'. They were taken aback by this outburst of emotion. Before dawn the next morning, Father went down the mountains and waited for hours outside the post office until it opened. He sent a three-page telegram to my mother, with words of contrition and apologies.

My mother had not only forgiven him. Her enduring love for him filled the flat. A larger than life-size photo of Father, the last taken of him before the Cultural Revolution when he looked youthful and handsome, his thick dark hair combed back and his big eyes sparkling, was hung in her bedroom, right next to her bed. When I first saw this picture, I was uneasy and felt that the image was too strong. I said to my mother, 'Mother, would this not make you think too much about the past?' She said softly, 'Don't forget your father.' Then, as if she thought her words might sound like a criticism, she added with a smile, 'I just want to talk to your father sometimes.'

One day, after an outing, when my siblings had gone to do their own things, Mother and I found ourselves near the front gate of the People's Park of Chengdu. We walked in and strolled along flowerbeds that had been resurrected and were being attended to. The paths led to an open space, which had been a dance floor in the 1950s, then a venue for mass denunciation meetings in the Cultural Revolution. The stage that had been built for the orchestra had become the platform on which the denounced were forced to stand. Now there were pots of spectacular chrysanthemums for a flower show. Horticultural events were coming back. My mother and I found a bench and sat down. She asked whether I remembered having come here with her for a denunciation rally at which she had been one of the victims. I remembered it well. It was in 1967, and perhaps the biggest denunciation meeting against her, with thousands of participants. As she was about to be taken away from home by Red Guards, my grandma struggled to suppress her sobs. My mother was suffering from haemorrhages from the womb, and violence could kill her. I offered to go with her and wait for the rally to finish and bring her home. My mother refused to listen: the scene would be too horrible for me, then fifteen years old, and the crowd might turn nasty towards me. But I insisted, and I went, sitting in a corner off the stage so I could get to her as soon as the rally was over. I saw my mother being forced to bend double, a large plaque hung around her neck by a thin wire. On it was written in giant characters: 'Down with the stinking wife of Chang Shou-yu!' – my father's name. My mother's rank was not high enough for her to be known to the crowd. She was put through the ordeal for refusing to disown my father. Next to me the hysterical crowd thrust their fists up, yelling bloodcurdling slogans. I buried my head in my knees, and pressed them hard together with my arms, to shut out the sight and sound, and to avoid participating, while getting ready to say if I was spotted that I was having a bad stomach ache. The rally was not violent but lasted a long time, and by the end of it my mother could not stand up straight, collapsing on the stage. Eventually, we managed to get home.

With our eyes now on the chrysanthemums, neither of us said anything about that event. We talked about my current job. After I got my doctorate from York in September 1982, I had been working as a consultant for a British television company that was making the first ever documentary about post-Mao China: *The Heart of the Dragon*. I told my mother that I enjoyed my work very much.

I had written to her about the job. From her replies, I had noticed some disquiet about the fact that I was acting as a 'consultant' on things to do with China. She had shown the same concern when I told her I had commented on China to the media, and was even going to Germany to give a China-related talk to a European institution in Donaueschingen, the town at the source of the River Danube in the Black Forest which I heard would be a sea of golden leaves at the time I was going, in early winter. Replying to my excited letter, my mother had said she was pleased, but that I must make sure what I said was 'accurate' and 'based on facts'. She was clearly worried about the reaction from the Chinese government, who cared a great deal about what was said about it in the West. Now she gently asked how I would handle my comments. I said that I would just say what I believed to be true, and 'always be honest, as you and Father taught us'. As I was happy and optimistic about the liberalisation that was happening in China, I felt there would not be problems. My mother did not respond; she just put her arm around me. Her hand, which was normally small and soft, seemed large and forceful as it gripped my shoulder, pulling me towards her as if to shield me from some danger. She knew, without spelling it out, that by being truthful, I would most likely be on the wrong side of the regime sooner or later. She did not ask me to be careful not to offend the government or to steer away from trouble. She was only assuring me that she would be there for me.

Soon after I left Chengdu, my mother took early retirement. She was fifty-two and energetic. She would lose not only a large portion of her salary and considerable perks, but also things to do. She decided to give it all up because she was already preparing for the day that I would offend Beijing. As her job gave her access to some 'classified' documents, she could easily be accused of 'supplying state secrets to foreign countries' – a deadly accusation that could be used to threaten her and put pressure on me to stick to the Party line. My mother wanted me to say exactly what I wanted to say and to live the way I wanted in the West, with no concern about displeasing the Party. So, from 1983, my mother ended her own career.

And I embarked on mine in Britain liberated from worry.

6

To Chengdu with Western Capitalists

(mid-1980s)

In the early to mid-1980s, the general secretary of the CCP selected by Deng Xiaoping was Hu Yaobang, the most liberal of top officials. Under him, monumental reforms took place that gave the whole Deng era a flying start.

The biggest, most significant move came in 1984, when the People's Communes were abolished. The communes, founded in 1958 and numbering some 26,000 in the whole country, had been the system through which Mao's totalitarian regime controlled China's 550 million peasants. I had lived for three years as a peasant in two different communes between 1969 and 1971, and I had seen how they dictated every aspect of the lives of the rural population. It was through the commune system that peasants were nailed to their villages to till the designated land, not permitted to do anything else. They could not change their occupation, or move out of their villages. With a few exceptions, they were made to remain peasants all their lives – a fate that extended to their children.

During the Great Famine (1958–61), most of the forty million people who died of starvation were peasants. City residents had food rations which, however inadequate, enabled them to survive; but peasants were not given those lifelines. They were even banned from looking for food elsewhere, including begging in the cities. The people responsible for keeping the peasants penned inside their villages, even to die there, were commune cadres.

I remember one day when I was about eight or nine, around 1960. I was walking in the streets of Chengdu with my parents when a woman in tattered clothes, cradling an emaciated baby, approached us and held out her hand. My mother looked incredibly sad and took out some money and food ration coupons and pressed them into her palm. The woman was about to fall on her knees to say thank you when my mother stopped her and told her to go away quickly. Afterwards my father said, without looking at my mother, 'You know there are strict orders for Party members not to give to beggars ...' My mother snapped back, looking straight into his eyes, 'So should I not have given?' My father murmured, 'I didn't mean that ...' We walked home in heavy silence.

The event stayed with me because my parents' exchange was unusually charged, and because there were hardly any beggars around. I realised much later that the woman must have been one of those who had managed to flee her home. But she was bound to be caught and taken back by her commune cadres who would have been contacted by the police.

Now the invisible door of China's vast 'camp' was flung open, and 550 million quasi-serfs were free – free to go to cities, free to set up enterprises, and free to flourish. In little more than a year, the hitherto poverty-stricken peasants had not only filled their stomachs, but also produced unseen everyday goods for urban dwellers, from folding umbrellas to cigarette lighters, from pocket calculators to handbags. Many things that I had been asked to bring home in 1983 were easily available on my next trip in 1985. The unshackling of those hundreds of millions of individuals, which released long-suppressed entrepreneurial dynamism, was the first fundamental move towards the country's economic take-off.

When peasants came to cities wearing smart Western-style suits and expensive watches, peeling off wads of cash, the urban population, who had looked down on the 'country bumpkins', were enormously inspired and wanted to better their lives as well. Every family seemed to be engaged in some business venture. 'Tomorrow will be better' was the strongest sentiment. While most were zestfully pursuing commercial deals inside China, those with overseas connec-tions, however tenuous, looked beyond the borders and tried to do business with the West. Many got in touch with my mother, imploring her to ask me to connect them with West-ern companies.

My mother sent me many letters, each containing requests. She was somebody who liked helping people solve their problems. In the past, she had helped bring together hus-bands and wives who had been sent to different parts of the country, and found a roof over their heads for newly-weds. Even though they were often not her responsibility, she had rushed around tirelessly. Once my father remarked that all those problems should be addressed through official channels. My mother retorted, 'But where *are* the official channels?' Her helpfulness was rewarded during the Cultural Revolution when people working under her by and large did not make her suffer. It struck me that had she been in a democratic system, she might make a good Member of Parliament as she was genuinely dedicated to tackling grassroots issues and derived pleasure and satisfaction from her labour.

One request came from a factory. Its engineers had seen footage of 'a yellow machine' in Austria which dug up huge hunks of earth with ease, swivelled round and deftly dumped the load on the other side of the road. The factory wanted to contact the producer of the yellow digger and learn to make it. A photo of the machine was sent to me. It would not be too difficult to make the connection, would it? my mother pleaded.

Some requests had nothing to do with business. The Sichuan Song-and-Dance Troupe was touring several European capitals and dearly wanted to come to London; my mother urged me to help obtain an invitation, describing their dancers' unusual skills in detail to try to rouse my interest: one twirling gorgeous huge fans and another throwing long colourful silk sleeves across the entire width of the stage, all of which, she enthusiastically suggested, would be unusual and interesting for a British audience.

By then I was working at SOAS (School of Oriental and African Studies) University of London, running courses that taught the Chinese language to young diplomats from the British Foreign Office and to executives of big companies going to China. (The television series I had worked on was completed at the beginning of 1984.) I was busy, had no interest in business matters, was not actively helpful by nature like my mother – and so was irritated by the demands. She sensed this, and the tone of her letters was apologetic. But her enthusiasm shamed me, as I knew I was those people's only channel to the West and it would be too selfish of me not to do something. It was even my duty to help if I wanted the door of China to open wider and wider. One day I expressed my exasperation to a friend I had met through the television series, Clive Lindley, an English entrepreneur who had built up a sizeable business.

Gracious and impeccably dressed, in sharp contrast to Frank, he was equally good-natured and totally decent. He had tremendous curiosity about the world, and was immediately excited about doing something in Sichuan, which was then still largely a hermit land. He said he could help link up businesses there with the West, and went to Chengdu with me in March 1985.

On this trip I did not stay at home with Mother, but checked into the smartest hotel in town at the time, the Jinjiang – the Silk River, named after the city's most famous product. It was easier to work with Clive who was staying there.

The highest building in Chengdu, with nine floors, the Jinjiang had been built as a government guesthouse in the early 1960s. Its elevator had been a wonder to us children, as we had never seen one before in a city that back then had had only bungalows and buildings of three or four storeys at most. Xiaofang, then a toddler, was mesmerised and got my mother to take him up and down again and again. Soon came the Cultural Revolution, and the Jinjiang, renamed the 'East Is Red' after the title of the main Mao-cult song, was turned into a quasi-prison for purged officials. My father was kept there for months in 1968, in what was euphemistically termed a 'Study Course for Mao Zedong Thought'. The pressure in the 'course' was so unbearable that several inmates committed suicide by leaping from the top floor. One of them was the father of someone I knew. When I heard the news, I raced there to try to see my father to make him feel loved and that life was worth living. No visitors were allowed, so I stood outside and yelled as loud as I could at the building, 'Papa—', hoping he would appear at a window. I had done this before when he had been detained in another location, a former 'college for health workers', and on that occasion I had seen my father gazing at me through a second-floor window of very thin glass, with immense excitement. Many other faces had also appeared at other windows, obviously hoping the voice belonged to their daughters. But at Jinjiang I was unable to catch a glimpse of my father as the building was too tall and faraway, and the windows were too thick.

The Jinjiang on the day in 1985 when I checked in was the first hotel to cater for the pioneering Western businessmen who came to Chengdu after China opened its doors. It was wrapped in thick layers of dust, which had settled on everything from windows to trees – thanks to the rush to build accommodation. Rain had turned the grey powder into mud, which our shoes carried into the hotel lobby. No amount of mopping by the staff could get rid of it. The carpets in the corridors were equally dirty. The rooms were cleaner – but when Clive pulled open the shower curtain, part of the ceiling collapsed in front of him into the bath. No matter, he said with undiminished good humour, let's go and have a drink. We went to the bar on the ninth floor, but found it still being decorated. I stepped out onto the terrace where years back detainees had leaped over the rail to end their lives. The memory of my panic at hearing about the suicides flooded back and I looked down at the faraway spot on the ground where I had stood almost hysterically yelling 'Papa—', hoping to catch sight of him. The old and the new 'ninth floor', now dominated by brand-new lighting equipment and sound systems in the bar for disco dancing, were so incongruous and caused such a total change of mood that I decided to talk to Clive about it another time. We returned to our floor to find that a queue had formed outside his room.

From that moment on, we had uninterrupted meetings with entrepreneurs, engineers and managers from seven o'clock in the morning, sometimes to eleven at night. People came to ask for what they would like to have, or what they had heard about. Could Clive, the first and only Westerner they had encountered, help them set up an airline? Build hovercrafts for the Yangtze? Mine the Himalayas for marble? Or construct an amusement park, like Disneyland? There were also less grand projects, such as importing dry-cleaning machines. In Chengdu, silk was an everyday wear, and washing silk garments was a big problem, which I knew too well. But my heart was in another peculiar request from a group of peasants. They grew a kind of grass from which some of the most expensive perfumes in the world were made; but they had been obliged to sell the grass for next to nothing to the state. Now that the communes were gone, the growers were eager to export their products to overseas perfume-makers direct.

Clive took down all the requests carefully, and started acting on them straightaway by telegramming his office in the UK, which was the only way to communicate in writing speedily. One morning Clive greeted me with an exaggerated long face. In his excitement, he had sent a telegram of 596 words, and had been woken at midnight by urgent knocks on his door: a bellboy stood there with a gigantic bill, which Clive was asked to settle at the front desk at once. The bill was so large that the hotel would only feel at ease with the money in its tills. Clive's subsequent cables were considerably shorter.

I shared Clive's exhilaration. In a postcard to friends in London, I wrote:

'Things have changed unbelievably . . . Making money is the order of the day. Shops look tempting, with goods ranging from "Japanese-made" Western suits to Chinese produced breast enlarging equipment. Loudspeakers are no longer blaring "Quotations of Chairman Mao" but disco music. Love and murder stories are the main attractions in newspapers and magazines.

'Chengdu is full of life. People are HAPPY & BUSY! Plenty of opportunities to bring out their initiative & talent. I can't help feeling excited & wanting to do something for them . . . Am terribly busy & force-fed like a Peking duck.'

After one sumptuous dinner as the guests of a local company, which had started at 5:30, Clive and I strolled out of the hotel, crossed the Silk River and walked along the bank. I was leading him to a spot that was unforgettable to me. Nearly twenty years before, in the summer of 1966, when I was fourteen years old, I had been there with a group of fellow pupils, to close a tea-house. A teahouse in Sichuan was like a café, or a pub, in other countries, the place people went to meet friends, to chat, to read, or just to sit. When the Cultural Revolution started, the teahouse was deemed 'bourgeois' and told to shut down. Schoolchildren were sent to be the enforcers. The mission of my group was to drive away the customers. When we arrived, some of them were sitting on bamboo chairs under a big Chinese scholar tree, drinking tea and playing chess at square bamboo tables. The boys started to mess up the chessboards and throw the pieces towards the river. We girls were told to go inside and get the customers to leave. One old man, puffing at his long-handled water pipe, berated me: 'Leave? Where to? Home? What home?' He shared a room with his two grandsons and when they were home he came to the teahouse for peace and quiet. 'Why do you want to take this away from me?'

His words shocked me and filled me with guilt and sadness. I turned away and walked out of the room. He, too, left. Teahouses throughout China were closed for fifteen years until the post-Mao reforms reopened them in 1981.

When Clive and I went in 1985, the scholar tree was still there, much grown. The same kind of bamboo tables and chairs were under the tree. We sat down and sipped our fragrant tea; people around us were playing chess. I felt so moved by this ordinary scene that a big lump rose to my throat. I told Clive about the old man. He asked how he could have managed when his two grandsons had grown into marriageable age. I said millions, or tens of millions, had managed – as there was nothing they could do. This was why everybody here had that thirst, that urgency and passion for their business ventures. Clive nodded, and was silent. Soon, across the river and above a row of hut-like houses, the moon rose, a somewhat dirty yellowish half-moon, nonetheless luminous, over a city which had little public illumination. Clive talked about our projects for a long time, not so much the business side but the people involved, wanting to know more about their lives.

One of the requests was to build a chicken farm, a concept that had just come to China and roused much excitement. Chicken was a tremendous delicacy, and a chicken-eating day was a red-letter day. When at the age of seventeen I had been exiled to the mountains and was ill with violent vomiting and diarrhoea, all I wanted was to have chicken soup cooked by my grandma. Clive was invited to inspect a possible site for building a farm. On the day a big entourage followed him, all keen to witness what could be a life-changing event. Everyone wanted to do something for him. One carried a hot water flask for making tea, another a teapot and a cup. A third had under his arms an umbrella, which he tried several times to open over Clive, though to shield him from what was unclear: it was not raining, and the sun, much yearned-for, stayed stubbornly behind heavy clouds. Yet another man hugged a stool, in case Clive wished to rest. Everyone was most impressed that this Englishman walked cheerfully, with no sign of fatigue. To them, foreigners were rich and rich men did not walk. They were amazed when Clive, surveying the site, touched the mud walls and felt the soil on the ground, like a farmer. Here was a big cheese not afraid of dirtying his hands – I heard admiration in their laughter. Clive sensed his success, and poked fun at himself with facial expressions, at which everybody roared with more laughter.

A venture that I had helped bring to fruition was the equipping of a factory in Yibin by the British chemical giant ICI. When the deal was done, one day the factory contacted my mother in panic: the British official coming to celebrate with us is the prime minister's younger brother! What is the appropriate way to entertain him? Please tell us urgently! I had never heard of Margaret Thatcher having a younger brother. Then it occurred to me that the 'younger brother' was Lord Young, the British Secretary of State for Trade and Industry. I informed the factory, and that put their minds at ease.

What this plant had, and most other aspiring Chinese businesses did not, was hard currency, which was in the tight fist of the state, which stipulated strict rules on how to spend it. No money must be spent on buying non-essential ready-made goods. Most enterprises were told to form joint ventures with foreign companies, in which they must only contribute land and labour, leaving their Western partners to supply technology and equipment. It was mandatory to insist on technology transfer. This very shrewd policy was another key to China's economic success.

My involvement in doing business with China lasted a couple of years. My heart was not in making deals and my mother could see this. She stopped involving me. I did not regret the whole experience as I witnessed the very onset of capitalism re-entering China, and even participated in the great move. In particular, I felt that I had done something useful by bringing people like Clive to China. In Chengdu, he was the first Westerner most people met. Certainly to me, he made an excellent ambassador for Britain. I remember that one day we were at a street market, and Clive bent down to select some apples from a pile for sale on the pavement. He felt his buttocks were being stroked, and thought, Wow, in China! When he stood up and turned around, two middle-aged women were clearly discussing the cashmere coat he was wearing. They obviously did not regard him as a human being. Clive introduced himself with a smile, using the little Chinese I had taught him: 'How do you do? I am *Ke-lai-fu* [Clive].' The two women were taken aback; they looked at him, looked at each other, and fled, giggling in embarrassment.

The decency and good humour shown by Clive and others I brought to Chengdu left a lasting impression on the locals who met them. People had a chance to see what Westerners were like and developed empathy with them. It was thanks to numerous encounters with people like them over the years that most of the Chinese, I feel convinced, do not and cannot be made to hate the West and Westerners, no matter how hard some of their leaders try to stir up anti-West fervour.

7

What Deng Xiaoping's
Stepmother Told Me

(1985–87)

Deng Xianfu, 'Auntie Deng' as we called her, was a half-sister of Deng Xiaoping, China's paramount leader after Mao, who started the post-Mao reforms that changed the face of the country. The Dengs came from Sichuan, and she worked for the Sichuan government. We were neighbours in the compound before the Cultural Revolution and got on well. About my mother's age, with a round, kindly face and modest manners, she was close to her half-brother, and her two children grew up in Beijing with his children, as her mother, his stepmother, lived with him and took care of the children of the two families together. Deng Xiaoping loved lots of children around him. At mealtime there often had to be two tables to accommodate the household. Auntie Deng visited Beijing frequently, and whenever her half-brother came to Chengdu, he brought her children along to see her. Once Auntie Deng's son, still a baby, threw up during the three-hour flight; Deng

Xiaoping took out his handkerchief and held the vomit with both hands.

During the Cultural Revolution, whenever we bumped into each other, Auntie Deng would tell us how much she admired my father for his courage, and we continued to greet her warmly even though her half-brother was branded by Mao China's Enemy Number Two and people who used to fawn over her avoided her. The friendship formed in those bleak times was enduring, and she was a most vocal advocate in favour of me marrying a foreigner and staying on in Britain. She was an unusually broad-minded person, very interested in the outside world, and keen to make friends with Westerners. When Clive was in Chengdu in the spring of 1985, she came with my mother to meet him and asked Clive many intelligent questions. We had a thoroughly good time.

Auntie Deng longed to visit Britain. But her administrative job did not give her the chance to travel in an official capacity, and personally she had no money to go abroad, like almost everyone else in China at the time, including her half-brother. To be the guest of a commercial company or a private individual would have been easy for her. Clive, indeed, invited her to stay with his family. But this would be considered inappropriate; she could only go with a delegation. She thought of an idea. Her husband, head of the Public Records Office in Sichuan, had already led a Public Records delegation on an exchange visit to America. Could something like that be arranged, and she be included in his delegation?

She mentioned the idea to my mother and me when I was in Chengdu again in the summer of 1985, and I consulted Clive after I returned to Britain. He thought it an excellent idea, and wrote to the Member of Parliament of his constituency, suggesting Britain issue an invitation, which he argued would benefit trade with Sichuan, China's most populous province, where his company was already doing business. In December, Counsellor Peter Thompson of the British embassy, on behalf of the British government, issued an invitation for a four-member delegation that included Auntie Deng. Britain would pay for the expenses of a week in the country and the delegation would cover their own international airfares.

Auntie Deng did not receive the invitation. I was puzzled and enquired at the British embassy, which confirmed that it had been issued, but nevertheless sent out another, copying in my mother. This second letter did not reach either of them. It was as if the letters had vanished into a black hole. Weeks went by and Auntie Deng was on tenterhooks, not knowing what was going on, and she asked my mother if I was having problems securing the invitation. I reassured her, but was disconcerted by the total silence and opaqueness, which gave me a sinister sensation. My mother suspected the letters had been intercepted, but doubted whether anyone would do this so flagrantly to Deng's sister. In a state of agitation, while I was in Beijing in February the following year, I went to the British embassy to see Counsellor Thompson. As I was entering the building, an elderly, kindly looking moustachioed doorkeeper came up and opened his arms to bid me welcome. At this show of easy friendliness, my nerves relaxed, and I felt grateful that I lived in Britain.

The counsellor issued the invitation for the third time, and again it seemed to have been dropped into a black hole. Before too long it was the Chinese New Year, and Deng Xiaoping came to Chengdu for a family reunion. All the letters to his sister were now produced in front of him. And he told her that she could not go: she was not working in the Public Records Office, and it would not do for her to be included as the wife of the head of the delegation. Auntie Deng accepted her brother's decision, and wrote to the British embassy to decline the invitation, claiming health problems.

I thought Deng's decision was right and proper. But I was disturbed that correspondence from the British embassy could be so blatantly seized; and that the letters addressed to one person – Auntie Deng – could be given to another (even if he was her half-brother), having been opened by a third unknown person – all without any explanation, as if this were the most normal way of communication. What upset me most was why the whole business could not be handled without causing Auntie Deng so much anxiety. What difference would it make if they let her have the invitation in a straightforward way, and then tell her not to accept it? That casual disregard towards an individual's feelings, the modus operandi of the regime, angered me again. I felt lucky that I had escaped that world.

Auntie Deng had proposed in 1985 that I write a book about Deng Xiaoping. She said she knew I wrote good compositions when I was in school (which was important in Chinese education). I was touched by her appreciation and said yes. I admired Deng for what he did to change China and my own life. If he had chosen to continue Mao's legacy, China could have been another North Korea. When I saw pictures of university students affectionately shouting 'Hello Xiaoping!' on National Day parade in 1984, my throat had tightened and I had wanted to cry out the same. Auntie Deng began giving me interviews, about her relationship with her half-brother, the Dengs' family life, and other interesting titbits. I took detailed notes. Occasionally she sighed with regret that in the Cultural Revolution she had burned the family albums, letters and other papers, for fear that they would be seized in house raids and used against her half-brother. She suggested I interview her mother, Xia Bogen, Deng's stepmother, who was only five years his senior and had been living with his family ever since the Communist take-over, bringing up his five children. She was so close to Deng and his wife that in 1969, when Deng was exiled to a provincial city, Nanchang, to work as a labourer in a tractor plant, one of the few requests he made to Mao was to take her with him.

As a child I had known her and called her Grandma Deng, when she came to stay with her daughter, which was quite often. She preferred Chengdu to Beijing because following Mao's wishes, Deng and the other leaders all had to live in Zhongnanhai, an old palace in the capital turned into a compound for the Chinese leadership, a bit like the Kremlin in Russia. There, like others, she could not go outside the gate at will, and socialising with other residents was discouraged. So she had no friends. Those living in Zhongnanhai 'are even less free than the ordinary people,' Auntie Deng observed.

In Chengdu, Grandma Deng often chatted with my grandma. They dressed alike: Chinese-style blue or grey cotton tops buttoned on the side, with matching trousers, which they made themselves. They made their own black cotton shoes, too. In fact, in Zhongnanhai, Grandma Deng's leisure time was largely spent making shoes for the family, including Deng. As our neighbour, she regularly invited me to her kitchen. One day when I was in my early teens, I came home from school after an indoctrination session at which a former farmhand had spoken tearfully about the 'exploitation and oppression by the landlords' before the Communists came. I burst out to Grandma Deng: 'How you must have suffered under the evil Kuomintang! . . . And the bloodsucking landlords! What did they do to you?' She answered, softly and calmly, 'Well, it wasn't really like that . . . they weren't always evil . . .' Her words hit me like a bombshell. I was confused and did not dare to tell anyone about them.

I only learned later that Grandma Deng's family had actually been classified as a 'small landlord', because it had hired a farmhand to help till the land. She herself had been an orphan of a poor ferryman before she married Deng's widowed father, who had died before Deng returned as the Communist boss of Sichuan and neighbouring provinces. Deng urged her to hand over the family property to the peasants, abandon her possessions and leave the village to go and live with him. In this way, he protected her from living the rest of her life as a 'class enemy' in a village and suffering endlessly in the years to come. In the Cultural Revolution, the authorities tried to deport her back to her village, which would have been fatal for her. Deng appealed to Mao, arguing that Grandma Deng could not live by herself as she was illiterate and could not even read the different ration coupons (in Zhongnanhai she never went out shopping). I was surprised to hear that Grandma Deng was illiterate, as she looked so intelligent and fine.

In September 1985, I went to the apartment in Beijing where Auntie Deng was staying, to interview her mother. Deng's car had brought her there, and she greeted me with her old easy and welcoming smile. At the age of eighty-five, she looked to be no more than in her sixties, with the same unlined face as twenty years before. (She would die at the age of 101 in 2001.) I was impressed by the understated strength of this former orphan of a ferryman, now linchpin of the family of China's paramount leader. She was the companion and confidante of Deng's wife, and was in charge of his large household with many children and grandchildren. As we started our interview and I took notes, I noticed how clear and sharp her mind was as she related family and political events precisely and expressed her views pithily. She was natural, relaxed and confident. To begin with, she spoke about Deng's life inside Zhongnanhai in the early period of the Cultural Revolution:

how, followed by guards, he and his wife spent hours every day reading wall posters denouncing him which covered the former palace including the courtyard of their living quarters; how, afterwards, they were under orders to sweep the courtyard, where fallen leaves from two big trees would fill a large basket daily; and how they did not talk to each other but wrote on pieces of paper – for fear of bugs. The Dengs had to go through the inescapable denunciation meetings inside Zhongnanhai, carried out by Deng's former subordinates, who shouted slogans at him, thrusted upward the 'Little Red Book' of Mao's quotations, and yelled: 'Bow your head!' Deng bowed his head obligingly. I asked if he had been beaten up; Grandma Deng shook her head: 'No. Some people said he had been, but in truth no. Once or twice, someone pushed his head down while yelling "Bow your head!", but no one struck him.'

She attributed this relatively lenient treatment to Deng putting up no resistance. 'He patiently endured,' said Grandma Deng. 'Unlike your father. Your father was too upright, too passionate . . . he did not bend, and spoke the truth as it was, and he ended up dying such a tragic death . . .' She sighed long and deep. Auntie Deng had obviously told her what had happened to my father so she knew that I would be my father's daughter and could be trusted. 'You and your brothers and sister must live decent lives and take good care of your mother. Your father died so tragically, he died for speaking the truth. Your father was too upright . . .' She repeated the word 'upright' (*zhi*) several times, before returning to Deng: 'Our old man just acted obedient and did what he was told – they asked him to bow his head and he bowed his head; they asked him to sweep the ground and he swept the ground. If he didn't act this way, he would not have survived to this day.'

Thus Grandma Deng vividly described a major quality of Deng Xiaoping: his ability to make compromises. During the

Cultural Revolution, he wrote to Mao nine times and, while making a few personal pleas such as to bring Grandma Deng with him to Nanchang, he subtly reassured the Great Leader of his loyalty and kept Mao's goodwill. The Chairman had no personal grudge against him and did not hate him with venom, yet he kept Deng in suffering. Deng did not grovel in those letters, which meant he was not broken, and Mao knew that behind the façade of tractability, Deng was tough as nails and would be a formidable opponent given half a chance. Mao would summarise Deng's character to his face: 'Hidden inside your cotton wool exterior is sharp metal'; 'You looked soft, but underneath you are all steel.' Indeed, having survived through making compromises, Deng emerged after Mao's death to shatter the mould that Mao had cast for China.

We paused our interview for lunch, and I was delighted to see my favourite dish: *kou-rou*, stewed pork with preserved Sichuan kale, which Grandma Deng remembered me liking in my childhood. She chatted about my grandma: 'Your grandma did so much for you children. I really feel for her. I remember how she tired herself out looking after your youngest brother – what's he doing now? Your grandma and I, we share the same lot in life . . .' Again she sighed, as my grandma did not survive the Cultural Revolution. Grandma Deng herself had been thrown out of Zhongnanhai with Deng's children and hauled to several denunciation meetings – until Deng was sent into exile and Mao nodded to her going with him.

After lunch she took a nap and urged me to do the same, offering half of her bed. I declined and rested on the sofa, going over in my head what I would ask next. At three-forty she got up, and after folding the light quilt unhurriedly and yet swiftly, she sat down with me again.

She talked till the evening, her voice tinged with bitter emotions. Anyone who had a heart could not but feel bitter. One of

Deng's sons, Pufang, had been abducted blindfolded by Red Guards in 1968 and had been much abused. Unable to endure the cruelty any longer, he threw himself out of a top-floor window, and was paralysed from the chest down. Deng and his wife were only told about it a year later, on the eve of their expulsion from Beijing to Nanchang, when they were given permission to see their children and say goodbye. Pufang, unable to move, could not come. The blow was so devastating for Mrs Deng that she wept by herself for days and was on the verge of a breakdown. When they arrived in Nanchang, she collapsed onto the floor, and had to be pulled upstairs – to her new quasi-prison, the top floor of a two-storey house. For a long time she kept saying to her mother-in-law that she wanted to die. Grandma Deng comforted her and asked her to think about her family, and look to the future, to the day when the nightmare would be over. Mrs Deng was pessimistic. Grandma Deng told me, 'Even now she is still saying, "I had no idea we would live to see this day." '

Mao eventually gave permission for Pufang to join his parents in Nanchang. Deng, working as a labourer on the factory floor, became the main carer of his paralysed and incontinent son. As Pufang was much bigger than he and Nanchang was unbearably hot and humid in summer, he had great difficulty washing his son and turning him over several times a day. Deng silently did all this, never showing anger. He showed no emotions when their prison warden barked insults at him and shouted at Grandma Deng 'you landlord cow [di-zhu-po]'. When at long last Deng was leaving Nanchang, summoned to Beijing by Mao, he invited the warden to a farewell dinner. The man was scared to death, fearing reprisals from the big boss to be. But Deng waved away his abject apologies, merely saying, 'It was your job.' Revenge did not stir in Deng's breast, and this contributed to his latter-day decision not to repudiate Mao.

After supper, Auntie Deng rang the Deng household for his car to come and fetch her mother. Grandma Deng told me that the family had strict rules that only Deng, his wife and she could use the car, but offered me a lift to my hotel. We departed together at nine-thirty that evening. The car was a Mercedes, with tinted windows. The young driver was all smiles, though he soon lost them as we sat in never-ending traffic jams and he realised that my hotel was a long way away in the opposite direction. I apologised, but did not offer to get my own transport as taxis were rare in those days, and I was unfamiliar with Beijing's public transport.

During the ride, Grandma Deng rested, and I ruminated on the long conversation of the day. The most striking impression I took away was anger against not only the Cultural Revolution but also Mao. I had already come across this sentiment in Sichuan. Now, and in the coming years, when I met more people in the top circles, including those close to Mao, the strength of feeling impressed me time and again. Nearly every one of the elites had suffered, most of them atrociously. I would gradually become convinced in those early post-Mao years that had Deng decided to renounce Mao, he would have been doing the popular thing as well as the right thing. There would have been more support for him than opposition at the top. But Deng did not choose this option. He decided to prop Mao up, and blamed the Cultural Revolution on the 'Gang of Four' led by Mao's wife, Jiang Qing. This was so absurd that to go along with it any thinking person would have to suspend disbelief. Auntie Deng did a rare thing of challenging it one day at the dinner table, when she asked Deng, 'All of you generals, marshals, so many of you – you beat the Kuomintang and seized China. How come Jiang Qing single-handedly beat down all of you?' Deng's chopsticks and bowl of rice paused in mid-air, and he stared at his half-sister without a word for a good few seconds – before silently resuming eating. (Auntie Deng put the same question to another top, and liberal, leader, General Zhang Aiping, whom she had known well from the old days, and he just said, 'I can't explain!')

I would eventually come to the conclusion that Deng was after all a lifelong believer in communism. As such he was committed to keeping the Party's monopoly of power, and his reforms were about making the Party rule better. In his long Communist career under Stalinism and Maoism, Deng had seen so many purges and atrocities that in the end nothing, however awful, even involving himself and his own family, would be too shocking and too unacceptable for him. Believers and apologists of communism often said: You can't make an omelette without breaking eggs. Perhaps this was Deng's mindset. He aimed only to break fewer eggs and break them less brutally than Mao.

As I was struggling to clarify my thoughts in Deng's car, I began to have doubts about writing about him. Any honest book I wrote would inevitably upset Auntie Deng or Grandma Deng, both of whom I loved. Mentally I put the project on hold and did nothing about it when I returned to London. Then, in the following year, when I saw how repeated letters from the British embassy inviting Auntie Deng to Britain were blocked, I realised her vulnerability and feared that the book, if written, could even bring her trouble. I made up my mind to say no to her. It was an easy decision to make as inside me there was no real desire to write at the time. I told Mother, and she agreed at once, visibly relieved.

My mother had been unusually cool about this project, unlike other things I was doing. She said nothing against it, which was characteristic. She had left it to me to reach my own decision. Now she said she entirely agreed with me. What my mother did not say at the time, for fear of undermining my confidence, and which only dawned on me years later, was that she knew my knowledge of the history of the Chinese Communist Party had been largely conditioned by the indoctrination I grew up with in China, and that I needed to do monumental research to undo the brainwashing in order to write a truthful book about a major Party leader. As I had shown no inclination to engage in such research – in which my interviews with Auntie Deng and Grandma Deng could only be a few drops in the ocean – she sensed that I was not ready to write about Deng. How right my mother was.

She volunteered to tell Auntie Deng about my decision to back out. Auntie Deng was entirely understanding. In fact, she had begun to feel the heat herself for being too free-thinking. With the arrival of 1987, an ominous political event rocked China. Hu Yaobang, the liberal Party chief Deng had hand-picked, was forced to resign by Deng himself after he was judged too tolerant of the sporadic student movements calling for more freedom, which the regime termed 'bourgeois liberalism'. Auntie Deng in her youthful days had lived near Hu and liked him tremendously for his liveliness, his open mind and warm heart. They had gone out a lot, dancing and watching films, together with several others who later became top officials. She admired Hu and identified with his ideas. In the general tightening up following Hu's downfall, she was told she needed permission 'from the Politburo' to meet any foreigner. Still, she was a woman with a mind of her own. On my next trip to Chengdu, with the man who would be my second husband and the love of my life, the Anglo-Irish historian Jon Halliday, she invited us to her flat and cooked us a dinner, all without Politburo permission.

8

My Mother Meets the Love of My Life

(1984–88)

I had been introduced to a strikingly gentle-mannered, scholarly looking man with pale-blue eyes behind delicate glasses one spring day, 1984, in the office of the television company that had just made the series about China, *The Heart of the Dragon*. He had come to ask for advice about getting cooperation from Beijing for a TV series about the Korean War which he was writing, and I was presented as someone who might be able to help. We exchanged a few words, and I noticed his full head of curly silver hair, which I later learned had been white since he was three. The next day he rang and invited me to lunch. I did not catch his name properly and wrote it down in my diary as 'John Hemingway'.

At lunch I was struck by the intelligence and charm of the man, who I now knew was called Jon Halliday. But there was something much more about him: he was the most sensitive man I had ever met. After we parted, I could not help turning round and watching his back receding from view. Wind had lifted the bottom of his raincoat, which opened like a fan as he walked swiftly, with a big file of paper under his arm, looking quietly assured. Something stirred inside me. I think it might be called 'love at second sight'.

As we became friends, he told me about himself. Born in 1939 – thirteen years my senior – he had spent his childhood in Dundalk in Ireland, hometown of his Catholic mother, where his father, a Yorkshire Quaker, had run a family shoe factory. In order to marry each other, his mother had to promise the Church that she would bring up her children as Catholics and his father had to sign a document with words to that effect. Later when the marriage became a sad one, they did not divorce because of her Catholic faith. Jon was sent to the most famous Catholic boarding school in England, Ampleforth, in Yorkshire. Meanwhile, his father's Quaker beliefs sowed some of the seeds for Jon's future principles.

Dundalk was on the border with Northern Ireland, and the IRA was active there when Jon was a child. His father treated his Irish employees fairly, nevertheless he was caught in the middle of the clashes, and had to employ IRA members to protect his family. One day on their way to a football match, Jon's guard stopped outside a grim-looking grey slate building, the Dundalk police station, and said to him, 'Master Jon, I want to show you something.' He took Jon inside to the first floor, where a row of barred windows looked onto a courtyard. The guard pointed to the wall at the end and said, 'That's where the British killed my friends.'

Jon grew up without militancy, only an insatiable interest in international affairs. By the age of four, he had become an avid newspaper reader. When he was five, one day when his parents were entertaining guests at lunch, he excitedly announced to the table the day's headline: 'Mussolini is dead! And he was hung upside down with his mistress!' Jon's mother was upset – not because she had any sympathy for the dictator, but because Jon, a tiny child, should not have known such a word as 'mistress', let alone pronouncing it in front of all the guests.

After Ampleforth, Jon went to Oxford to read Greats, the study of ancient Greek and Roman history, literature and philosophy. There he gained the ability to think deeply and unconventionally, and to acquire encyclopaedic knowledge on subjects that were also interesting to me. His curiosity took him around the world and to many unusual places. In 1968, in his twenties, he had gone behind the Iron Curtain to a conference in Bulgaria, to deliver a message for the philosopher Bertrand Russell, urging Moscow to withdraw its invading army from Czechoslovakia. To his exasperation, as soon as he opened his mouth, his host pulled the plug of his microphone out of the wall socket.

At the time I met him, Jon had just been to Russia, China, and South and North Koreas for the Korean War series he was writing. He had previously taught history in universities in Mexico, Italy and other European countries, and had written about the German/American film director Douglas Sirk, as well as the Italian director Pier Paolo Pasolini. He had co-authored a book on Japanese history.

Yet what attracted me was that he bore his achievements lightly and was never pompous – nor was he ever pedantic. As a friend commented, 'Jon doesn't do dull.'

Jon introduced me to the writer Emma Tennant, who was commissioning a series of short books for Penguin, the publishing house, about notable modern women. What about writing one on Mme Mao, Jiang Qing? Emma asked. At the mention of the name my mind flashed back to an extremely painful period of my life. In 1967, after my mother petitioned

Premier Zhou Enlai and secured my father's release from prison, the Tings, my parents' nemeses and the bosses of Sichuan, appealed to Jiang Qing, their patron, to put my father behind bars again. Mme Mao, they told the Red Guards, rose to her feet and said with tremendous indignation, 'For the man who dares to attack the Great Leader so blatantly, imprisonment, even the death sentence, is too kind! He must be thoroughly punished before we have done with him!' As a result, although my father was not rearrested, he was subjected to more brutal denunciation meetings, and served up to thugs who just wanted to beat up people for fun. At one of those beating sessions, half a dozen of them set upon my father, kicking him ferociously, forcing water into his mouth and nose and then stamping on his stomach until he passed out. Afterwards the organisers told my brothers and me to go and collect our father, and we borrowed a cart that was normally used for transporting coal to pull him to a nearby hospital.

No, I told Emma and Jon, I don't want to write about her. I did not tell them why: in those days I avoided talking about the past as I often could not hold back tears. But I could see that they understood. Emma asked: Is there another Chinese woman you would like to write about? I thought of Soong Ching-ling, wife of Sun Yat-sen, pioneer of republican China. She herself was the first modern Chinese female politician from the early 1920s. Emma said fine, and Jon offered to help with the writing.

In fact, I had no passion to write, but this was an opportunity to be with Jon. In that year when we were working together, my mind was more on Jon than on Ching-ling, fascinating though she was. I did my research quickly and superficially and gathered readily available information. In the name of writing the book, I drove to Jon's house almost every other day. Each time I hated the journey for being too long. Once when I arrived, in great haste to park the car, it just would not go into the space. When I finally pressed the doorbell, Jon appeared with a lovely teasing smile, 'I saw you were here twenty minutes ago.' I was not adept at driving and would give it up before long. The moment that clinched my decision was when I got into the driver's seat in Jon's car and, not having driven his car before, I asked him, 'Which pedal is the brake and which is the accelerator?' Alarmed, he delicately asked me to move over to the passenger seat.

In spring 1986, my small book was published. As it had received so little attention from me, it quite rightly received little attention from the readers. But it brought me closer to Jon.

During those months, I held back my feelings for him as I was married (and Jon had a girlfriend, a photographer). But the fact was that my marriage had become an increasingly unhappy one as Yee and I found ourselves having more arguments than laughter. Shortly after the publication of my little book (about which Yee offered some hurtful, but perfectly fair, remarks), we had another distressing exchange, and I suggested separation. He agreed, saying that perhaps we were both too headstrong and uncompromising to live under one roof. If he had sensed my feelings for Jon, he never mentioned it. We went out and had a very friendly meal, and were separated. I moved to a small flat in Notting Hill, then already vibrant but not yet trendy. We were later amicably divorced.

Soon after my separation, I went with Jon to Rome, his favourite city, where he had worked for a magazine and learned to speak perfect Italian. For our trip in summer 1986, he booked the Forum hotel overlooking the vast ruins. We arrived when it was dark, so I could not see much. During the stiflingly hot night, I got up to peer out from a window trying in vain to decipher what was hidden in the moonless darkness. Drowsily in the morning, I went up to the roof terrace for breakfast and all of a sudden saw Jon sitting bathed in sunshine at a corner table, with the magnificent Forum behind him, its heyday as the heart of Rome back in the seventh century BC still resonant. Instantly I fell in love with Rome.

Jon took me to the places that had been a part of his life. Every morning he had walked from his riverside flat in Traste-vere, the colourful and buzzing quarter of the city, crossed the Tiber, passed the great octagonal Temple of Hercules Victor and the humorous Bocca della Verità, to his office near Michel-angelo's Piazza del Campidoglio. I am in paradise! he had exclaimed to himself, As he swept me along from one splendid church, fountain, piazza to another, I felt the same. The cob-blestoned alleys threading Rome turned up marvels at every corner, and we could only express our excitement by embra-cing each other. I felt wildly happy, only occasionally letting a sense of guilt prick me as I had just ended a marriage.

Rome meant so much to me also because I saw in it the elu-sive ghost of vanished old China. Over there, most visible signs of Chinese civilisation had been erased from the face of the earth, without even ruins for imagination. Many of the destruc-tions were deliberate and recent – some I had witnessed myself. When I was very little, I had climbed up some big antique copper animals in a park in Chengdu; those animals disappeared when I was six in 1958, fed into furnaces to make steel as per Mao's order. When I entered my middle school in 1964, China's oldest public school still had a grand temple, a pair of carved and towering stone slabs, and many little statues of animals on dainty bridges over a small canal across the campus. Two years later, all the treasures were destroyed right in front of my eyes after Mao called for 'smashing up the old culture'. Also gone was the beautiful two-thousand-metre moat surrounding the ancient palace along which I had walked every day when I was in primary school. In the Cultural Revolution, it was drained of water and turned into an air-raid shelter against imagined attacks by 'US imperialists and Soviet revisionists'. Moreover, following Beijing's order to erect giant statues of Mao all over China in cities and towns, even the surviving parts of the palace, including the centuries-old lofty gate tower in the centre of Chengdu, on which I had stood with my family to watch a fireworks display, were wiped out. Bulldozers roared day and night, and bricks and tiles were cleared away wholesale, with not a speck of the old splendour left – so that Mao stood mighty on a vast empty space as if surveying the cultural void he had created. Having lived through the wrecking of one civilisation, I found solace immersing myself in another in Rome.

My mother spent much of 1987 dealing with all the procedures connected with a visit to London then. She had to get permission from her work unit (even though she had left her job by taking early retirement), to apply for her passport and exit visa from various government offices, and to obtain a hard-to-get visa to Britain.

At last, in February 1988, she arrived at London's Gatwick Airport, after a twenty-four-hour flight. As she wheeled out her luggage cart, her hair pulled tightly back, in a black silk jacket with mandarin collars and traditional knot buttons opening in the middle – a typical outfit for the 1980s – I rushed over to hug her. Jon took her cart and offered his newly acquired Chinese greetings: 'Mama, *nin-lei-ma* [are you tired]?' My mother thought he was asking her whether she was cold (*nin-leng-ma*), and pointed to her forehead, saying, 'Look at the sweat.' After this initial little misunderstanding, I noticed they had many things in common. Watching my mother unpack, I was amused that, like Jon, she wrapped her shoes in newspapers and put the inky package right next to her white shirts. To both of them, the papers seemed pristine clean.

I longed for my mother to have the best time and took her to all the tourist sites. Naturally we went to Harrods and other fancy shops. A decade of open-door policy had given the Chinese a taste of Western consumer goods, and the craze for them was overwhelming. I assumed that my mother would be delighted to see them on full display and that she would be thrilled to go shopping. But she followed me past rows of clothes hardly giving them a second glance. I thought this was because she didn't want me to spend money on her. In those days the Chinese had no hard currency, and while I was more than happy to do what I could for my family, my mother was always conscious that she and her other children should not be a financial burden to me.

One day I took her to Oxford Street, and when we got near its western end, her body language suggested a strong reluctance to go further. I said, 'Mama, are you really not interested in shopping? You are not just trying to save money for me, are you?' She replied, 'No, I am really not interested. You have already shown me the shops, I know what they look like, and that's enough.' She asked if I remembered ever going shopping with her in my twenty-six years in China. Indeed, we had never done that. It was true that there had not been much to shop for; but there had always been something. I would learn that my mother had shunned shopping for pleasure initially because it was associated with the limited life of women such as her mother, who were supposed to be contented with just wandering in shops. Then, after she joined the Communists, she had to adapt to their puritanical lifestyle (she was criticised by her comrades for using face creams), and positively steered herself away from shops. Yet my mother cared about how she looked, and always dressed attractively. She encouraged my sister and me to enjoy shopping and look pretty.

My mother knew I liked looking at or buying beautiful things if I could afford it, and now she apologised for being a 'spoil-sport' as we turned away from the edge of Oxford Street and walked into Hyde Park. I remarked that it would have been wonderful if Grandma were here; she would have loved the shops and would have had such fun in London. I vividly remembered going shopping with my grandma as a child. Before we set off, she prepared herself. First, she changed her clothes, even if they were all more or less the same; then, with a special expression of concentration, she looked into the mirror and drew her eyebrows ever so lightly with a charcoal pencil, before rubbing the tiniest amount of rouge on her cheeks. That was all she could do in those days as make-up was effectively banned. But my grandma compensated for what she could not do on her face with the way she did her hair. She had a carved wooden comb which she soaked in a bowl of water boiled with pomelo seeds. With the comb still moist she ran it through her long, thick hair, which seemed to grow soft and shiny as the comb slid through. Watching my grandma, I was mesmerised and always breathed deep to draw in the faint aroma of the citron fruit blossoms. After she twisted her hair into a bun at the nape of her neck, another scent, equally delicate and delicious, wafted over as she tucked into her hair a pair of unopened ivory-coloured magnolias, or a wide-open snow-white Cape jasmine. Until the Cultural Revolution, street vendors had sold those flowers for women's hair, and the few errands I had run for my grandma were to buy them.

My grandma never used shampoo, as she regarded chemicals as unnatural and harmful. Instead, she used dried fruit of the Chinese honey locust tree, which she would boil and rub until a sparkling white lather filled the bowl, and she would drop her mass of black hair into the brilliant froth. She bought the fruit in Chinese medicine shops, and also asked me to collect the fallen ones from a big honey locust tree in the compound. I loved picking up pieces of the fruit and rubbing them in the water, feeling blissful as the soft white foam rose to submerge my hands, which would remain faintly fragrant for a long time. Having my hair washed by my grandma in that heavenly lather was one of my most pleasurable childhood experiences.

I liked going out with my grandma. With flowers in her hair, and eyes smiling, she looked different, and people turned to admire her. She had a knack for spotting beautiful and unusual things. In the shops in Chengdu, occasionally, there were clothes that had been made for export but had been rejected because of flaws and were being sold on the domestic market. They were lustfully coveted and once my grandma grabbed a sky-blue cashmere cardigan for my mother. It had padded shoulders, which at first baffled me: Chinese beauty standards prescribed sloping shoulders, as a sign of feminine delicacy, and infant girls' shoulders were swaddled downwards tightly so that they would grow into the desired shape. As a baby, I had refused to allow my shoulders to be so restricted and had bawled incessantly until the binding was loosened and my arms and hands were let out. As a result, I have square shoulders, which were supposed to be masculine and unpretty, and for which I was much teased at school. The cardigan intended for export comforted me: in other places women even exaggerated the width of their shoulders!

Most things in the shops required ration coupons. Once, using all our family's available textile coupons, my grandma bought some pink floral cotton and made a dress each for my sister and me. The dresses were identical, but my sister's had a pocket and mine did not – the material had run out. I cried, and my grandma found some white cloth and made a pocket for me; but it did not look good, and I cried even more bitterly. It was one of the very few emotional outbursts from my early childhood that stuck in my memory. I later realised that the crying was not because I cared so much about the pocket, but because I feared that Grandma did not love me.

My love for my grandma grew more intense when I lived through the bleakest years of the Cultural Revolution with her and saw her anguish as my mother was put through endless abuse. I watched her faint twice, each time after hearing bad news about my mother, and each time in the most frightening way. One day our former maid, Hua, who had helped bring up my siblings and me, came to see us and said she had seen my mother. Grandma asked where and under what circumstances, so urgently that she shot up from her chair and gripped Hua's hand tight. Hesitantly, Hua said that she had seen my mother being paraded through the streets with a dozen others, wearing a white armband and a dunce's hat on her head (both carrying insults written in black ink). Victims being marched through city streets and country roads were another common sight in those days and always drew gangs of children who hurled stones at them. Before Hua finished, my grandma's whole body stiffened, and in front of my eyes, she fell backwards like a plank, the back of her head hitting the wooden floor with a loud bang. Hua and I were thrown into utter panic and screamed by her side 'Grandma! Grandma!' until she came to. In 1969, at the age of sixty, my grandma died of undiagnosed and untreated pain all over her body. When I was nursing her, I felt she seemed to be suffering all the pains that had been inflicted on her daughter. Later, when I recalled this episode, Jon observed that the falls very probably had done damage to her brain.

At my mention of Grandma on our walk in Hyde Park, sadness spread over my mother's face. She had been in detention when her mother was dying, and had been allowed home for only two days before Grandma died.

I kicked myself for bringing up the subject and started talking about the park, and how much I loved it. We were walking at the end of February when the giant trees were bare of foliage, their stark arms extending far and wide, filling me with awe. We reached the Italian Gardens, where around a group of fountains there were many urns. My mother paused, and pointing at a big flat round stone on the ground, perhaps the base of an urn that had come loose, exclaimed, 'Look, this looks just like a millstone! This was the kind of stone they used to put on a baby girl's feet to create the "three-inch golden lilies"!'

My mother's mind was clearly still on Grandma, whose feet had been cruelly bound into the so-called 'three-inch golden lilies'. Staring at the stone, I felt shocked, as I had never known exactly how foot-binding, the traditional Chinese practice for women, had been carried out. My mother began to explain. When my grandma was two years old, her mother, my great-grandmother, had put a millstone on top of her feet to break the bones of four toes, leaving only the big toe intact, and then, bending the four toes under the arch, she bound the feet tight with a long piece of cloth to stop the broken bones from recovering. The unendurable process lasted many years. My grandma could not crawl away from the stone or the excruciating pain; between moments when she passed out she begged her mother to stop, but my great-grandmother only wept and told her that unbound feet would ruin her life as she would not be able to find a husband when she grew up.

My mother's description petrified me. I had seen my grandma's feet naked when I was a child – after we had gone out shopping. The first thing she always did as soon as we got

Top: My parents in Communist uniforms en route from Manchuria to Sichuan, 1949. My mother, aged 18, would soon miscarry her first child due to the hardship of the cross-China march. **Right:** Her father Gen. Xue Zhiheng, chief of police in Beijing in the early 1920s. My grandma was his concubine. **Below:** My mother (left) with her mother and stepfather, Dr Xia (seated), c.1939. With them are Dr Xia's son and grandson, the only members of his large extended family not to have disowned him for marrying a former concubine.

My childhood. **Top:** Aged one (wearing a hat) in 1953, with my paternal grandmother to my left, Father's youngest sister behind, and Grandma to my right. My mother, smiling, holding my 2-year-old sister Xiaohong, and Aunt Junying cradling my one-month-old brother Jinming. **Below left:** Aged 6 and 12. **Below right:** Aged 14 in 1966 (standing first right), on pilgrimage to Beijing to see Mao with my friends, on Tiananmen Square, wearing our Red Guard armbands and all holding the Little Red Book.

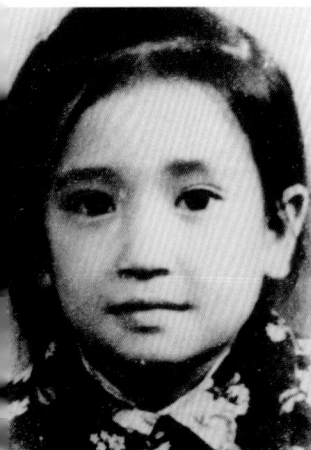

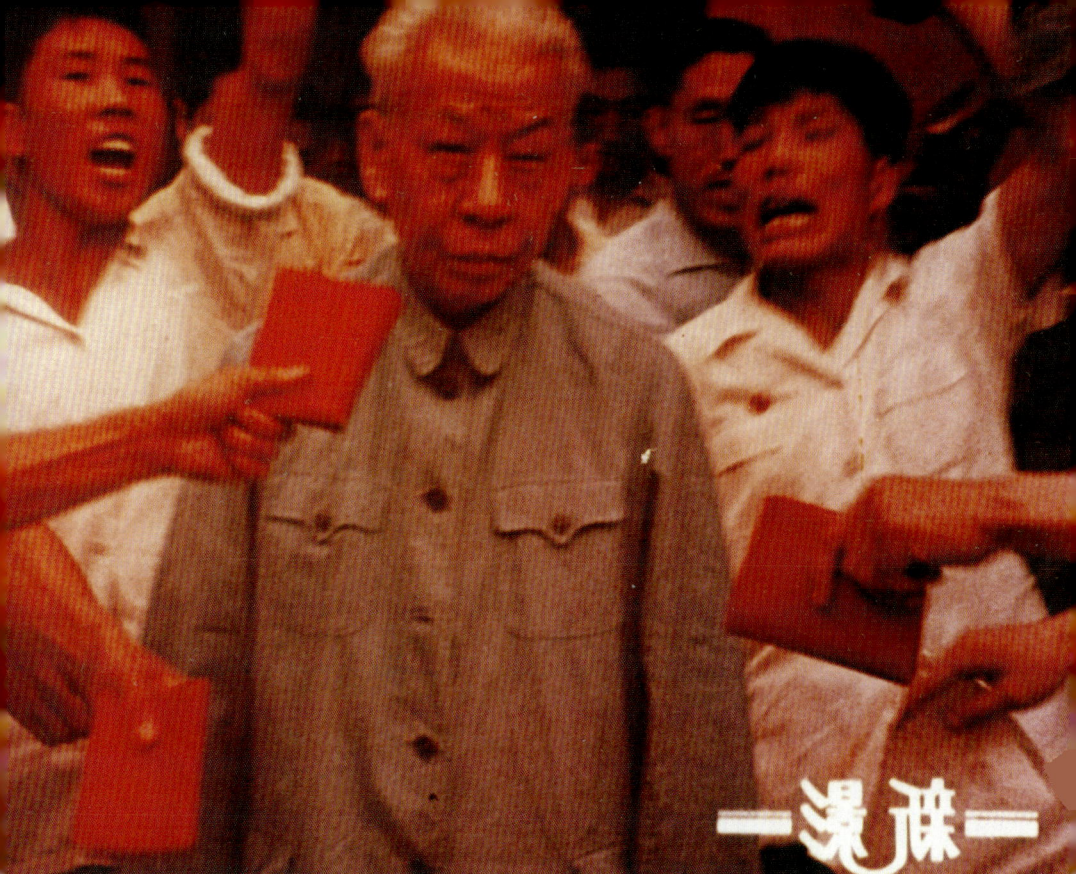

Top: President Liu Shaoqi, Mao's no. 1 target in the Cultural Revolution, being struck by crowds waving the Little Red Book. **Below:** Execution of 'counterrevolutionaries', watched by organised crowds.

Top: A denunciation meeting, a common sight during the Cultural Revolution. The victim was forced to bend double, his hair grotesquely cut as an insult, with words of condemnation on the plaque hanging from his neck. My parents were subjected to many such brutal meetings.
Below: My parents in quasi-labour camps in late 1971. My much-abused and much-aged father, with my brother Jinming, said, 'If I die like this, don't believe in the Communist Party any more.'

Top: At my father's funeral, 1975, supporting my mother with Jinming. Opposite us from left: my brother-in-law 'Specs', my brothers Xiaofang and Xiaohei, my sister Xiaohong. **Below:** My mother and I in her bedroom with Father's portrait. **Insert:** About to be expelled to the edge of the Himalayas in 1969. Me (second from right) and my siblings with Grandma and Aunt Junying (seated to the left and right), both of whom would die within a year.

Top left: Ancient Chengdu's last surviving gate tower, bulldozed to create a giant Mao statue and a vast empty square. **Top:** In 1989, the square would become the site of student demonstrations like Beijing's Tiananmen Square. **Below left:** With my mother on the eve of leaving China for Britain in 1978. We were both wearing 'Mao suits'. **Below right:** My Mao suit was replaced in London with clothes I bought from a jumble sale; wearing a dress from that sale at Marx's tomb, 1979.

Sichuan, my province, in the years after Deng Xiaoping started the reforms in 1978.
Top: Before private cars came into people's lives. **Middle:** Tea houses reopened in 1981 after being shut for 15 years. **Below:** A stall at a country market selling ingredients for Chinese medicine. A village dentist at work.

Insert: I gained a PhD in linguistics from the University of York in 1982 and became the first person from Communist China to obtain a doctorate from a British university. With my supervisor Professor Bob Le Page. **Top:** I returned home to Chengdu in 1983 and enjoyed newly permitted dancing with my family in my mother's small flat. From right: me, Specs, Xiaofang, my mother, Jinming's then girlfriend and Xiaohei. **Below:** Rowing in the Lake District. I found freedom and happiness in Britain.

home was to soak her feet in a bowl of hot water, when she would close her eyes with a big sigh of relief. Her feet were horrendous to look at. Only the big toes were normal; the other toes under the arch were limp as if there were no bones in them. Once I saw her flipping the lifeless toes up and cutting the toenails that would have been digging into the flesh of her soles. My grandma said to me, 'People say you will get over the pain. But you never get over it.' And yet, on those crippled feet, my grandma hobbled busily all day long, looking after me and the rest of the family. Listening to my mother in Hyde Park, recalling how my grandma had died in unbearable pain, I felt a surge of overwhelming emotion. I was ashamed that I knew so little about her life, and pressed my mother to tell me more.

My mother had in fact been longing to tell me about the life of my grandma and about her own life. In the last few years, having left her job, she had had time to think and had thought a lot about the past. She knew that when I was a child I liked writing, and was hoping I would be interested in writing the story of my family. But when she tentatively suggested the idea a couple of times, I showed no enthusiasm, and instead grumbled that I already had so many things to do and that I had no free time. Deep down, I think, I did not want to revisit any painful memories. I wanted to forget about the past. My mother said no more. But I noticed that she was not having the time of her life in London as I had hoped. I had put it down to her not speaking the language and not having friends, and tried to think of ways to entertain her. She put on a cheerful face, but I detected something subdued in her mood.

Now I understood that she had been hurt by my apparent indifference. The moment I showed interest, my mother sprang to life. She started talking, and could not stop. I told

Jon some of her stories and he was riveted, telling me that they were truly extraordinary. He asked many questions, which sparked off more curiosity in me and brought out more details and stories from my mother. One day Jon came to my flat with the photocopy of a page from a *Who's Who in Republican China*. It was a photo of my grandfather, General Xue Zhiheng, police chief of Beijing in the early 1920s, in full regalia of the time. My mother was overcome by excitement: she had never seen a picture of her father and did not know what he looked like (he had died when she was two years old). Looking at my grandfather's photo, I felt more intrigued about the past, and bought a tape recorder, which I installed on my black dining table, next to a bunch of early daffodils. Spring had quietly arrived while we were engrossed in our conversations. My mother sat at the table all day long, speaking into the recorder when I was out working. The stories must have churned in her head for a long time, as they came out perfectly organised and fluent. By the time she left London, she had left me sixty hours of recordings.

While I was listening to my mother, I noticed in particular that despite her having lived a life of suffering and torment, her stories were never depressing. Underlying them was a fortitude that was uplifting. It also seemed to me that my mother knew writing was where my talent, and my heart, lay, and was encouraging me to fulfil myself by supplying me with material.

And so a long-suppressed passion was stirred. I realised that I had always loved writing, and wanted to be a writer. It was just that when I was growing up, nearly all writers were condemned, and I could not even dream of being one. I recalled writing my first poem on my sixteenth birthday and having to destroy it by flushing it down the toilet. But I also remembered that the desire to write did not leave me. In the years that followed, when I was in the countryside working as a peasant, and in a factory as an electrician, when I was spreading manure in the paddy fields and checking supplies on top of electricity poles, I was always writing in my head with an imaginary pen. Now, inspired by my mother, I felt an urge to put pen to paper.

In August 1988, my mother left for Chengdu. I had asked her whether she would like to live with me in London, and she had said no. She told me that as she spoke no English, and as she was too old to learn (she had tried and had failed), she could not live a proper life here. Without the language, she felt she would have to be dependent on me. Life for her had to be active and independent.

When we were saying goodbye, my mother told Jon and me that she was grateful to Jon for being so interested in our stories, and that she was sure with his help I would write a good book. She had spotted Jon's tremendous strength underneath his gentle exterior and noticed his exceptional sensitivity. She had commented to me that it might have had something to do with his childhood relationship with his mother, intense and protective, an experience she could identify with – and Jon had said that my mother was right. He was touched and embraced her long and hard. I rarely felt so fired up as, immediately after my mother's departure, I settled at my desk with her sixty tapes by my side.

9

Wild Swans Taking Wing

(1988–91)

M y mother's recordings were superbly clear and struc-
tured, and I translated them directly into English. Based
on her memoir, and on my own first twenty-six years in China,
I wrote a synopsis with Jon's help for my book, eventually titled
Wild Swans: Three Daughters of China. It is the story of my
grandma, my mother and myself through China's turbulent
twentieth century. The publishers Simon & Schuster in America and HarperCollins in Britain bought the rights to the book
and scheduled to publish it in two years. When my mother
received my jubilant postcard, she was as elated as I was and
hardly slept that night. What made her most excited, she told
me, were the words Jon had added on the card, that ours would
be 'a great book'. My mother shared with me a deep trust in
Jon's judgement. We all agreed that I should give up all my
commitments except my teaching job at SOAS, University of
London, to concentrate on writing. She would help: answering
my questions, finding additional information and securing

witnesses for interviews when I came to China. She offered to go to all the main locations to set things up.

I was glued to my desk for most of the next two years. But in the evenings, when Jon came over, we lay together on the sofa after supper, watching old movies. I was busier than ever, yet never more contented. I wrote to my mother every few days, and she supplied more information fulsomely and promptly. She gave me one crucial piece of advice: to keep to personal stories and not attempt to write a history book. She told me that my knowledge of the history of modern China had been heavily influenced by indoctrination, citing as an example one of my questions to her in which I had used the phrase 'the three-year Natural Calamity'. Meaning bad weather, this was the Party's standard euphemism for the Great Famine of 1958–61, in which tens of millions of people died. Although I already had some idea that the cause of the famine was not bad weather, my understanding was woolly, and I was still using the regime's term out of habit. My mother, who knew more about the truth than I did at the time, was afraid my book might be marred by propaganda.

Thanks to her wise counsel, I stuck to our lives in *Wild Swans*, and kept background information to a minimum. Later, after I had spent more than a decade researching a biography of Mao, with Jon, and had revised my previous conceptions drastically, for a moment I got into a panic thinking that I might have to revise *Wild Swans*. I reread the book, and was hugely relieved that it was truly a book of personal stories, and comments about the general background were few and far between, none of which needed rewriting – although a few expressions could have been rephrased. My mother's wisdom helped to ensure that *Wild Swans* would stand the test of time.

*

In January 1989, I was granted British citizenship. By the previous September I had lived in Britain for ten years, which had qualified me to apply. I had immediately handed in my application, and it was soon approved. To this generous and kind country I owe my happy life, and my first and foremost feeling towards it was – and is and will always be – gratitude. Jon went with me to the Passport Office to collect my new passport, and outside the building, in beautiful sunshine, he took a picture of me beaming as I held up the passport.

In April, we went to China to research *Wild Swans*. At the time we were not yet married. My mother was worried that marriage to a foreigner might be an obstacle to getting interviews from some people: a former boss had turned her down when she mentioned Jon. While people in big cities like Chengdu had begun to accept, even desire, marriages to Westerners, in small towns or less open provinces, fear of contact with foreigners was still commonplace. My mother had another concern, that people who had opposed my marriage to Yee seven years before might gossip and stir up trouble if they knew I was divorced. Divorce was frowned upon back then. She did not want to draw attention to the issue of my marriage, so that I could conduct my research smoothly.

Still, my mother agreed to Jon staying with me in her flat, even though as a foreigner he was supposed to stay in a hotel. She just asked him to remain in our bedroom when visitors turned up. One day Auntie Deng, Deng Xiaoping's half-sister, came for a chat and stayed for over two hours. Jon was cooped up in the bedroom dying to use the toilet but could not as he would have to pass through the sitting room. Afterwards we decided to introduce him as my husband. I was pleasantly surprised that few people seemed to care about my divorce or remarriage. Everybody was now busy making money, with immeasurably more things to occupy their minds. As for Auntie Deng, the moment she heard about it, she invited us all – Jon, me and Mother – to dinner that evening. Her flat was in the old compound, and like a true auntie, she spent most of her time in the kitchen and came to the table only to urge us to eat, and eat more. It was late when we finished, and she courteously insisted on seeing us to the compound gate to say goodbye. As we walked along the path in the dark, a figure appeared in the distance coming towards us. Auntie Deng lurched like a shot into the shadows of the trees, and, reappearing a few moments later, she said that she was sorry she could not go further with us as there were bound to be more people nearer the gate. 'I can't be seen with a foreigner,' she said ruefully. We said a hasty goodnight. Afterwards my mother told us about the injunction that Auntie Deng needed Politburo authorisation before meeting foreigners.

The Party was very much on our minds as Jon and I had come to China on the eve of a historic moment. Student demonstrations were about to break out at the announcement of the death of Hu Yaobang, the former general secretary of the Party (and old friend of Auntie Deng), who had been forced to resign two years earlier for being too tolerant of people demanding greater freedom. Hu had died of a heart attack on 15 April, four days before we arrived. And we saw demonstrations building up in Chengdu, as they did in other cities across China, especially in Beijing. The huge empty square below the giant statue of Mao, created by destroying a grand old palace gate tower, now became the perfect place for crowds of protesters to gather, and there they mourned Hu, venting their anger at his sacking and expressing their aspiration for more liberty.

On 26 April, while out on a bike, Jon saw large numbers of agitated youths in the square. As he watched, a middle-aged local man turned and spat forcefully at him. Probably the man was not a supporter of the students and hated what he regarded as 'dirty linen' being paraded in front of a foreigner; or he might have thought that Jon as a Westerner had had a hand in stirring up the students – which was the Party's standard assertion. That evening Jon and I went to a friend's for dinner, and when we returned home, quite late, my mother was waiting in the sitting room. She said in an urgent voice that Jon must leave her home, as his staying was against the rules and could cause him trouble. That day's *People's Daily* editorial, which everyone knew was the voice of the Party, had condemned the students. As the newspaper alleged that they had been manipulated by the 'black hand', which often meant Westerners, Jon's presence in Chengdu was bound to draw unpleasant attention. My mother said that she had organised a car to take him to the Jinjiang Hotel. The hotel was on a boulevard extending from the Mao statue and the square straight down to the south, but with many roadblocks along the way, the car had to go round and round through alleyways. When he finally arrived, it was after midnight. To his immense relief, and no small surprise, the hotel receptionist asked no questions, not even about the fact that he had no luggage. The old tight control that had been loosened by a decade of reforms could not be reinstated at a snap of a finger.

The next day my mother and I were waiting for Jon outside her block of flats, when a woman approached me with a piece of paper, apparently asking the way. I was about to take it when my mother snatched it from her hand, positioning herself between us, and saying to her, 'She [meaning me] doesn't live here. Give it to me.' I saw some incomprehensible squiggles on the paper and the woman grabbed it back and walked away. Afterwards my mother warned that I must not take any paper from a stranger, especially now that I had become a British citizen: there was the danger of being accused of receiving state secrets. My mother never relaxed her alertness about my safety in China.

While the students started more emotional demonstrations, enraged by the condemnation of the *People's Daily*, we had to leave Chengdu for Yibin for the next leg of our research. Before we left, my brother Xiaohei gave Jon and me a parting gift, taking us to the No. 1 People's Hospital to see a doctor – not for health reasons but to have our futures divined: the doctor was a fortune teller. Above the hospital's main entrance hung a banner: 'Keeping state secrets is every citizen's duty!' Even sick people had to be vigilant – although it was never spelled out what constituted 'state secrets'. By the side of the entrance stood a billboard telling people about AIDS with illustrations of 'Don'ts', one of which read: 'Don't use blood and blood products from overseas.' (And 'Strictly ban homosexuality.')

As we went into the doctor's room, he stood up to greet us, in his white doctor's coat, looking worried when his eyes fell on Jon. Hesitantly, he said, 'I don't know about telling the fortune of a foreigner; it could get me into trouble. I have already got into big trouble before, telling the fortune of . . .' Mao, as it turned out. In 1968, at supper with an old friend, after precious alcohol (strictly rationed) had loosened his tongue, he had told his friend that Mao would die in 1976. Back home the friend told his wife, after swearing her to secrecy. A few days later, the friend and his wife had a big row, and she went straight to the police and denounced her husband. The doctor was thrown into prison – until 1976, after Mao died (and his prediction was proved right). He cautiously and vaguely muttered a few words about our future lives, telling us nothing interesting or ominous.

About one hundred and thirty miles to the south of Chengdu, Yibin, my father's and my birthplace, was a lush region with tea groves and terraced rice paddies, which captivated Jon. We hired a four-wheel-drive car, a Cherokee, new in the country and hugely coveted as roads were bad. The young driver was immensely proud of his vehicle, even though it was not his – there were no private cars yet. He cleaned it assiduously at every opportunity.

The city's population had grown to over two hundred thousand, and there were no student demonstrations. Instead we went to a most tranquil place – the Bamboo Forest, or the Bamboo Sea, as the locals call it, where bamboos of all types densely cover miles of mountains, their continuous swaying along the contours of the undulating peaks and valleys indeed looking like the waves of an emerald sea. Jon said he had not seen anything so magical, and that 'someone must come and shoot a film here'. Years later, the Oscar-winning film *Crouching Tiger, Hidden Dragon* did shoot some memorable scenes in the Bamboo Sea.

We had emotional meetings with my father's family, friends and former colleagues who told me many things about him that even my mother did not know. My father had been born into the family of a well-to-do textile manufacturer, as my paternal grandfather, together with his brother, had a flourishing business. But the two brothers' former employer, for whom they had worked when they were children, accused them of stealing money to start their own factory, and brought a lawsuit against them. The case lasted many years, and everyone connected with the court demanded bribes. Their business went bankrupt, and both brothers died young from mental and physical exhaustion. Their children had to struggle to make their own living. At the age of thirteen, my father left school and started doing odd jobs. Like most child labourers euphemistically called 'apprentices', he worked long hours and received no pay, only a bed and meagre meals. He was hungry all the time, and one day ate a cold sweet potato in his sister's kitchen. The sister, who was married to a schoolteacher and was supporting their mother, was poor herself, and she scolded my father: 'It's hard enough for me to support our mother. I can't afford to feed a brother as well.' My father was so hurt he ran out of the house and never returned.

His loathing of corruption drove him to the Communist underground in Yibin, after which he travelled to Yan'an, Mao's headquarters during the war against Japan, in northwest China near the Gobi Desert. A decade later, in 1949, my father returned to Yibin as the first Communist governor of the region. Leaving home poor and put-upon and returning a powerful man: this was the fairy-tale dream for Chinese men and their families. But my father alienated all the members of his family by carrying to an extreme his determination not to do them what he regarded as 'favours'. Soon after he had refused to transfer my mother to a better hospital to deliver me safely, he gave away his family house to a school that needed accommodation for its teachers. The house was large, as it had been built for the households of two brothers, and it had a big garden at the back – I could tell how huge the grounds were as our car drove for quite some time around and outside the walls. During the drive, my mother pointed out the areas inside the wall, where there had been a field of winter plums, where groves of bamboo had grown, and where a turtle lived in a pond with lotuses. She had stayed there when she first came to Yibin from Manchuria in early 1950, and had been enchanted by the place. It was where she had gone to kowtow to and make friends with the spirits of the plants.

I longed to see the garden, and I wished I could go back in time and take just a peek at the house itself, with its latticed windows and elegant furniture made of deep-red padauk wood. My mother said, 'Your [paternal] grandmother and Aunt Junying loved the house so much. There was not a speck of dust anywhere, and all the windows were gleaming.' I thought of the heartbreak they must have felt when they moved out after my father had given the house away. His argument had been that it was unjust for such a big house to be inhabited by only three people – even though they were his mother, an unmarried sister, Aunt Junying, and a disabled brother. My mother had been infuriated, and my father's large extended family were enraged. They told him that it was he who was being unjust. The house was home to all of them; they all adored it, and had not sold it even when they were starving. My father had no right to give away what was theirs, they complained. But a Communist boss had that power. While the teachers and many other locals were delighted, my paternal grandmother moved into a small house that my father had found for her, unhappy but uncomplaining.

In Yibin in 1989, I had a feeling that the family had long stopped being angry at my father about the house. The decades in between had shown that they would not have been able to hold on to the property and would have had to give it up sooner or later. All private houses had in effect been taken over by the state at different stages. In the post-Mao era, when China seemed to be embracing capitalism and allowing private ownership, some former owners tried to get their properties back; but virtually none succeeded. The few who did were largely because the local governments wanted them to pay for the costly repairs, after which they often came under pressure to 'donate' the houses to some good causes. When we were in Yibin, in fact, a rumour was circulating that we had come back 'to reclaim old family property – with a foreigner', which implied that some foreign power was backing our 'claim'. To avoid any misunderstanding, my mother did not ask to see the house, although I was very disappointed.

My mother thought of everything and took all precautions to keep Jon and me safe. In that area, few people had ever set eyes on a foreigner, and Jon was a colossal object of curiosity. One day we visited a bustling country market, where for the first time I saw a big variety of odd-looking dried worms for Chinese medicine. In bamboo baskets, fat pigs were being carried on shoulder-poles by peasants to the slaughterhouse. There were even dead rats on display, serving as advertisements for packs of poison on sale which had killed them. Jon exchanged a few words with a much-wrinkled elderly man wearing a turban – a local necessity against the sun and the damp air – and a long apron to protect his brand-new blue 'Sunday best'. They were both laughing. But the staring of some other people was less friendly. My mother kept explaining to the crowds, raising her voice: 'A foreign friend – this is a foreign friend', while conducting us as swiftly as possible towards the office of the local government, which stood on raised ground up a flight of stairs. We sat outside the main gate, and the peasants below came close to watch Jon. A few bold children climbed up the steps and touched his nose. He good-humouredly played with them, which the crowd seemed to find highly amusing.

Out of the blue I heard loudspeakers on moving trucks. This had been a familiar sound during the Cultural Revolution, announcing that 'criminals' were being paraded as a warning to onlookers. I had seen my father on such a truck one day, his hands tied behind his back and a plaque hanging from his neck declaring that he was a counterrevolutionary. Two men behind him were trying to push his head down, and my father was struggling to lift his head – a scene that had given me such a piercing pain in my heart. Now I stood up to see what was happening. A line of the same kind of open trucks were driving through the market, again parading 'criminals', each with two men behind holding their guns at the ready. This time, judging from the signs around their necks, they were smugglers of opium, women or children, en route to be executed. China used the death penalty actively, but I was surprised to see that it still exhibited people in this way before their execution, given that many other barbaric customs had been abolished in the reforms. I picked up Jon's video camera. My mother slapped my wrist hard, almost causing me to drop the camera, and hissed, 'What are you doing? Do you want to die here?' She was right: the crowds could easily become volatile and even turn nasty against us. As it happened, they took one look at the trucks and turned back to Jon, who was obviously more of a novelty.

Our next destination was Lulong, some hundred and fifty miles east of Beijing, where my grandfather, General Xue, came from. We travelled fifteen hundred miles north by train. Our compartment was called 'soft sleepers', the equivalent of first class. This comfort was reserved for officials above the grade of 14, which my mother would normally not have been entitled to as she was Grade 15, thanks to my father's earlier anti-corruption crusade. Every time she encountered such dis-crimination, she felt anger towards my father, even as she loved him. On this trip she had no problems: all the privileges enjoyed by high officials applied to foreigners. The three of us had the soft sleeper carriage all to ourselves while the Chinese masses were packed in the carriages of the 'hard seats', with the slightly less disadvantaged in the 'hard sleepers'. As my mother settled luxuriously into her soft seat, with fragrant tea steaming from a fine porcelain mug, and with all sorts of delicious food to boot, she laughed to Jon and me, 'There are after all advan-tages to being associated with a foreigner!'

Only with a foreign son-in-law (and a daughter) could my mother stay in a hotel room with a private bath, which was not available to people of her grade and below. But the baths were not what one might expect. In Lulong, our hotel was the best there was. The county had been officially 'opened' to foreign-ers the year before, but Jon was probably its very first foreign visitor. After leaving our luggage in our rooms, we set off to call on our relatives. My mother had set up the meeting the year before when she had come to prepare our trip. On seeing

Jon coming out of the hotel with us, the local boss had a very troubled look on his face and whispered to my mother, 'You see, it's not convenient for a foreigner to come with us. You know the conditions of the home of your cousin . . . It's not good to let a foreigner see – you know, see the dark side of socialism.' Jon was annoyed when I translated for him, but resignedly went back upstairs to our room, saying to himself, 'I will have a bath instead.' He opened the shower curtain and saw a bathtub filled with rubble and yellowish dirty water with cigarette stubs, and said to me later: 'Talk about the dark side of socialism, it is right here in our room.'

Compared to the undulating hilly greenness of Yibin, Lulong was a land of brown-yellow earth, flat, drab, boundless, interrupted only by clumps of poplars, whose part-green, part-silver leaves shimmered in the sun. General Xue, my grandfather, born here in 1876 into the family of a schoolteacher, and rising to be the police chief of Beijing, had designed and built an enormous mansion outside the town. My mother and I were taken to it, driven on hard, stony roads, coughing as the sandy dust whipped up by our car flew into our faces. Like virtually all of China's private houses, the mansion had been confiscated and divided up to accommodate multiple households over many years and was now largely uninhabitable for lack of repairs. Only one corner was lived in – by our relatives. For their connection with General Xue, categorised under Mao as an undesirable 'warlord', they had been treated as 'class enemies'. Even without a foreigner, they did not invite my mother and me into their home, which, judging by what we could see outside, was no more than a hovel. Instead, they came out, greeted us and showed us around, describing the place with such nostalgia that I could vividly picture its old grandeur: two armed guards standing on each side of the front gate, next to a pair of large stone lions; and in the square in front, eight other statues for tying up horses, carved in the shapes of elephants and monkeys, animals lucky for the sounds of their names.

It was to this place that, in 1932, when he was dying, General Xue had summoned my grandma, his concubine from Manchuria some two hundred miles away, to bring their one-year-old daughter, my mother, to see him. When my grandma arrived, her daughter was taken away from her and she was told the child would call the wife 'Mother' – as was the tradition for the children of concubines. My grandma realised that she could lose her daughter forever, and one night 'kidnapped' the baby and fled the mansion, travelling back to Manchuria.

My mother had told me in London about my grandma's escape, but only here did I fully register just how difficult it had been for my grandma: the well-guarded mansion, the long, hard road strewn with sharp rocks to the nearest railway station – and her crippled feet. I saw my grandma in my mind's eye, a petite, frail figure, struggling to walk in the most inhospitable environment, sustained by one thought: not to lose her daughter. And I understood better how the Cultural Revolution had killed her by torturing my mother.

Our relatives showed us around the grounds, now a large, grassy field encircled by tall poplars, surprisingly green amid the brown-yellow earth. A large pond lay in the middle. It was like an oasis in a desert, and I imagined horses or even camels drinking and strolling there. The North China Plain to the east ends here, and visible at a distance to the west was the silhouette of the mountains on which the Great Wall stands. One day we all, including Jon, went to climb to the wall – not the part outside Beijing that had been smoothed out for tourists, but the savage, awe-inspiring remnants in the wild rocky mountains. We were accompanied by a dozen escorts, one of whom, a young man, walked closely behind Jon. I spotted a pistol on his hip when he was climbing. What did they think

Jon might do? Call for a revolution on top of the Great Wall in the wilderness, with not a soul in sight?

From Lulong going north, we crossed the pass where the Great Wall sweeps down to meet the sea, and entered Manchuria. We stopped first in Yixian, birthplace of my mother and grandma, a county with a population of perhaps a hundred thousand; and afterwards in neighbouring Jinzhou, where my mother grew up, an industrial city whose inhabitants exceeded 1 million. In both places, I was shocked by the depressing monotony of greyness, by the overwhelming sand, dust and debris, which made the cities look like giant abandoned building sites. All the old houses my mother had lived in were decrepit, including the elegant house General Xue had bought my grandma, in which she had given birth to my mother in loneliness, and the huge house inhabited by the extended family of my step-grandfather, Dr Xia, where as a child my mother had been bullied mercilessly because her mother had been a concubine. While the sorrowful memories were still fresh, the houses had deteriorated beyond recognition. 'Well, it's just as well everything is gone,' my mother said.

She took us to see the mud hut in Jinzhou where she first lived with her mother and Dr Xia after the doctor had left his family and moved there. As Dr Xia had given all his possessions to his children, he could only afford a room in a slum. The mud hut was no longer there, but the site gave me a fright as it was below the level of a big river on the other side of a high bank, suggesting a permanent threat of being swallowed by floods, especially in the spring when the ice thawed. And yet, living there had been the happiest time for my grandma, as Dr Xia loved her, and she had her daughter with her all the time. My mother was happy, too: there was warmth all around her and no tension. Standing on the bank and looking down at the abandoned slum, my mother said that my grandma had told her, 'If you have love, even plain cold water is sweet.'

We went to visit Grandma's brother, Yulin, and his wife. They had just been allowed back from twenty years of exile in the northern wilderness, where they had been sent because Yulin had had an identity card showing he was a Kuomintang intelligence officer. In fact, my grandma had bought him the card so that he could escape being conscripted into the army in the civil war, and he did nothing for the Kuomintang. But he was still punished. Now he and his wife were back, and were given a home that was an earthen hut next to a rubbish dump. It consisted of two tiny rooms and we went into one. My grand-aunt, whose sallow and ravaged face matched the street scene outside, declined to meet Jon, even though he was right there. She was terrified that she might one day be accused of 'associating with foreigners', a deadly accusation of Mao's time, still casting a black shadow. My mother spent a lot of time persuading her, promising that, if there was any trouble, she could say she had been 'conned' into the meeting by my mother. Grand-aunt finally agreed, and Jon joined our conversation. We talked about my grandma.

Dr Xia was an excellent doctor with a high reputation, and soon after he came to Jinzhou he was able to set up his own clinic and the little family moved into a bigger house. My grandma invited her kid brother to live with them and helped him find a wife. While Yulin worked in Dr Xia's medicine shop, his wife did much of the work around the house. As my grandma ran the household as its mistress, my grand-aunt felt put upon by her sister-in-law. When the Communists took Jinzhou, they urged everyone whom they defined as an 'employee' to speak up about 'oppression and exploitation' by the employer, and my grand-aunt's grudges against my grandma were given a political framework. In 1951, in Mao's first political campaign after seizing power, 'the suppression of counterrevolutionaries', a former suitor of my mother, Hui-ge, was publicly executed for having been a colonel in the local Kuomintang army. (My parents had gone to Sichuan by then.) My grandma, who had liked the young colonel and would have preferred him to be her son-in-law, went to the place of his execution to collect Hui-ge's body. It was a freezing winter day and the ground was white with deep snow, stained dark red by the blood. She had brought a long piece of red silk in which to wrap the bullet-riddled corpse, and had hired professional undertakers to give him a decent burial. My grand-aunt denounced her to the authorities for harbouring sympathy towards the Kuomintang and making complaints about the Communists. The Party gathered the neighbours to 'struggle against' my grandma. Luckily, the neighbours were nice, and my grandma had a Communist daughter. She was let off the hook easily. But the relationship between the two sisters-in-law was wrecked.

My grandma had related this episode to my mother after joining my parents in Sichuan. When my mother left Jinzhou, she had been worried sick about her daughter, and so had travelled alone across China to be with her. On the thousand-mile-long journey, she had taken train, boat, trucks, whenever possible, and walked when there was no other transportation, hobbling on her crippled feet, and narrowly dodging bullets several times as the civil war still raged.

My mother had told me in London the story about Grand-aunt. I did not bring it up in my interview with her. Slightly to my surprise, Grand-aunt talked on about how kind my grandma had been to her and her husband, giving them shelter and jobs, so they never had to starve (she had come from a poverty-stricken family). There was not a hint of a grudge. Clearly the subsequent decades of suffering had put the hardship of heavy housework in context. My mother asked me to give them some money at the end of the visit; I did, of course, as generously as I could.

During the conversation, Grand-aunt started to relax with Jon. She showed us into the other room, their bedroom, most of which was taken up by a big brick bed – the *kang* – heated from below to cope with the severe Manchurian winter. One side of the *kang* was the outer wall itself with a window, and my mother crouched down on the other side to demonstrate how the family had used the beds as shields against the rain of bullets when the Communists were attacking Jinzhou in a key battle in the civil war in 1948.

My mother, then a seventeen-year-old student, had been working for the Communist underground and had organised student demonstrations inside the city in coordination with the assaulting Communists. She was taken to the Kuomintang martial law headquarters and told to 'confess' to her Communist connection and name names. She shook her head. Her captors tried to scare her by taking her to a torture chamber, and even putting her up against a high wall in the weed-strewn backyard of the headquarters, telling her they were about to execute her. Still she refused, surprising her captors that she was not scared witless.

The man responsible for my mother's arrest had been the Kuomintang political supervisor of her school, who then fled to the island of Taiwan, where Chiang Kai-shek had set up his new base after he was defeated by Mao. In 1988, when my mother was in Jinzhou staying with Grand-uncle to prepare for my trip, she spotted him walking out of a smart new hotel, just across the street, a stone's throw from Grand-uncle's hovel and the rubbish dump. He had come for a visit from Taiwan, and was surrounded by fawning locals, to whom he was showing off photos of his fine house and shiny car.

During our trip, my mother stayed with Jon and me in that hotel, which was deemed fit to receive foreigners. Every day local officials laid out banquets to entertain potential investors from overseas, who they hoped would help transform the city. Westerners were rare, and the businessmen mostly came from Taiwan, former Kuomintang personnel like the political supervisor of my mother's school. All over China, they were returning as honoured guests. As the Kuomintang period was called 'Before Liberation' and Communist rule 'After Liberation', a popular jingle emerged:

'Forty years of march forward After Liberation,
We march back to Before Liberation.'

In early May 1989, my mother, Jon and I left Manchuria and travelled south to Beijing. Unbeknown to us, we were about to witness 'Tiananmen' – the biggest ever student demonstration in Communist China, crushed by rolling tanks. When we arrived in the capital, there was no hint of upheaval or violence. We had no greater preoccupation than our camera being against the sun from a window when I tried to take a picture of our dinner with my mother's friends. As the two parts of the curtain would not stay closed to shut out the sun, Jon leaped to his feet, darted to the window and held them together for our photo-taking, straining to keep his arm out of the picture. Everybody burst into appreciative laughter, exchanging remarks to the effect that my foreign husband was a lovely man. My mother laughed with pride. Then, like true tourists, Jon and I went up the newly opened Tiananmen Gate, on which Mao had hailed the masses on the square. For fun, Jon posed in front of the balustrades above the giant portrait of Mao, and waved to me, while down below tourists milled about on Tiananmen Square.

In a few days' time the square would be transformed. Mikhail Gorbachev, president of the Soviet Union, was scheduled to visit Beijing on 15 May to normalise the frayed diplomatic relations, and the global media would be there. Leaders of the student demonstrations decided this was a golden opportunity to publicise their demands to the world. They occupied Tiananmen Square and began a hunger strike there on 13 May. On Chang'an Avenue that led to the square, we saw students on bicycles racing in that direction, some wearing white headbands with black-inked words 'Hunger strike!'.

My mother, who had led student demonstrations herself forty years before, saw disaster coming. The occupation of Tiananmen Square by a massive crowd, which forced the government to relocate the ceremony for Gorbachev's state visit, would seem to suggest to the world – and the Chinese people – that the Party was losing control, an impression it would definitely not wish to convey. The Party would want to assert its control, by whatever means, certainly harsher than those of the Kuomintang. 'The Communist Party is not made of tofu [symbol of softness],' she said to us with apprehension as she boarded a train for Chengdu the day after Gorbachev's arrival.

Jon and I headed back to England that same day. In London I commented on BBC and Sky TV about what was happening in Tiananmen Square and expressed my support for the demonstrators' aspirations, which boiled down to political reform. After the regime sent in tanks – which I learned was on the orders of Deng Xiaoping and which caused the death and injury of hundreds and perhaps thousands of students and other citizens – on 4 June, I condemned the bloody act in the strongest language on television. This terminated my hitherto amicable relationship with the Chinese embassy, whose door I never crossed again until almost twenty years later, when another event compelled me to go in. Mindful that what I said could bring trouble to my family, I stopped writing to them for a long time. (Meanwhile, in disgust, my friend Clive Lindley ended all his business ventures in China.)

In spring 1990, I was diagnosed with breast cancer. I hid the news from my mother, but she heard it from a visitor. She fainted on the spot, and while falling knocked over a cupboard. She told me afterwards that she felt as if her soul were floating out of her body, which apparently is a kind of sensation some people feel when they are scared to the extreme. This was the only time my mother felt so frightened. When she came to, she was in agony, blaming herself for making me work too hard. She telephoned me, using up more than a month's salary. I explained to her that my cancer was of a mild type and had been caught early; I had had surgery and was having radiotherapy; I was not anxious about it. My optimism and calm voice reassured her. She gathered her wits and gave me very useful advice. My mother was knowledgeable about health matters, having grown up in a medical family.

The most important thing my mother did for me was to remove my anxieties, which she seemed to have a knack of sensing. She knew I was worried about what might happen to her in China after the publication of *Wild Swans*, which would not please the regime. After Tiananmen, the political climate changed for the worse. Student leaders went on the run. General Secretary Zhao Ziyang, successor to Hu Yaobang and another liberal leader sympathetic to the students, was sacked and put under house arrest. (It was when Zhao was the boss of Sichuan that my father had been rehabilitated in 1978.) Still, my mother told me emphatically not to think about her safety: 'Even if your book offends somebody, I don't believe they will put me in prison. The times are different now. Deng Xiaoping is not Mao Zedong. I have been through the worst, and nothing can be as bad as that. In any case, I am not a fragile and quivering little blade of grass. You must banish all concerns and write exactly how you want to. That's the only way to write a good book.'

She also asked me not to give any thought to whether *Wild Swans* would do well. As far as she was concerned, she said, writing the book had brought us closer, and that was enough for her. Last but not least, I must not think about whether *she* would like the book or not: 'You and I are bound to look at some things differently. I don't expect to agree with your book a hundred per cent. In fact, I expect not to agree with parts of your book. So please, don't show me the manuscript of the Chinese translation. It's better if I don't know.' (Eventually, after the Chinese translation of the book was published, I gave her a copy, but we never discussed it.)

With those reassuring words, my mother put my mind at ease. I wrote *Wild Swans* and received cancer treatment with a light heart.

Jon assured my mother that he would take good care of me. But he was already giving me the greatest care possible through helping me with the writing of *Wild Swans*, which made a world of difference to me physically and psychologically, and to my book. In our joint effort to create *Wild Swans*, I was touched by his generosity time and again and fell more deeply in love with him. We were married on 26 July 1991, in a London register office, with two friends – Maggie Keswick and Charles Jencks – as witnesses.

Afterwards Maggie, author of a seminal book on Chinese gardens (who would also found the cancer care charity 'Maggie's'), gave a reception for us in their home, which had been designed by Charles, an American architectural theoretician. I knew how much he loved its special floors, and asked our guests not to wear stilettos. Just before the event, for which I had bought my first designer dress, long and red by Karl Lagerfeld (wedding dresses are red according to Chinese tradition) with matching shoes, I took out the outfit and noticed the shoes had high heels, even though they did not look to me to be too thin. In a fluster, I telephoned Maggie. This most warm-hearted friend laughed: 'Oh Jung, no matter how high or thin the heels, your shoes are NOT stilettos!'

On the day, the sun came out for us, radiant on the emerald lawn of their beautifully crafted garden. Two of my brothers came, along with Xiaohei's wife, Rong, all of whom were studying in Britain. Xiaohei, now a writer, would gain a master's degree; Rong, a mathematician, and Jinming, a physicist, each a doctorate. They would settle in the West. Xiaohei and his family in Britain, and Jinming and his family in Canada. At our party, Jinming made an impromptu speech, which was very touching. Afterwards Clare Peploe and Bernardo Bertolucci, friends and film directors, asked about our dinner plans. We had made none. So Clare cooked a most delicious meal and we all ate merrily in their cosy kitchen. Bernardo had made the Oscar-winning film *The Last Emperor*, for which I had translated the initial 'treatment' into Chinese.

We didn't have a honeymoon but went straight into preparations for the publication of *Wild Swans*, which came out in America first, in September, and then in Australia and Britain and then all over the world. To date it has been translated into nearly forty languages and read by tens of millions of people around the globe – except in China, where it has been and is still banned. I have received thousands of letters from readers, many of them expressing admiration for my mother. Although she could not experience the full joy of reading those letters as it was impossible to translate all of them to her, she felt profoundly moved and rewarded. Many times she wrote me about her gratefulness to the readers, to Jon and to me, telling me that I had made her a truly happy woman.

10

Joy and Sadness in the Days
after *Wild Swans*

(the 1990s)

My mother had asked me not to think about her safety in China when I was writing *Wild Swans*. But she agreed to leave the country when the book came out, to avoid any risks. She was impatient to see me anyway, to convince herself that my cancer was really gone as I had been telling her. Since getting a visa to Britain was time-consuming, we decided to meet in Russia, which issued visas easily. A doctor friend of hers had opened a clinic in Moscow and invited her to stay. As usual, there were problems. This time her application for an exit permit was initially denied, with the 'reason' that the government had not given permission for parents to meet their children abroad 'in a third country'.

While she was fighting her battle, Jon and I arrived in Moscow in late August 1991, on the day after the coup against Gorbachev by Communist hardliners had failed, and Gorbachev had been set free from house arrest. We admired him.

One day I spotted him walking below our hotel window at the front of a colourful parade, and rushed downstairs into the street. 'Hello, Mr Gorbachev,' I shouted, waving my arm enthusiastically at him. He waved back with a big smile, looking genuinely pleased with this show of support. The Russians around either did not pause to look at him, or watched him with expressionless or even hostile faces. But the great changes to the USSR he had started could not be stopped. When Jon and I took an overnight train to 'Leningrad', we woke up in the morning arriving in 'St Petersburg'.

My mother joined us when we were back in Moscow. It was over two years since we had seen each other, and she scrutinised me, telling me I looked abnormally tired, and attributing it to intensive work on *Wild Swans*. She asked no questions about its forthcoming publication, and we just went sightseeing, mostly without Jon so I did not have to translate for them. My mother's worry about my health, and my lack of energy, made our being together in Moscow somewhat subdued.

Wandering around the Russian capital, I was struck by just how bare the shops were, as deprived as China's had been at its worst time under Mao. There were long queues for a loaf of bread or a handful of sorry-looking vegetables. Once we saw a small crowd of women battling to get to a counter inside a shop. I had no idea what they were fighting for, but joined them nonetheless, while my mother looked on. When I was finally pushed to the front, it turned out that on sale were some linen tablecloths, napkins and aprons, the latter reminding me of female collective farmers' outfits in old Soviet movies. I asked for a few aprons, which I wanted to give to friends as souvenirs, but was told that each person could only buy one. When my mother saw it, she shook her head and said, 'No wonder the Soviet Union is in turmoil. Its economy is in such unbelievably bad shape.' She did not evince optimism about a democratic Russia emerging, saying instead that once the economy got better, the old Communist ways would reassert themselves. A country that had been ruled for so long and so thoroughly by the Party could not easily cast off its past, she said. I thought she was being unduly pessimistic. Today, after Vladimir Putin's invasion of Ukraine, it seems to me that my mother was far-sighted.

One day we visited a monastery, and saw that at the far end of its grounds, in a corner half-hidden by a big tree, a vendor had set up a little store with Russian dolls and Red Army fur hats – the most common merchandise for tourists. He was absorbed in a book, cutting a solitary figure in a rather romantic setting. My mother observed, 'He is certainly in a beautiful spot. But he seems to be hiding from the customers – so he can read his books.' We laughed, one of the few times on that trip. My mother went on, 'How much money can the man make? No Chinese would set up a store in that location. When it comes to making money, really few can beat the Chinese. I would say that the Chinese craving for getting rich – and richer than others – is unequalled.' Her words reminded me of a question Jon had once asked me: whether there was a Chinese equivalent of the English saying 'Keeping up with the Joneses'. I had not been sure. Now I thought of an expression that was close, but different: 'Overtaking the Joneses' (pan-bi).

Soon Jon and I had to leave for America for the publication of *Wild Swans*, and we asked my mother to stay on in Moscow just in case. We did not know that Deng Xiaoping was very concerned about the Chinese economy after the Tiananmen suppression, which he himself had ordered, and was trying to do something about it. It had nosedived, hit by the combination of political repression, the loss of entrepreneurial momentum, and Western sanctions. By the end of that year, 1989, GDP growth had dropped to 3.9 per cent from 11 per cent the year before. My sister had joined a friend's clothing company in the mid-1980s, and it had nearly gone bankrupt. Deng wanted to revive the economy, and his plan was to channel his people's energy away from politics into money-making. Control was being relaxed. My mother sensed no danger and returned home at the end of 1991. Before long, in early 1992, Deng embarked on a well-publicised tour to south China, during which he assured the population that the reforms would go on. His emphatic encouragement unleashed an explosion of economic initiatives, along with which came greater freedoms. My mother was unmolested. In fact, she found herself something of a star, visited by readers of *Wild Swans* from all over the world and all walks of life – from backpackers to diplomats, tourists to businessmen. While some arrived through government departments and accompanied by officials, in which case the atmosphere was often stiff, and the conversation formal, others came knocking on her door and had lovely chats with her. She mentioned to me a young woman from Israel, who had studied Chinese and who described her experience in a kibbutz, which greatly interested my mother.

In the following years, my mother was invited to many countries, signing books with me after I gave talks. When the BBC made a TV documentary about the writing of *Wild Swans*, it brought her to Britain. Jon and I had just moved into a house together, and my mother immediately put her energy into the rather neglected garden. She went with me to a nursery to buy plants, and there I found she was far from uninterested in shopping. So many things caught her eye and made her linger, and it looked to me as if she wanted to buy the whole shop. And she truly knew an immense amount about plants. One day she said pleadingly, 'Please will you give your plants some water? Your garden is too dry.' I replied, 'But nobody waters their garden here' (which I did not know but assumed to be the case). 'It rains all the time in England.' My mother said, 'But English rain is not real rain', a remark over which Jon and I had a good giggle. It turned out she was not wrong. A gardener later told me the same: that my garden was too dry, and that one did need to water the garden even with the English rain.

During the filming, I was impressed by my mother's complete ease and fluency to camera: she seldom needed a retake, whereas I often had to do more than one. On one of our trips to Japan, she gave a talk in a large auditorium in Tokyo, and wowed the audience with her soft-spoken concise presentation and her choice of appropriate and amusing Japanese expressions. (My mother grew up under Japanese occupation in Manchuria, an experience I described in *Wild Swans*.) One day in a smart restaurant, a waiter came over carrying on a silver tray an exquisite handkerchief, asking for our signatures. The waiter pointed at a table across the room, and a woman dressed in a kimono gracefully rose and bowed to my mother – and my mother bowed back. In Holland, we were driven a long way to a windswept town by the sea, where a large group of women greeted us with warm hugs. My mother laughed with them, and engaged in such rapid exchanges that the interpreter ran out of breath. In Hungary, President Árpád Göncz invited us for tea, at the end of which he had a picture taken with us, each arm linking one of ours. He joked about the photo, 'If China were to invade Hungary, we would now know why!'

We travelled in Ireland, Jon's homeland. In Dublin, and at the literary festivals, my mother saw long queues snaking around the venues, waiting for our talks and book-signing, and she was almost moved to tears. One day, on the road, she felt something wrong with one of her eyes. Not wanting to upset the scheduled event and let down our readers, she made no fuss and played down her symptoms, and we did not pause to have her eyes checked. It was discovered later that she had suffered a detached retina, and the delay of treatment had left her with permanent eye damage, which could not be put right by an operation or wearing glasses. It worsened to the stage that she could not correctly gauge the distance to the edge of steps, which caused her to fall several times in her old age. I often kick myself for not pressing her to have her eyes checked in Ireland, but my mother never expressed regret.

For me, book tours could be emotional rollercoasters. Warm, appreciative readers moved and exhilarated me, but speaking about the past was draining, especially at the beginning. In particular, I found that when I talked about my grandma, I just could not help tears choking me despite my best effort to push them down. Jon noticed and said to me that the story of my grandma seemed to be too upsetting, and maybe I should keep it to the minimum. I agreed – also because I did not want the atmosphere of my talks to be sad.

I asked myself why I had this strong reaction about Grandma, and thought perhaps it was because I had seen her suffering murderous pain in her last years, and yet when she died, in 1969, I had been unable to get to her deathbed – and so perhaps there was an unexorcised regret. I had looked after my grandma in a hospital, sleeping under her bed on a bamboo sheet that I had brought from home, and night after night had listened helplessly to her efforts to stop herself from crying out. Doctors could not diagnose the pain: X-ray machines and other instruments for examination had all been broken as a result of the upheaval of the Cultural Revolution. All she received were painkillers, which after a while stopped being effective, and she was discharged. As no public transport was working, and my grandma was in too much pain at the base of her spine to sit on the bicycle my brothers and I had borrowed to bring her home, I supported her and we walked. With the pain and her bound feet, it took us nearly an hour to get half-way, and then it started to pour with rain. We were instantly soaked. A violent wind slashed against us, and for the first time in her illness, my superhumanly stoic grandma let out a tearful cry: 'Oh heaven, let me die! Let me die!' I don't know how we could have got home had there not been a kind-hearted young man riding a pedal-cart who gave us a lift. He had also been to the hospital to fetch his father. When he came over and carried my grandma onto the open cart, I cried heartily with relief, not bothering to hide my sobs as the wind and rain drowned them.

I had at that time been allocated to a remote village in Ning-nan on the edge of the Himalayas, and was struggling to get myself transferred to another village near Chengdu, in Deyang County. This was a daunting task, and to arrange the necessary papers I had to get back to Ningnan first. The journey would take several days one way, and there was a deadline for the transfer. On the day I had to leave, I went to say goodbye to my grandma at her sickbed. She wept and said she did not know if she would ever see me again. I stroked the back of her bony hand and pressed it to my cheek, promising her that I would be back soon. But I was delayed by one problem after another, and when I finally returned to Meteorite Street, there was only her empty bed. It was excruciatingly painful to listen to my sib-lings' account of her last days. Her body had become lifeless bit by bit, until one day she seemed to be dead. But her eyes were still open, looking around expectantly. She would not close them until she had seen her daughter. My mother was in deten-tion nearby, but was not permitted to visit her dying mother. My siblings went to her place of detention repeatedly to implore the authorities. At long last, my mother was allowed home. She stayed by Grandma's bedside for two days and nights before my grandma closed her eyes.

When I came to write *Wild Swans*, it was my grandma's death that was the most painful to recall and to write about. Today, after more than half a century, when I had to read those passages to check my memory for this book, I found myself having to drag my eyes to the pages and hastening to leave them as soon as I could.

Shortly after the publication of *Wild Swans* in Britain in 1992, it was discovered that my cancer had returned. I was working on the Chinese language edition of the book, which my brother Xiaohei had translated. (I love writing in my mother tongue and would have translated the book myself, had I not been preoccupied with my cancer treatment and the publication of *Wild Swans* in other languages. I translated all my subsequent books into Chinese myself.) Being absorbed in the editing cushioned me from the blow. I was on the hospital bed with the manuscript tinkering over an expression when the nurses came to wheel me into the operating theatre. The operation this time was drastic, and I was under general anaesthetic for nine hours, which left me feeling permanently tired for many years.

My sister flew over from Chengdu to look after me, staying with Jon in his flat near the hospital. (Jon and I were yet to buy our house together.) Every day she brought me appetising food like stewed chicken which she cooked in his small kitchen. I was munching a chicken leg one day when the surgeon came in. I tried to put my napkin over the pile of bones on the plate, and he smiled, 'Don't. This is the best thing to get you back on your feet!' The weather was hot, and the hospital bed had a plastic under-sheet which did not breathe. The mattress sagged in the middle, and I could not turn easily with many tubes sticking out of my body. The hardest thing was the waves of nausea, a side effect of the long general anaesthetic. To make me more comfortable, my sister massaged me and fanned me ever so gently. I was able to leave the hospital in one week, having been scheduled to stay for two.

The ground-floor flat below Jon belonged to some friends, and they kindly lent it to us, so I could step into the communal garden easily. Every morning I walked there and did the pre-scribed exercises, determined to get well as soon as possible. One day, between shivering and sweating, I could not get the temperature right and was cross. Jon bent over me with such anxiety on his face and such panic in his voice – 'Hot or cold? Hot or cold?' – that I burst into laughter. Being well looked after enabled me to return to a normal life quickly, despite the fatigue.

I was 'monitored' for twelve years before being given an 'all clear', and in those years I decided to indulge all my unfulfilled hankerings. My home province, Sichuan, was landlocked, and before I came to Britain, aged twenty-six, I had seen the sea only once, when my fellow students and I were sent to the tropical port of Zhanjiang to practise our English with foreign sailors. There we were only allowed to dip our toes on the beach once, briefly, as the authorities feared that we might swim away and 'defect'. To swim in the sea had been my dream. Now, as my doctors told me that I must swim as much as I could to ensure the muscles damaged by the operation would not stick together the wrong way, I spent quite a few holidays with Jon by the sea, where I learned to snorkel and fell in love with the underwater world. I even made friends with a little black fish off the Caribbean island of Martinique. One early morning I was in the water and with one hand holding on to a rock, gazed down at shoals of fish wriggling in and out of the rocks and seaweed. A little black fish approached me. It gave my fingers gripping the rock a nibble or two and then shot away, before turning and gliding over most gracefully to stroke me with its fan-shaped tail. This dance of flirtation went on for quite a while, and I was enchanted, telling myself that this fish was fond of me. The next morning, and the mornings after, I swam to the same spot, and sure enough the same little black fish appeared, now staying with my hand and kissing my fingers again and again – until I got cold and swam away. It was with such regret that I left Martinique.

In spring 1993, I returned to Chengdu for the first time since 1989: the aftermath of the Tiananmen suppression, my work and illness had combined to prevent me from making the journey. My mother had been worried sick about my health. As there was little Western medicine could do to help, she consulted doctors practising Chinese medicine, and made stews of herbs and other ingredients for me. But they produced no perceptible improvement, only filling her flat with a bad smell. I said let's forget it, and she advised me to take ginseng, which did help.

At the time tens of millions, if not hundreds of millions, of Chinese were mad about a type of breathing exercise called *qigong*, whose masters had huge followings. Even the official papers carried news about the alleged supernatural powers of some of them. My mother suggested I see one renowned master in Chengdu who had the reputation of curing cancer patients. He had worked in an osteopathic hospital that had come under her department before the Cultural Revolution. It was to this hospital that, in 1967, my brothers and I had taken our father after he had been beaten up by Red Guard thugs, and his tender handling by the doctors had greatly moved me. The smell of the hospital-made paste, which the doctors had used to make plasters to apply to injuries, has remained with me ever since.

The *qigong* master who came to my mother's flat in 1993 did not look like a doctor – he looked more like a clerk in a government office, with a Mao-era blue jacket, a battered soft-cover 1980s briefcase, and an excessively (to me) attentive manner. He asked us not to tell him about my health problems – declaring that *he* would tell *us* after the session. On his instruction I lay face down, and he took a long breath and started to move his hands, palms down, over my body without touching it. He said I should be able to feel the flow of *qi*, air, from his palms to my body, and now that he mentioned it, something did seem to be going on there. Soon I dozed off – and woke up feeling better. My mother was ecstatic. The *qigong* master then gave her his diagnosis: that I had had breast cancer and two operations. Since she had not told this man about my cancer, my mother was awestruck, and I was also impressed.

He came for several days and each time I fell into a light snooze and felt brighter afterwards. My mother commented hopefully that perhaps he really deserved his reputation. After one session he told us he could feel from the flow of the *qi* that I still had cancer cells inside me, perhaps in the liver, perhaps in the kidney . . . At this my mind went blank, and my mother's face took on a frightened look that I had never seen. The *qigong* master said that he felt the 'positive *qi*' from him could drive out the cancerous *qi* from my body, but it would take time, and it was a pity that I was leaving Chengdu in a few days. Anxiously, my mother asked whether he would consider going to London to stay with me and clear me of all the cancer cells. He bent his head as if in deliberation of a problematic proposal, and finally with an air of resolve said that although this would involve abandoning his clients in Chengdu and staying away from his family, he felt he must go as he had so much respect and gratitude for my mother who had supported the osteopathic hospital when the authorities had wanted to close it down (on the grounds that what it offered was not a proper medical discipline). My mother jumped up from the sofa and said we should get going organising his visas, exit and entry. The *qigong* master picked up his battered briefcase, put it on his knees, and pulled out a file of documents, which I needed only to sign as his financial guarantor before he started making the arrangements.

There was no doubt to me now that the man was a crook – and an unspeakable one at that, as he preyed on people made vulnerable by sickness and love. It also occurred to me that it was actually quite easy to find out about my health problems in Chengdu. I politely threw him out and then, turning to my mother with exasperation, cried: 'Mother, how could you possibly believe this utter and obvious rubbish?'

Of course I knew well that my mother fell for the *qigong* master's trick because of her love for me. Her desperate fear about my life had made her lose her normal clear-headedness and shrewd judgement. It was also true that my mother, while always on her guard vis-à-vis the regime, was trusting and almost naive when it came to dealing with conmen, which was a new experience. Ever since she was an adult, she had lived in a totalitarian environment in which petty conmen had not had the liberty to thrive. There had also been little to con for, while now there was a lot. In the coming years, my mother would be taken in by other crooks. After the episode with the *qigong* master, a new feeling grew in me towards my mother, a feeling of protectiveness.

Before Chengdu, I had been on a long book tour to some Pacific countries, and visited Taiwan, where the Chinese language edition of *Wild Swans* had just come out. I had been there twice before, the first time in 1985, when the island was a dictatorship under the Kuomintang and anti-Communist slogans were everywhere, using very similar language to that in Communist China against Chiang Kai-shek. On the sheets of stamps that I bought for sending postcards, a warning read: 'Do not collect stamps of the Communist bandits!'

But 1985 was also the year when things began to change. Chiang Kai-shek's son, Ching-kuo, who had succeeded him to be the president of Taiwan when he died in 1975 (a year before Mao's death), made the first move towards democracy by announcing that no member of his family would be his heir. Ching-kuo had been taken to Russia by a secret Communist agent at the age of fifteen and kept as a hostage by Stalin for eleven years. The harrowing experience, including labouring in the Gulag, led him to reject the system of dictatorship, and he became Taiwan's Gorbachev.

Jon and I were in Taiwan again, to research for *Wild Swans* in 1989, and by then the island had an opposition party, the Democratic Progressive Party. People were shedding fear. Former Kuomintang generals gave us frank interviews about Chiang's rule on the mainland, about which their disenchantment was plain. Their perspective helped me understand my mother's student days as an anti-Chiang activist.

A new era was definitively dawning in Taiwan at the time of the publication of *Wild Swans* in Chinese in 1993. The first general election was on the horizon. My publishers, who had recently returned from America, were eager to publish books in the Western way, free of the old thought control. I could feel exciting vibes reverberating throughout my stay.

Then I flew to Chengdu, and was met with a similar buzz. Although here the CCP was holding tight to its dictatorship and the energy and dynamism were mainly directed towards making money and seeking opportunities, inevitably, people were breaking old Party rules and pushing for more freedom. In that spring I felt there was more freedom there than ever before in my memory. Copies of the Chinese edition of *Wild Swans* had come in with travellers, and were doing the rounds. The Sichuan television station recorded an interview with me, talking confidently about airing it 'on Sunday'. A friend offered to be my 'agent for the mainland market', and went with me to Beijing to find a publisher. In the capital, several publishers got in touch, most very keen, and we settled on the Friendship Publishing House. It asked for permission to omit certain comments in the book, to do with Mao, but promised to print on the pages 'The following xxx words have been cut.' I agreed. A ceremony was held for the signing of the contract, filmed by the Japanese broadcasting company, NHK, which was making a short documentary on *Wild Swans*. A renowned Chinese writer reviewed the book in the leading literature magazine in China (*Du-shu*), and a major reformist, post-Mao editor-in-chief of the *People's Daily*, Qin Chuan, carried the first chapter in a periodical he had just produced, with plans to serialise other chapters in the following issues.

And yet, that spring was brief. After the first issue, Qin Chuan's periodical was ordered to fold. My interview with the Sichuan television was never aired. *Wild Swans* Beijing edition was cancelled having gone to its second proof-reading. Some years later, I met a retired head of the state censors' office, and, astonished by how liberal he was, I blurted out, 'I wish you had been in charge at the time when my book came out. Then it would not have been banned.' He gave me a wry grin: 'It *was* when I was in charge that your book was banned – after it was nearly published, though.' He was of course only a functionary who had to carry out orders. Yet people like him were constantly trying and pushing the boundaries. Sometimes they almost succeeded, but the regime caught up and clamped down.

The ban on *Wild Swans* was stringent, especially when it came to making a film or television series out of it, in which case it would reach a much larger audience. Ever since its publication in the early 1990s, numerous people have tried hard, some extremely hard, to dramatise *Wild Swans*, and quite a few have explored the possibility of shooting it outside China, hoping that this would bypass the Chinese government. But Beijing has been adamant, and all attempts have failed. Beijing has a stranglehold: the indispensable distributors, and streaming platforms, which have faced the threat of their other films being boycotted in China and their lucrative *products* that are sold with the films being banned from entering the Chinese market.

While thus preventing *Wild Swans* from reaching most Chinese, the regime was less draconian regarding travellers bringing the book into the country, and, for a while, pirated editions were being sold on street pavements. The book was known to a lot of people, and readers were not afraid to come forward. One day, when Jon and I were walking in the streets of Beijing, a car – a private car it seemed: people were beginning to have cars – sped around the corner and braked next to us; the window wound down and the woman driver poked her head out: 'I love your book!' she shouted and then drove off. On another occasion, after Jon and I had eaten in a restaurant, when he was about to pay the bill, he was told that it had already been settled by a young local man, who said he had learned about his country's past 'from your wife's book'. This 'fame', combined with the relative relaxation in China in the 1990s, thanks to the fact that the country desperately needed the West for its economy, made it possible for Jon and me to embark on our next book together.

11

Getting to Mao's Inner Circle

(the 1990s)

With the publication of *Wild Swans*, I became a writer. I left my teaching job and decided to write a biography of Mao. Years before, when Emma Tennant had suggested a short biography of Mme Mao, I had declined as I dreaded revisiting the past. Now, after the cathartic experience of writing *Wild Swans*, I found myself contemplating Mao with detached curiosity and fascination. I had also learned that much of the received wisdom about the history of the Chinese Communist Party was false, and was ready and keen to clear out the threadbare and rickety mental furniture and equip my mind with solid fresh facts. I knew that much digging would be needed to find the truth, and wanted to be that detective.

Jon was also interested in Mao, and we started working on the biography together. We divided our research roughly by language: I dealt with the Chinese language sources, and Jon, who speaks many languages, was landed with the rest of the world. Most importantly, he speaks Russian, and was able to work in the Russian archives, which turned out to be a treasure trove. Moscow had been the boss of the CCP for over three decades and after that had kept a close relationship. Jon had learned Russian when he was a child in Ireland, in a village near Dundalk, where he grew up. A Russian émigré, Count Mikhail Kutuzov-Tolstoy, a great-nephew of the novelist Leo Tolstoy, had settled there and was giving Russian lessons. Jon had read *Anna Karenina*, which had inspired him to learn the Russian language. For several years, when he was back home for holidays from his boarding school, his mother drove him to the teacher. Tolstoy had a large painting of the River Neva in St Petersburg in his study, and he would recount stories about the palaces on the banks of the river and their occupants, as well as other tales about Russia, in Russian. Jon was enthralled. His tutoring stood him in good stead now in the Russian archives which President Boris Yeltsin opened for public access in the 1990s. Many of the files have since been closed by Putin. Jon and I were lucky to have caught that window of opening.

We were fortunate with the timing in China, too, as many people in Mao's circle were still alive and lucid. For a decade from 1993, I went to China a couple of times a year to research the biography. The regime issued a warning against talking to me, but only to a small number of top people, and the order was not vigorously enforced, unlike the ban on writing about or publishing *Wild Swans*. So, while some people opted to avoid trouble and declined my interview requests, most talked. There were so many things people longed to get off their chests, and the Chinese also had a deep-rooted sense of duty to history. Ironically, the warning itself helped, as people learned about me and *Wild Swans*. They could see that my future books could reach an international audience, and that they would not be following the Party line – which was a huge incentive for people to speak. I gave all my interviewees *Wild Swans* as an introduction, filling my large suitcase with dozens of copies on each trip. I hoped that they could see that I was an honest writer and would trust me with their memories. So many reacted as I hoped, to my immense delight.

The regime was of course watching me, but the surveillance was discreet. A friend who was helping me set up interviews told me his boss knew what he was doing and one day warned him. But when I asked him to distance himself from me, he said he was not afraid and would go on as before. He said he would argue if asked that since the government let me into China and did not prohibit me from seeing people, it was not up to him to censor himself. People like him grew even bolder when they saw that nobody seemed to have got into trouble for talking to me. In the 1990s, the authorities wanted to avoid heavy-handed repression unless they felt a direct threat (like from the Falun Gong, a powerful religious movement). They needed the goodwill of the West, to help the Chinese economy take off. Beijing's calculations gave me a chance.

In that decade massive amounts of original documents to do with Mao and the Party's history were also available in China (even though, sadly, they were little used). The country had been publishing collections of archive material since the early 1980s, when the post-Mao leadership was at its most liberal and gave orders to archives in Beijing and the provinces to compile and publish their documents systematically. Even the most secretive Central Archives published at least six collections, each dealing with a major historical event. Those publications had initially been marked for 'restricted circulation', but were quickly on sale in specialist bookshops. The bookshop that I visited the most was the one attached to the 'Central Archive Documents Publishing House', where I bought dozens of books every time I was in Beijing.

At the recommendation of friends, I stayed mainly in the

Palace Hotel, to the east of Tiananmen Square. An imposing landmark building under classic Chinese roofs with bright-green glazed tiles, it was the very first Western-style luxury hotel in the centre of the capital. When it opened in spring 1989, Jon and I had gone there to have a drink. In 1993, the Palace was probably the city's most prestigious hotel and it was not prohibitively expensive. Friends who were helping me contact interviewees argued strongly for me to stay there: 'So people could combine seeing you with browsing around the shops nearby.' And: 'If you stay in a nameless hotel, nobody will come!'

The Palace had a large swimming pool, which was a luxury in Beijing, and was useful for doing my exercises prescribed after my last operation seven months earlier. But the most valuable service the hotel provided was to post back to London all the books I bought. Its porters carted them off to the nearby post office and I did not even have to pack them. I was told the priceless service might have to do with the government order to watch out in case 'state secrets' got out of China. But none of my books had the stamp 'secret' on them.

Friends warned me from day one that my hotel, like other big hotels, was under surveillance by the State Security, and that a suite was filled with monitoring equipment. But my friends, interviewees and I would rather that Big Brother know what we were talking about than not know and be suspicious. We were not plotting but exploring historical facts – I only asked people to give me the facts they knew, never their opinions – and anyone was welcome to listen in.

One of my first meetings in that hotel heralded a most productive decade. A friend I had made in London, a liberal official of my father's age, who had returned to China, came for lunch. I gave him a copy of *Wild Swans*, and said I was working on a biography of Mao. He asked who I wanted to see, and whether he could help. Knowing my friend was from Hunan, the same province as Mao, I said I wanted to start with Mao's early friends who were still with us. He asked such as who, and I mentioned a Hunanese, Mr Yi Lirong, who was relatively unknown to the general public but who I knew through research had been a close friend in Mao's youth – perhaps even the closest. At the mention of the name, a broad smile spread over my friend's face, and he said, 'You are asking the right person. He is my father.' I had had no idea of the connection as my friend had taken a nom de guerre, a common practice among old revolutionaries. He told me his father, four years younger than Mao and now ninety-six, was still physically healthy and mentally alert. Indeed, when I met Mr Yi, he talked in full flow for over an hour without any sign of fatigue, every now and then walking about the room making hand gestures to stress his points.

Mr Yi was the key witness to Mao's early involvement with the Communists. When Moscow founded the CCP in summer 1920 in Shanghai, Mao, then a freelance journalist, had not yet professed a belief in communism. But he was in Shanghai at the time, and happened to visit one of the founders, Professor Chen Duxiu. The professor liked the young radical and offered him a job: starting a bookshop in Hunan selling Communist and left-wing publications – activities that were perfectly legal in those days. Mao loved reading and needed money. He opened the bookshop at once – and in so doing entered the Party and was picked to be a delegate to the first Party congress in July 1921. Mao invited Mr Yi, his most dependable friend, to be the bookshop's manager.

Yi became Mao's first recruit into the Party. When Mao returned from the first congress in Shanghai, he came to the bookshop and signalled to Yi to go outside with him. Leaning on the bamboo fence in the courtyard, Mao asked Yi to join the Party. Yi was reluctant, telling Mao he had heard that the Russian revolution had been very violent and resulted in a huge number of people being killed; but Mao reassured him that it would not be like that in China, it would be a 'civilised revolution' without bloodshed. Yi had always regarded Mao as a big brother. 'He asked me to join and I did.'

Moscow immediately started funding the Party branch and the bookshop. Yi told me: 'I collected the funds and was in charge of the spending. To start with, we received sixty silver dollars a month, later the amount was increased to a hundred and sixty dollars. I managed the expenditure, and I answered to Mao Zedong.'

With the Moscow funds, Mao rented a house at the foot of a lush hill, surrounded by green fields, with a crystal clear pond in front. Yi was the nominal owner and paid the monthly rent: 7.2 silver dollars. Mao lived there with his second wife, Yang Kaihui, a beautiful and extraordinary character whom Yi admired immensely, like other young men in their circle. Yi told me that Mao had written of his passion for her in a wistful poem, which Mao had shown him. He wrote a few lines for me on my notebook in his still strong handwriting. But he also mentioned that while Kaihui loved Mao with all her heart, Mao was having affairs, and, dipping an index finger in the tea, Yi wrote on the table two big ideograms, *bu-zhen*: 'unfaithful'.

After the interview I wrote to Yi from London with more questions, and he took great care answering them – verbally to an assistant, who wrote the answers down and copied them out in large characters for Yi to check their accuracy. Yi had a steel-trap memory partly because he had been grilled so many times over the years, especially during the Cultural Revolution in Qincheng, the prison for top officials, and the questions

inevitably involved Mao. He had also given interviews to official historians after Mao's death, but they understandably
stayed away from areas such as Mao's personal life. Yi's meticulous testimonies which I received by post were historical
gold dust.

Whenever I thought of Mr Yi, I felt and still feel a stirring of self-reproach, as when I first went to see him, I arrived
hopelessly late. His son, my friend, was downstairs looking out
for me in case I had lost my way. To my profuse apology, he
smiled gently and said, 'Not to worry, everyone knows how
bad the traffic in Beijing is nowadays. My father is resting
anyway.' As Beijing is sprawling, travelling over an hour in
heavy traffic to get to my interviewees was the norm. They
kindly overlooked my lateness as they could see that I was run
off my feet. Through friends, old and new, I assembled a long
list of people who were willing to talk to me, and I was in the
lucky position of straining myself to manage. I usually did two
or three interviews a day: one in the morning and afternoon,
and often another over dinner. Afterwards I sorted out the
tapes and the notes and prepared for the next day's appoint-
ments. This meant I went to bed very late and was too tired to
get up early enough to meet the Chinese schedule – work starting at eight and lunch could be as early as eleven. I mostly
skipped breakfast and grabbed an apple for the taxi journey. At
lunchtime I tried to hasten back to the hotel for a lie-down,
without which I found it hard to function for the rest of the
day. Taxis in Beijing were now easy to hail, very different from
the 1980s. In this way, over the years, I was able to interview
some one hundred and fifty major historical witnesses, some of
them many times, including family members, friends and staff
of Mao and his colleagues.

I brought my interviewees and people who helped me souvenirs from Britain which were unavailable in China: a bottle of perfume from Harrods for women, and a bottle of Scotch whisky for men, for instance. Of all the people I interviewed, only one man asked for a not unreasonable sum of money as his 'fee', and I paid him willingly. Once I offered to pay a young man who was making introductions for me; he was offended and berated me for not treating him 'as a friend'.

Some of my interviewees gave me presents: a pretty sweater, an eggshell light porcelain vase, calligraphies with poetic lines, saying very kind things about *Wild Swans* – and in the case of one man who had been at the top briefly in the early years of the Cultural Revolution before incurring Mao's ire and plummeting into Qincheng, the poems he had written behind bars. Accepting them always reminded me not to let down their trust.

I did several revealing interviews with Mao's daughter-in-law, Liu Siqi, widow of his eldest son, Anying, who had been killed in the Korean War in an American air raid. Mao had five known children, three sons (one had died in childhood, and the other had mental problems) by his second wife, Kaihui, a daughter by his third wife, and the youngest daughter, Li Na, by the notorious fourth wife, Jiang Qing. But Siqi's closeness to Mao pre-dated her marriage. She had already been practically a member of Mao's household, having spent a great deal of her childhood and youth around Mao, who affectionately called her 'Daughter'.

A reader of *Wild Swans* from Hong Kong had mentioned my book to Siqi, and when I asked to see her, she readily came to the Palace in autumn 1994. A poised but low-key woman of my mother's age, she answered my questions factually and exactly, often searching for the right words in order to be precise. My impression of people in the top circle was that they were extremely careful with their words. As Mao never talked about politics with the children in the family in her days, she answered my questions about Mao's family life, and gave me an evocative, intimate picture of Mao and his household.

In that family, Mme Mao did not like Siqi, and when the Cultural Revolution started, she condemned her and her mother at a Red Guard rally as 'spies' and 'time bombs' in the Mao household. Siqi was almost trembling as she pleaded with Mao to stop his wife making groundless accusations. Mao did not respond. Li Na, Mao's youngest daughter, also entreated her father to restrain her mother. Mao again remained silent. He did seem to have done something afterwards, Siqi informed me, as Jiang Qing made no more accusations in public. But he did not intervene when Siqi and her mother, and even Siqi's second husband, were later thrown into prison and suffered physical abuse. I sought an explanation for this treatment. Siqi said she did not know. Like other interviewees, she never speculated. To me, the most likely explanation was that Mao did not want to rein in his wife too much: the role he had assigned her in the Cultural Revolution was to attack and bite like a ferocious 'dog' – a role Mme Mao spelled out during her trial after Mao's death. Mao knew his wife was full of venom: he once told Siqi, 'Jiang Qing is deadly poisonous, worse than a scorpion', and he wiggled his little finger to imitate the tail of a scorpion. He meant to exploit that venom, not subdue it. And he needed to let her carry out her own vendettas.

Mao's only daughter with Jiang Qing, Li Na, came to a dinner a friend gave for my birthday on 25 March 1993. It was in a smart hotel, and she sat next to me, polite and bearing herself with quiet dignity. In her early fifties, she was soft-spoken, and talked slowly and thoughtfully. I asked if she wished to visit Britain. Her reply surprised me: 'There is no chance of me going. They would never let me out – look what happened to Svetlana!' She was referring to Stalin's daughter, who had defected to the United States (although later returned to Russia). I was struck that she should make the comparison, and talk about it so frankly.

Li Na had much in common with Svetlana: they both adored their fathers, and they both studied heavily political subjects because of the wishes of their fathers, who were grooming them for future assistance. Stalin's daughter studied history and political thought, although her own passion was literature and writing. Li Na was a student of modern Chinese history – a highly politicised subject which, she told me, she did not particularly like, but took because the Party wanted more children from Communist families to become historians. ('So our children will write our history,' as the Party put it. Indeed, in Beijing I came across quite a few Party historians of Li Na's generation who were high officials' children.)

When he started the Cultural Revolution, Mao began giving Li Na assignments. One was to purge and control the army newspaper, which would help him control the army. Under her, the entire editorial and managerial boards were packed off to prison, and over 60 per cent of the staff suffered appallingly. Among the many people ferociously and repeatedly beaten up under her regime of terror was an old friend of hers, who was accused of opposing her just because he had uttered some minor disagreements, thinking that they were good friends.

I interviewed that friend of Li Na, a very congenial man, some days later, and saw him several times over the years. He said that in that period, when Li Na had unlimited power, and having been taught to 'rule brutally' (*ba-dao*) by her father, she became a different person from before. She had been kind and courteous, but would now scream abuses like 'How I want to have you shot!' at the drop of a hat, at the staff, many of whom were older people she used to address as 'uncle' or 'auntie'. And she appeared to be indifferent to the ghastly torturing that was going on around her on the newspaper's premises.

Li Na's next assignment was to help her mother run the Cultural Revolution, and in that post she was indirectly involved in more atrocities. But at the peak of her power, she collapsed into a grave mental breakdown – until after Mao's death. Mao, who had intended for her ultimately to be the boss of Beijing and control the capital for him, gave up using her. Slowly, she recovered. In the 1980s, the congenial friend bumped into her at an art exhibition. She showed him great joy and warmth, as though nothing unpleasant, let alone horrible, had happened between them. He found her the friend he had known long before, only a little slow, possibly the side effect of her medication. After listening to her cheerful chattering for a while, he could not pretend any longer and asked, 'Do you remember what happened to me at—?' and mentioned the boiler room in which he had been imprisoned. She went pale and murmured, 'I am sorry. I apologise. I can't remember anything from those years . . . I have forgotten all the things in the past . . .' And she bowed to him deeply.

I did not ask Li Na about her mother, Jiang Qing, with whom she was said to have had a love–hate relationship. I had been told it was too painful a subject for her. Mme Mao had committed suicide two years before in Qincheng, the prison to which she and her husband had sent so many people, and she herself was sent after Mao died.

At the dinner, Li Na wore a faded Mao-era blue jacket, which, through its shapelessness, made her look rather frumpy.

A fellow guest, who worked in a ministry and was clearly an old friend, berated her for dressing 'out of date', telling her, 'You should change out of that garb and go with the times. Look, you look so dumpy! You really shouldn't be looking like this.' After our dinner, at the end of which I cut a birthday cake, the official herded us all into the hotel's boutique, and tried to select a jacket for Li Na. As he picked one after another, all seeming to me to be too colourful, even gaudy, she gently but firmly declined.

Over dinner, our host had asked the man from the ministry to lend Li Na a hand: her only son was working as a servant cleaning guest rooms in a hotel, and could he help getting him a managerial post? The friend's look suggested this was difficult, and he said he could try to get the young man a managerial job, but only in a three-star hotel; it would not be possible in a five-star one. Li Na silently nodded to the answer, neither surprised nor upset. Perhaps she had had similar experiences before.

I was a little taken aback that Mao's grandson worked as a servant in a hotel and that people were reluctant to do his family favours. It seemed to me that this reflected how the regime really felt about Mao at the time: it was only propping up Mao's God-like status out of political calculation, rather than genuine devotion. It may help explain why nobody seemed to be making serious efforts to stop me from carrying out my research.

Another daughter with a tortured soul was that of Marshal Lin Biao, Mao's number two and controller of the army in the Cultural Revolution. It was thanks to Lin's backing that Mao was able to launch his giant bloody purge in 1966. A few years later, in 1971, they fell out, and Lin Biao, his wife and son, Tiger, escaped from China in a plane.

Lin Biao also had a daughter, Doudou, who was a little older than her brother and twenty-seven at the time. She loved her father, and he doted on her, but he and his wife had come to the conclusion that their daughter was thoroughly brainwashed and would regard fleeing China as 'defection' – high treason – so they had decided to leave without her. But Tiger cared very much for his sister and thinking of the disaster awaiting her after her family's flight, told her the plan and asked her to go with them. As her parents had foreseen, Doudou was terrified and fiercely against fleeing, even though her brother had pointed out that their father, who was in very poor health, could not survive for three months in Mao's prison. After the conversation, Doudou went to the guards and denounced her family.

This doomed the brother who loved her, and her parents. When they realised that she had disappeared, they left for the airfield at once – which meant that Lin Biao's plane had no time to refuel. Planes in China were allowed only the minimum fuel on board, to prevent anyone from using them without authorisation. While they were out of China over Mongolia, en route to Russia (then Mao's number-one enemy state, even ahead of America), the plane ran out of fuel and crash-landed, exploding on impact, killing the three members of the Lin family as well as everyone else on board.*

Doudou was not spared prison even though, as Zhou Enlai observed, if she had not informed on her family, Lin Biao

---

* Mikhail Kapitsa, Stalin's chief adviser on China and deputy foreign minister of the USSR, told Jon the Russians were relieved that Lin Biao did not make it to Russia as the Kremlin did not want to have a super-hot potato on its hands. Lin Biao seems to have anticipated this attitude, as his first choice of destination had been British Hong Kong, a plan that had to be abandoned at the last minute as the flight would have to be in Chinese air space more than twice as long.

could well have landed safely in a foreign country and done untold damage to the regime. Doudou tried, unsuccessfully, to commit suicide, and had lived in torment ever since. I assumed she felt guilty for being instrumental in her family's demise.

A mutual friend, who knew the Lin circle well and had introduced me to several of its members, invited me to his home for supper with Doudou. She came in, as lightly as a floating ghost, thin, apparently timid and very reserved, her voice sometimes verging on a whisper. She answered my questions neutrally and placidly, even when they were about her father's unspeakable role in the Cultural Revolution, which she excused by claiming he had been ill, mentally as well as physically, and so knew little about the terrible things that were happening. Strong emotions flared only when it came to her father's escape from China. She insisted that it was not his wish, that he had been 'kidnapped' and 'forced onto the plane' by her mother (with whom she did not get on) and her brother, Tiger. I was struck that to Doudou, fleeing China, even for survival, was the most unpardonable crime, of which she must do her utmost to have her father cleared. Doudou's anguish, it occurred to me, may not have been due to her sense of guilt at having been an informer and caused the deaths of her family, as I had thought before, but perhaps due to her regret that she had not been able to prevent his family's 'defection', and her shame for belonging to a family of 'defectors'.

Over a decade before, in 1982, when I had decided to stay in Britain, I had faced the potential accusation of being a 'defector'. My mother had supported my decision, and, while doing all she could to head off the deadly charge, she had made every effort to claim responsibility for it. Listening to Doudou's desperate attempts to exonerate her father from this 'crime', I felt renewed admiration for my mother.

Doudou's brother, Tiger, who organised his family's escape from China, had resisted brainwashing and was blessed with a free mind, which was partly due to his access to Western science magazines, one of the many privileges of being Lin Biao's son. The West that emerged from those publications wowed him. (Western achievements in science and technology opened my own brother Jinming's mind too when he was a child. After reading a simplified science journal, one day he declared to our family at dinner that he thought America was fantastic. My father was lost for words and, stroking his head, said to my mother worriedly: 'What are we going to do? This child is going to grow up and become a Rightist [intellectuals classified as enemies of the state].')

Tiger saw through Mao's tyranny – even though his father had done more than most to perpetrate it – and with some air force officers he made a plan to assassinate Mao. He chose the codename 'Project 571' for their plot, because '571' – *wu-qi-yi* – has the same pronunciation as 'armed uprising'. The plan had to be aborted: Mao's security was watertight and some of Tiger's team members panicked at the last minute.

I interviewed several of Tiger's friends. What I found most extraordinary was that so many officers had been involved with the assassination plot, still more people had known about his scheme to flee China, and yet no one had denounced him. I asked one of the group how come. He replied in a matter-of-fact way, 'Why, one doesn't rat on one's friends. That's all.' And he quoted a traditional code of honour, *zhang-yi*: loyalty to friends, a concept that had almost been eradicated as the regime tried to destroy anything that might compete with the Party for allegiance. I was elated to see that decent values were still practised by normal people such as those air force officers, but was depressed to ruminate that they were able to be 'normal' only because they were less in the grip of fear thanks to being under the shelter of Lin Biao's wings.

After Lin Biao's death, the officers were put in a quasi-prison. With them was one woman, Tiger's fiancée, Ning. His mother had sent trusted staff all over the country to find her beloved son an ideal wife – and she and Tiger had chosen Ning. I interviewed her in 1995 in New York, where she had moved, having married an American Chinese businessman, who bore a striking resemblance to Lin Biao. Perhaps this resemblance had made him feel like another 'son' of Lin, and he had written to her from New York to China to propose marriage. Ning impressed me particularly with her character: intelligent, fun and gutsy – the qualities Tiger had undoubtedly appreciated. She listened to 'decadent' rock music with him, and giggled at his nickname for Mao: 'B-52', the American heavy bomber. Tiger had said that Mao had a big belly full of nasty ideas, each of which, once dropped, would kill masses of people like a bomb. Most people, certainly Doudou, would have been scared to death hearing such irreverence towards the Great Leader. After Tiger's death, Ning resolved to kill herself in the de facto prison. Short of options to bring about her own death, one day she raced head on towards a solid door, plunging her head into a huge brass nail. She hurt herself badly, and survived to suffer more for her association with the Lins. But when I met her in New York, she made light of what she had been through, describing horrible experiences amusingly, even making me laugh.

Another brave woman I interviewed was Wang Guang-mei, widow of President Liu Shaoqi, another number two of Mao's and the predecessor of Marshal Lin Biao. None of my friends knew her well enough to introduce me, and I decided to write to her. I had her address, and left a letter requesting an interview at the concierge of the apartment building where she lived, along with a copy of *Wild Swans*. A few days later, she called through her assistant to my hotel room, inviting me to her home the next day, which I later realised was the day after her seventy-third birthday. I asked if I could bring Jon, who was with me in the room, looking expectantly at the phone in my hand. After a pause, she said she was sorry but for her to see a foreigner there had to be authorisation from 'the Organisation'. Jon was disappointed but had encountered too many such reactions to be upset.

I went, and to my fury with myself was late again. Cursing Beijing's traffic, I hurried to her door, which, unlike others in the building (I had been to that building many times as several interviewees lived there), had no steel grille. She had had it removed, as it had reminded her of the door of her prison cell, in which she had spent more than a decade. When the door opened, I saw her standing at the end of a corridor, welcoming me with a gracious gesture and an understanding smile. A physics graduate from a missionary university in the pre-Communist days, she had a reputation for being elegant, as people could see from the pictures of her accompanying her husband on overseas visits. Her elegance was still there, but years of ordeal had left their ruthless mark on her once beautiful face. Her home was utilitarian and spartan, as if she were in no mood to beautify it. I sat down, was offered tea, presented my gift – a bottle of perfume by Dior – and started to ask questions. I preferred to keep pleasantries to the minimum.

Liu Shaoqi had been handpicked by Mao to be his deputy for about two decades. Undoubtedly, he was a ruthless man. But he had a breaking point, which came during the Great Famine of 1958–61. Liu knew that the famine was the result of the regime exporting food to the Soviet bloc to pay for the military industries Mao needed urgently in order to turn China into a superpower so he could dominate the world. Liu wanted China to become a superpower, too, but he balked at the price of starving tens of millions of people to death. He argued that some of the purchases could be made later when the country had become richer. But Mao was in a hurry to become, ultimately, the master of the planet.

In spring 1961, Guangmei went with her husband to his home village in Hunan (which was near Mao's home village). By then over thirty million people had died of hunger, as Liu himself told Soviet ambassador Stepan Chervonenko whom Jon interviewed in Moscow. Seeing the suffering of the villagers with his own eyes drove home what that figure meant. The Lius saw people had virtually nothing to eat and heard their gut-wrenching stories of how their loved ones died one after another. Liu's own brother-in-law had died of hunger and abuse, whose horrific details Liu's sister, ill herself, related to them. Even a man with a heart of stone could not fail to be affected, and while Guangmei was in tears, Liu bowed to the villagers and apologised to them.

The trip changed Liu, and he made up his mind to stop Mao's policies. In January 1962, at a congress of seven thousand principal Party officials from all over the country, he made an unexpected speech that rallied the attendees, all of whom were against Mao's policies not least because they and their families were also starving. Mao was forced to halt some imports of military industries and cut down on food exports, and the famine stopped. Mao was furious – he hated being thwarted, and he hated being outsmarted even more. He had read and endorsed Liu's speech as it had been written beforehand, but he had not reckoned that Liu would say something completely different once he stood on the platform. To Mao, it was 'a surprise attack', the only thing that could potentially dislodge him. He urgently summoned Marshal Lin Biao to the conference to speak in support of him on behalf of the army, which steadied his position. From that moment on, Mao hated Liu with a vengeance and would exact revenge in the Cultural Revolution, in which Liu would be his number-one target.

Even the officials in the conference hall could feel the charged atmosphere, as Mao made thinly veiled threats against Liu. My father was there, and when he returned home, he said to my mother, 'I am afraid there are going to be disasters for Comrade Shaoqi.'

When I told Guangmei this, she said, 'It's really something that your father should say those things to your mother. He must have loved her very much.' In those days one could only discuss something so dangerous with one's spouse when they truly loved and trusted each other. Not many couples were in that position. I asked Guangmei whether she felt what her husband did was a turning point for him, as Mao would never forgive him. She said she knew; in fact Liu, a man of few words, had murmured when he saw Lin Biao making his unscheduled speech singing the praises of Mao and threatening Mao's opponents, 'Lin Biao comes, and talks like this. Trouble.'

Knowing that Mao was coming after you was frightening, and quite a few wives in a similar situation urged their husbands to beg Mao's forgiveness. But Guangmei encouraged her husband to stand up to Mao and supported him throughout. I asked her what they did to protect themselves in the years before Mao pounced. After all, Lin Biao would flee – as had Mao's two other chief opponents in the past: Zhang Guotao to the Kuomintang and Wang Ming to Russia; but what did the Lius do, as they did not try to escape? She seemed pleasantly surprised by my question. 'Oh, you are interested in this . . .' she smiled. I said, 'It is unthinkable to me that you would just sit and wait to be crushed without putting up a fight.' And so I learned from Guangmei some extraordinary details which inspired me to find out more, and enabled me to piece together the unknown story of the Lius' fightback.

What Liu tried to achieve was to make it hard for Mao to purge him, and further, to pressure Mao into being a figurehead, leaving the running of the country to others. To achieve these goals, Liu went about gathering support from key officials around China, especially the heads of the provinces. He was quite successful. Even Mao's most faithful followers appreciated Liu's efforts to stop the famine and get the country back on its feet, and joined the groundswell of opinion that Liu should run the country and Mao retire to an honorary post. In 1965, Liu got himself re-elected president, after he had convened the National People's Congress against Mao's explicitly expressed wishes. Liu and his supporters then used the occasion to promote him, putting his portrait on the front page of the *People's Daily*, side by side with Mao's, and organising mass parades which carried Liu's portraits. There was even a suggestion to hang Liu's portrait on Tiananmen Gate instead of Mao's on re-election day – an idea Liu had to veto at once. So although Mao boasted to Liu, 'Who do you think you are? I can wag my little finger and there will be no more you!', it was not so easy for Mao to make good his threats. And he was in real danger of being forced to be a figurehead – which was why Mao needed a purge as mammoth and as horrendous as the Cultural Revolution.

Among the things Guangmei did to assist her husband was to make friends with the wives of Mao's devotees in critical positions, which helped secure their husbands' support for Liu. In their circle, it was referred to as 'the Diplomacy of Wives': *fu-ren-wai-jiao*. Although in the end the Lius failed, they had at least taken the plunge and fought.

Mao had liked Guangmei in the past, and had said rather personal things to her, such as he was having health problems which might be due to 'male menopause'. Now he hated her as much as he did her husband – for her guts, and for their love for each other. At a denunciation meeting inside Zhongnanhai, the Party headquarters, the Lius were punched and slapped by crowds. But at one point Guangmei tore free and gripped a corner of her husband's jacket; for a few moments the couple struggled to stand up straight holding hands tight. Their defiance, sustained by their love, could not have been clearer to Mao, who had ordered the whole thing to be filmed and watched it. While he made Liu die a painful slow death, he had Guangmei thrown into Qincheng under the ludicrous charges of being a spy for the CIA – and for the Japanese and Chiang Kai-shek, for good measure.

I knew how ghastly life in prison had been for Guangmei and what superhuman strength she had needed to survive. In fact, she could have got out easily, if she had disowned her husband. But she refused to do so. Once, Mao, acting magnanimous, gave permission for her children to visit her. She turned the offer down: 'I said I don't want to see my children – not until I am cleared of the charges.' I was nonplussed, and asked, 'But why not?' She answered, with just a hint of sadness in her expression, 'You don't know this, but once you see your children, your willpower will weaken, and you just want to do anything to get out.' She stayed in prison for over a decade until she and her husband were fully cleared after Mao died.

We had talked for well over two hours. And it was lunch time. Guangmei said she was only going to eat some leftovers, but if I did not mind, I could join her. It was the simplest meal I had during all my stays in Beijing: a hotchpotch of mostly rice and vegetables. And it was one of the most delicious.

*

When Mao was purging his colleagues, he liked to say it was the wishes of the Red Guards, whom he then used to torment them. In the case of the Lius, he selected a student by the name of Kuai Dafu, leader of the Red Guards of Tsinghua University, one of the top universities in Beijing. Kuai was designated to announce to the country that the president of China had fallen into disgrace by organising a demonstration through the streets of Beijing shouting, 'Down with Liu Shaoqi!'

Nearly thirty years later, in October 1995, I met Kuai in Shenzhen, a new city that had been created from paddy fields by Deng Xiaoping after Mao's death. Deng had intended for the place, which borders Hong Kong (Jon and I had been driven over from Hong Kong by car), to model itself on the then British colony and pioneer China's economic reforms. Today it is one of the most populous cities and an impressive metropolis, but the Shenzhen I saw was still an immense building site – except that ambitious entrepreneurs had already begun converging there from all over the country to try and make their fortunes. Kuai was one of them.

He came to my hotel and gave me a candid interview. Wearing a commonplace blue jacket and looking equally unremarkable, this former Red Guard leader had in fact had nationwide fame and a big following in the Cultural Revolution – for which he was made a scapegoat and sent to prison for seventeen years. On the day he was released, in the 1980s, cars with his former fellow Red Guards at the wheels were waiting outside the prison to greet him. He related that scene to me with unconcealed pride, before informing me, also proudly, that he had been invited to America to take part in a forum discussing the Cultural Revolution. I asked how the trip went; he shook his head and said he did not go. The police, which kept him on a tight leash, told him not to, promising instead to help make his business ventures profitable. He did make a lot of money.

During our several-hour-long interview, Kuai gave me a blow-by-blow account of how he had been stage-managed to persecute the Lius, frankly, unapologetically, with some satisfaction because Mao had considered him useful. He related in detail how Premier Zhou Enlai, Mao's envoy, had first approached him: he was woken in the middle of the night and found Zhou in front of him; he was too awestruck to sit properly and perched on the edge of a sofa for their conversation. Kuai repeated Mme Mao's telephone call to him just before the denunciation rally of three hundred thousand people he was staging against Guangmei, saying, 'Jiang Qing was telling me explicitly, in effect, to humiliate Wang Guangmei . . . We could insult her any way we wanted.' And so they did, following Jiang Qing's precise instructions. He did not offer any reflections, and I did not quiz him. My interviews were about facts, about what happened. I never asked my interviewees to reflect.

But Kuai offered his observation: facing the huge crowd calling for her blood, Guangmei acted with great bravery, which he talked about with admiration: 'She stood straight, and refused to bow her head when ordered to. Our students went at her with force, tremendous force, and pushed her down to her knees . . . But instantly she stood up straight. Wang Guangmei would not be cowed.' This so much reminded me of my father at denunciation meetings that for a second Kuai's face began to blur. I quickly looked away and gazed at my little tape recorder. The steady running of the tape inside the silver case restored my equilibrium.

12

Navigating Peril in Sichuan

(the 1990s)

When I started the biography of Mao with Jon, my mother stopped playing a big role in my working life. She was in her sixties, and spent a lot of time with her friends. In the 1990s, as Beijing blocked people's political talents and encouraged the whole population to make money, millions of unfulfilled and clever officials and intellectuals abandoned their careers that were not going anywhere and went into commercial ventures. This phenomenon had a name: 'Getting into the sea' – *xia-hai*.

My mother did not 'get into the sea' herself, but she had friends who leaped in at the deep end. And they needed money. I had been sending her some of the royalties from *Wild Swans* because they were also her rewards. The sums were substantial, especially in the Chinese currency. Many people knew this, and some coveted her cash.

My mother had a visceral disregard for money. She had grown up knowing that her mother had had a luxurious yet sad life as the concubine of General Xue, and was then poor and happy when married to Dr Xia. With those childhood lessons, she in her adolescence rejected rich suitors and chose to train to be an ill-paid schoolteacher. Under the Communists, my family's lifestyle was largely unrelated to the salaries of my parents, but was dependent on the privileges doled out by the Party. I was brought up to regard 'money' – *qian* – as a dirty word. As a child and reading a spy story in comic-strip form, I could not comprehend why the spy was motivated by money. How bizarre! I thought. After I came to Britain, unlike most Chinese mothers who would wish their daughters to marry wealthy men in the West, my mother cautioned me against 'becoming a Nora', who, in Ibsen's *A Doll's House*, had a rich husband but an unfulfilled life. With this dismissive attitude towards money, my mother was ill-suited to the new money-worshipping society China was becoming.

When she was in London one year, the novelist Martin Amis and his sharp-witted first wife, Antonia, invited us to dinner. Our conversation turned to the rise of corruption in China, and the author of *Money* asked my mother what one would have to give for a favour to, say, the governor of Sichuan, our province, which was the size of France. My mother hesitated, and said tentatively that probably a carton of '555', then the most expensive and desirable cigarettes. Martin chuckled, 'This is like slipping Mitterrand a fiver.' To my mother, even expensive gifts were inappropriate. She was a total stranger to the world of greed and corrupt practice involving obscene sums.

She would find out through her own painful experience the power of money. Among those who visited her with an eye for her cash were two men who had been kind to my father and to her in the Cultural Revolution and had suffered as a result. My mother was deeply grateful, and mentioned them (not by name) in *Wild Swans*. They saw from the book the depth of her

gratitude, and came to beg her to 'invest' in their 'most promising business ventures'. She found it hard to refuse. Their
'ventures' cleaned her out of all the money I had sent her over
the years. One 'venture' turned out to be a scam that targeted
retired officials with good pensions, some of whom also had
devoted and successful children. The main conman was sentenced to fifteen years' imprisonment for financial fraud. The
victims lost every cent they put in, most of them their homes as
well, which the fraudsters had mortgaged. Three elderly people
killed themselves by leaping from the roofs of their apartment
buildings. Those casualties of Communist China's introduction to capitalism highlighted the plight of many who were
ill-adapted to a money-oriented society, and who were vulnerable to the sharks that thronged the country's capitalist 'sea'.

My mother was lucky to have kept her apartment, which, as
people began to be allowed to buy properties, we bought in a
new property development. It has a picturesque name, the Village of Green Poplars, and my mother gave her old flat built in
the 1980s to my sister.

The frauds were heavy blows to my mother, not only in
terms of financial loss, but also to her confidence in her own
judgement. She reproached herself harshly and felt she had let
me down. She did not tell me about it, and just tried to save
money in all sorts of ways. I only heard about it indirectly and
sent her more money. I never brought up the subject, but
wanted to tell her that I loved her more for her all-too-decent
weakness in trusting even the wrong people. I wanted to say to
her jokily that since she had so little regard for money, money
perhaps just did not want to stay with her. Eventually, she proposed a solution: that I transfer the money to my sister, who
lived in Chengdu and could pay bills for her. So, to friends who
came to solicit 'investment', she could honestly say that she
had no money to spare. While her daily life was taken care of

by her state pension, I would pay for her two most costly expenditures: a live-in domestic to look after her, and her medical bills. My mother was besieged by health problems and her medical bills were large, even though as a retired official, she enjoyed some privileges.

Medical care in China was, and still is, cripplingly expensive, and a major illness, such as cancer, could bankrupt a family – which is why people save. A close relative was diagnosed with rectal cancer, and the cost of having it treated was nearly half a million yuan, the equivalent of roughly 70,000 US dollars, far beyond her family's savings; so several relations, including me, contributed. In hospital the patients' families were routinely asked to choose between medicines made in China, cheaper but not so effective, and those imported from Western countries, much superior but many times the cost. It is a heart-rending dilemma for poor families.

My mother was a stoic woman. Once, I was startled to see that one of her index fingers was so crooked that it was almost in the shape of an L, and I asked her about it. She said quite nonchalantly that she had once fallen on that finger at a denunciation meeting when pushed to the ground, and it had been broken. With so many troubles preoccupying her, an injured finger seemed trivial, and she never bothered to have it looked at. As she got older, it had grown into that shape. I could not bear to look at the finger, and yet my mother paid it no attention.

As she was entering old age, my mother's greatest joy was having her youngest son, Xiaofang, around. He was about a decade younger than her other four children and had always been the apple of her eye. When he was a baby, he had been the centre of attention in the family, and we all played with our kid brother as if he were a big toy. As an adult, he was the life and soul of parties and family gatherings, his amusing repartee and off-the-cuff wisecracks constantly having us all in stitches. Xiaofang had studied French in Sichuan before earning a master's degree from the University of Strasbourg III, France. After graduation, he worked as a freelance representative for a French company, and chose to live in Chengdu to be near our mother. It is impossible to exaggerate the comfort he has brought to her and the relief to me as I live at the other end of the world.

At the end of 1993, by chance at a friend's dinner, Xiaofang learned that there was an opportunity to mine gold in the remote mountains of northeast Sichuan. There had been a major mine there, operated by the armed police of the state, who had largely exhausted its reserves. Before the place was to be flooded and turned into a reservoir, the government allowed individuals to mine and sell their output to official agencies. Hundreds of people got rich. Xiaofang and a few friends decided to try their luck. My mother had apprehensions. She had looked into the venture and knew that Xiaofang could lose his life or be badly injured. Mountains had to be dynamited by amateurs to create the mines, which were inevitably primitive and could easily collapse and bury him. The mines were up to eighty metres deep, and large rocks or heavy baskets of soil hopefully containing gold had to be pulled up by ropes, which could snap and crush him. Local gangsters, seasoned spotters of gold, would be waiting at the mine entrances to try to seize the output if it looked promising. If Xiaofang was lucky enough to strike gold, he might be forced to get into a fight with the gangsters, or other envious miners. Murders over mined gold and gold-rich mines were commonplace.

I urged my mother to persuade Xiaofang not to go. 'The gold is not worth his life,' I said to her on the phone.

(International calls were increasingly easy and inexpensive.) I knew my words were gratuitous as 'gold' meant nothing to my mother. But she said not a word to discourage Xiaofang. As always, she never interfered with the decisions of her children. Like a mother eagle, who nudges out her eaglets and sends them flying, my mother never held her children back when they were keen to test their wings.

Xiaofang and his friends travelled a whole day over hundreds of miles by train and car to get to the site, which was surrounded by looming mountain peaks lit only by a feeble moon. The landscape was bleak. Under a yellowish electric bulb, they were entertained by local government officials. They paid for a plot of land vouched for by their prospector, hired a group of labourers, purchased dynamite and equipment – and last but not least, bought guns, including a machine gun, all of which were deemed necessary for self-protection and were for sale. Like his partners, Xiaofang acquired two bodyguards. He started to hear, and to see, gunfights.

He was in those mountains for five months, and only contacted my mother once to tell her that he was safe and to ask her to send him more money urgently. To make the phone call, he had to walk for two hours on treacherous mountain paths to get to the nearest post office, where he and my mother had to shout to hear each other on the line. He sensed her worries, even though he played down the risks. Still, she never asked her treasured and indispensable youngest son to leave the mines.

In the end, Xiaofang came home in one piece but without gold. His mine had been poor in quality, and he and his partners made hardly any money after their expenses. Because of his bad luck, no one harassed them. It was those who struck gold who had to fear for their lives. The owners of a good mine with whom they had made friends had escaped one moonless night with sacks of gold-rich soil on their backs. When Xiao-fang told this story at our family dinner table, my mother said that she could well imagine how fearful the successful gold-miners were as they groped their way along the edges of the dark cliffs, and she was only too pleased that Xiaofang had not been under those gold-rich sacks.

During the years when I was researching Mao in China, I visited my mother every year, but my stays were short, as the witnesses on my interview list lived elsewhere, mostly in the capital. But one spring in Chengdu, I met a former high official of the province, Chu, who had been in Yan'an at the same time as my father, in the early 1940s. At the time tens of thousands of young people like my father travelled from Kuomintang-controlled cities to Yan'an, Mao's headquarters during the war against Japan, to pursue their ideals, which they thought Yan'an embodied. I had met quite a few of those former young volunteers in Beijing, and invariably they talked about their disillusionment after they settled in what they had regarded as their 'Mecca'. 'Equality', one main ideal that had attracted them, turned out to be non-existent. Food, clothing, accommodation, medical care ... were all strictly graded according to Party ranks, often unfairly. There was a popular crack that went, 'In Yan'an, only three things are equal to all – the sun, the air, and the [equally stinking] toilets.'

Facing widespread discontent, Mao decided to use terror to scare the young volunteers into obedience. In 1943, he launched a 'spy-catching' campaign, practically accusing all of them of being Kuomintang spies. Yan'an was turned into a tightly sealed prison. The volunteers were herded to frenzied mass rallies at which they were under horrendous pressure to con-fess to being spies, and to denounce others. Those who stuck to their innocence could be trussed up on the spot and dragged away to mock execution. The fear generated by those rallies was unbearable. A close colleague of Mao's remarked at the time that the rallies were 'an extremely serious war on nerves. To some people, they are more devastating than any torture.' The Communist underground in Sichuan, which my father had joined before travelling to Yan'an, was condemned whole-sale as a 'spy organisation', and its leader committed suicide. The campaign lasted two years and found no spies among its victims, but the terrorisation turned the young volunteers from spontaneous and passionate advocates of justice into 'cogs' in Mao's machine. That experience marked my father, then barely twenty years old, for the rest of his life. During his insanity in the Cultural Revolution, when I was staying at home to look after him, there were a couple of nights when he talked obses-sively about the 'spy-catching' rallies, his eyes exuding strange, intense emotions, not least fear. I had never seen that expres-sion and was so scared that I pulled the sheet up to cover my head. At the time I had no idea what my father was talking about. I still had no idea when I was writing *Wild Swans*. It was only during the research for the biography of Mao that I began to learn, and to comprehend, what my father had been through to become a devoted member of Mao's Party.

I asked Chu about his experience as a victim of the terror campaign. To my surprise, he chortled, 'No, I was not a victim. I was one of the victimisers!' It turned out that in Yan'an he was working for the security apparatus, then called the Social Department, and was an interrogator of the volunteers. I was taken aback, and was keen to know more about his work. There was not enough time to talk on that occasion, but he readily agreed that when I returned to Chengdu that autumn, I could go to his home to do a proper interview. And so I did.

As my questions became probing, Chu paused and asked

who I had interviewed in Beijing. Trying to be honest without offending him, I answered that I thought it would be best for everyone if I did not discuss my interviewees' identities. This was what I had told people who asked the question, and they had all been satisfied with it. But this time things were different. The congenial avuncular figure sitting across the desk was suddenly transformed into an ogre, bearing down on me with tremendous force conveyed by his eyes as well as his body language, his voice not raised but charged with inexplicable power and authority. He pressed me for an answer: 'Who have you seen? Who have you seen?!' Despite all my experiences of confronting odious people and sitting through denunciation meetings in the Cultural Revolution, I had not felt such unsettling pressure directly on me. I was shaken and for a moment felt confused and compelled to produce an answer. After a quick mental calculation that concluded that the widow of the former president was the least vulnerable, I mumbled, 'For example Wang Guangmei.' As soon as I said the words, I regretted it and felt as if I had betrayed Guangmei's confidence – although she had never asked me to keep our conversations confidential. Like other interviewees, her trust in me was implicit. I was in agony.

As suddenly as it had appeared, the ogre disappeared, and sitting across the desk from me was that congenial avuncular figure again, now with a grin on his face, presumably from seeing the effectiveness of his little interrogation technique. I calmed down and went on with my questions, learning about the existence of the secret prison caves of the Social Department in the yellow-earth canyons outside Yan'an, which I would visit the following year. I had had a tiny taste of the ferocity and devastation of the interrogations, and my heart went out to the young volunteers like my father, who had been subjected to much, much worse pressure to admit to being 'spies' and to implicate friends as members of 'spy rings'. They would have been completely unprepared because of their youth, their innocence, and because they had come to their 'Mecca' with the purest intentions. When I read later that in the terror campaign hundreds of young people went out of their minds and dozens killed themselves, I understood now how it would have happened.

After I left Chu's house, I wandered the streets of Chengdu to calm myself down and was still tense when I returned home. My mother asked what the matter was, and cleared my confusion, putting me at ease instantly, by saying: 'What harm could Chu possibly do to the widow of President Liu Shaoqi even if he wanted to? And he would not want to as he had talked to you himself! Stop worrying unnecessarily.' She told me that she had in fact just paid Chu a visit. After I left, she had a premonition that the former interrogator might spring some unpleasant surprises on me. So she took off to Chu's. He was most amicable, and, informing her that I had gone, entertained her to tea, during which he praised me, saying he was glad I had achieved success by writing books, rather than doing business like others. My mother thought he was trying to be friendly. I put my head on her shoulder and embraced her, feeling all safe again.

In September 1997, while I was in Chengdu, I mentioned to my mother that I wanted to visit the Luding Bridge over the Dadu River, some two hundred mountainous miles to the west, and in Sichuan. The bridge was legendary. In May 1935, during the Long March, when Mao and the Red Army had been driven out of their bases in southeast China and were moving to a new base with Yan'an as its centre in the northwest (in order to 'get close to the Soviet border', according to Stalin's instructions), they crossed that bridge. Built at the very beginning of the eighteenth century, this suspension bridge between cliffs was over a hundred metres long and three metres wide, paved with wooden planks on top of nine iron chains. Under the bridge the river flowed fast with treacherous waves, especially in May, when it was swollen with melting snow from the Himalayas. The American journalist Edgar Snow, who played the biggest role in making Mao and the CCP attractive in the West, had used this dramatic setting and produced a description of the Red Army crossing the bridge in his classic book *Red Star Over China*. Based on the stories told to him by Party propagandists, he wrote: 'Half the wooden floor had been removed [by the Kuomintang], and before them only the bare iron chains swung to a point midway in the stream. At the northern bridgehead an enemy machine-gun nest faced them . . . who would have thought the Reds would insanely try to cross on the chain alone? But that was what they did.' Under his pen, Red Army soldiers were being shot and falling into the raging river, but the rest continued to crawl on the bare chains 'on their hands and knees, tossing grenade after grenade into the enemy machine-gun nest'. This scene, worthy of a Hollywood adventure movie, caught people's imagination, and the bridge became the symbol of the Long March, which at thousands of miles long and full of hardships was easily presented as a heroic epic. I just had to go and have a look at that iconic bridge.

My mother came with me. Snow's book had influenced her when she was a teenager, and had helped draw her into the CCP. Neither she nor any other fellow left-wing students knew that the Party had not only provided him with the descriptions but also organised the translation of the book into Chinese, changing the title to a less 'red' *Journey to the West*, to give the impression that it was a neutral book written by an objective American.

My mother made the travel arrangements. An office manager she knew enthusiastically provided a four-wheel drive, and my mother invited his wife to come with us. I also invited a Party historian I knew from the history research institute of Sichuan, Teng. The drive, often on hairpin-bend mountain roads, took the best part of a day. Along the way, Teng, a middle-aged lean and lively man, who had researched the Long March in Sichuan and found out many unknown facts, talked non-stop as I expressed great interest and switched on my tape recorder. Party historians often itched to talk, because they had a lot of knowledge about the true history of modern China, thanks to their sanctioned access to first-hand sources, from documents to eyewitnesses. And they were deeply frustrated because they could not write about the truth, or discuss it with other people. With an eager, trustworthy listener, they came alive. The presence of the driver and the manager's wife did not bother Teng: the historical events he was talking about were unfamiliar or uninteresting to non-specialists – at least that was the impression I got.

With Teng as a guide, my visit to the Luding Bridge proved most fruitful. It was late when we arrived, and we stayed the night in the town, a stone's throw from the bridge. I rushed him to it the next morning as soon as breakfast was over, and for a moment I stood marvelling at both the river, which was a turbulent mass even in autumn, and the bridge, magnificently suspended between bridgeheads that looked like entrances to grand palaces. We stepped onto the planks of the bridge and started walking, and the bridge swayed over rushing waves below. I felt dizzy and had to hold on to the chain on the side to steady myself. The chain, identical to those below, defied my attempt to grip it with my hands: it was too slippery from the vapour of the river. I tried to imagine crawling on it and decided that was impossible, because the chain was far too small for a human body to lie on, and there was a gap of over thirty centimetres to the next chain. It could not be clearer to me that Snow's description of the Reds crawling along the chains was sheer fantasy, still more outlandish was their tossing hand grenades while crawling. The Red Army soldiers were no Spidermen, they were flesh-and-blood human beings, famished, exhausted, having been on the march through untold hardships for eight months.

We visited the museum that commemorated the Red Army crossing. Those 'Red Museums', dotted around China where milestone events in the history of the CCP had taken place, were invaluable sources of information, as I had by now learned. Not only did they often sell collections of documents from the local publishing houses, they contained exhibits that showed the facts and thus revealed the truth. In this museum, among the maps, photos and documents was a copy of issue number 186 of the mimeographed Red Army newspaper *Soldier* (*zhan-shi*), published just after the crossing and with it as the theme. In the issue, skirmishes along the river, a crossing by boats elsewhere, and the forced march of dozens of miles to the bridge, all made headlines – but not that latter-day world famous 'battle of the Luding Bridge', which took up just two sentences. There was a mention of the twenty-one soldiers who were the first to go over the bridge. They were all safe and sound at the other end.

A local historian I met at the museum took me to interview some locals. A ninety-three-year-old woman had run a beancurd eatery next to the bridge, and she remembered the Red Army well, as some soldiers had been billeted in her house. She described the crossing as orderly, with no fighting. Some of the planks of wood on the bridge had to be reinforced for the march of an army, so Red soldiers borrowed the doors from her and her neighbours. After the Reds were gone, she went to collect her door.

I sat chatting with her under a picture of Christ. The locals were mostly Catholics, and the Red Army had set up its headquarters in the nearby church, which was a grand cathedral. Mao had stayed a night there, in the quarters of the French priest who had fled. At least partly because of this Mao connection, Beijing had issued funds to renovate the church. When I went to see it, I found its walls well-mended, Romanesque windows restored to their old shapes, and on the huge thick front door, carvings of Bible stories carefully retraced. Only it could not be used. Instead, the locals were allowed to hold religious services in the home of a middle-aged woman, who showed me the altar, with a wooden cross, an assortment of colourful pictures of Christ, and lots of silken flowers. Outside the house, under the wide eaves where bunches of golden corn and bundles of motley firewood were stacked, she pointed to distant peaks in the clouds and said there had been a leper colony, run by foreign nuns, until the Communists expelled them.

Talking to the locals and Party historians, I realised just how crucial the Luding Bridge was to China. It was the key link between Sichuan and Tibet, and it was irreplaceable, because it was extremely difficult to build another one. Attempts at building an alternative bridge under various regimes had all failed. I saw a discarded iron bridge rusting away in the wilderness like the skeleton of a steel dinosaur. Engraved on the imposing bridgehead was a star that would have been painted red but had by now faded to colourlessness. That abandoned bridge was built by the Communists in 1950–51 for the purpose of marching into Tibet, and was ultimately abandoned. The Luding Bridge remained the only passage for many more decades. Chiang Kai-shek, ruler of the country at the time of the Long March, would not have wanted to risk damaging it by making it a battleground.

Discovering that there had been no battle on the bridge did

not feel to me like a big deal, as the myth was so outlandish, and so easy to prove false. I also thought that anyone studying history seriously would know that any wartime propaganda, by however worthy a side, was bound to exaggerate and had to be taken with a pinch of salt. So, when Jon and I started writing our biography of Mao, I wanted to put the disproof of the 'battle on the Luding Bridge' in a footnote. Jon, who knew better how much and how many intelligent people cherished that Maoist symbol, prevailed on me to give it more space. To my (perhaps naive) astonishment, when our biography was published, we were much attacked by supposedly serious academics for daring to say there had been no battle on the bare chains – until a historian dug up a conversation between Deng Xiaoping and the US president Jimmy Carter's national security adviser Zbigniew Brzezinski, who visited the bridge – such was its fame – in 1982. When Brzezinski talked admiringly (even he!) about 'a great feat of arms', Deng smiled and said that 'It really wasn't that much of a feat, but we felt we had to dramatise it.'* It fell to a Communist leader to shatter an obdurate belief in Communist propaganda.

When I left the Luding Bridge for Chengdu, I had no inkling of the storm my discovery would one day cause. Nor did I ever imagine that people would be so fixated on one battle as proof of the Red Army's heroism. After all, what did it matter if there was no fighting on that bridge – there were other ugly battles in which Red soldiers endured tremendous batterings and showed great courage. I had in fact discovered just such a

* Brzezinski speech at Stanford, 2005, p. 3. See https://fsi-live.s3.us-west-1.amazonaws.com/s3fs-public/evnts/media/Brzezinski_New_Asia_03_2005.pdf

battle – that of Tucheng, which took place a few hundred miles to the southeast of the bridge in January 1935. The Red Army was at another river, the Red River, which separated two provinces, Sichuan to the north and Guizhou to the south. The river ran the colour of blood because of the red sand it was carrying, and because the dense green forests on both banks presented a stark contrast. Trying to cross the river into Sichuan, the Red Army suffered enormous casualties. Four thousand men, a tenth of the total Red force under Mao, were killed, or wounded and left behind in the wintry forests – mostly to die in heavy snowfalls. Tucheng was unknown even to those who thought they knew the history of the CCP, and I only learned about it during my investigation. It was taboo because the battle had been initiated, insisted on, and conducted by Mao, against the opposition of virtually all other leaders, after he had seized control of the Party that month. Tucheng subverted a primal myth about Mao – that he had saved the Red Army when it was on the brink of extinction, which was why he became the undisputed leader of the CCP. The truth was that right after he seized power he led the Red Army to its biggest and most devasting defeat on the whole of the Long March.*

Among the Red Army men who had been wounded and left behind, few survived. But there was a survivor in a village

* Mao initiated the battle of Tucheng knowing the Reds would be beaten by the famously ferocious Sichuan army. He used the defeat to stop the Red Army from going into Sichuan, which had been the agreed – and unavoidable – route. Mao did not want to go into Sichuan because he did not want to join forces with another branch of the Red Army there, led by Zhang Guotao, the rival he greatly feared. Mao was afraid that once the Red forces joined up, Zhang would take over the leadership as he was regarded as much better qualified for the job. For the details of Mao's Machiavellian power struggles, which made the Long March about a third longer and generated untold suffering for the Red Army, see the Long March chapters in Jung Chang and Jon Halliday, *Mao: The Unknown Story*.

not far from our route, and we made a detour to visit him. Niu, a sprightly man aged around eighty, sporting a goatee over a faded blue Mao-era jacket, had been a low-ranking Red officer when he was hit by a bullet in the leg. He now lived as a peasant in an ordinary house with mud floors. We sat on low benches, which gave me a close view of his old gunshot wound, when he rolled up his trouser leg to show me. It bore the marks of bad infections. His comrades had left him with a family in a mountain village when they had to move on, and he told the villagers that he was not even a soldier, but had been roped in to be a porter. The family was kind to him. I asked how the local Kuomintang force treated him. He said that they had come asking for his 'gun and bullets'. He told them he did not have any weapon; they did not believe him and, after trussing him up, they hung him from the beam of the house and started beating him, threatening to beat him to death. The family that took him in pleaded, 'If you are going to kill him, please put in writing that it was you who did it. Otherwise, when the Reds come back – they said they would – they are going to kill us for revenge.' The local force relented and released Niu, taking away his bedroll, which had been left for him by his comrades and was valuable.

Later, he fell in love with and married a woman he met and went to live with her family down the mountains, which was where we visited him. Our conversation got to when the Communists finally came back fifteen years later, when they took power. I remarked, 'You must have been so excited—' He retorted, 'Excited? What are you talking about? My wife's family was classified as a "landlord" in the Land Reform, just because they had hired a couple of farmhands . . .' Their house and possessions were confiscated. Fortunately, he was not treated too badly because he had been a Red officer. Still, life was hard, as it was for other peasants – until 1979, when

Author photo for *Wild Swans*, the story of my grandmother, my mother and myself. Its publication in 1991 changed my life; I became a writer.

Top: My mother and I stand in front of a window display of *Wild Swans* in London. The Chinese characters on the glass read 'Waterstones', the name of the bookshop. **Below left:** The writer Martin Amis and I exchanging our newly published books, 1991. Martin's book is *Time's Arrow*. **Below right:** Receiving an award for *Wild Swans*.

Top left: Jon and I at our wedding reception with our families, 1991. From left: Jon's older brother David Halliday, his wife Gerti, Jon's younger brother Fred, his wife Maxine, Jon, me, my sister-in-law Rong, my brothers Jinming and Xiaohei.
Bottom left: Collecting my British passport in January 1989. To my adopted country I am full of gratitude. **Below right:** Lady Thatcher presenting me with an Honorary Doctorate as Chancellor of the University of Buckingham, 1993.
Top right: Camel-riding on holiday in Egypt.

CLIVE HOUSE
Public entrance

'94年10月20日

Top: My mother and I on our research trip for *Wild Swans*, 1989. **Middle:** Me researching Mao, talking to a peasant in 1994 in the Great Leader's birthplace Shaoshan. **Below:** Sitting on the edge of an enormous wooden bed of Mao's. Half of it would have been piled a foot high with books, so he could easily read in bed, which was his favourite pastime – even though he denied books to the Chinese population for over a decade in the Cultural Revolution.

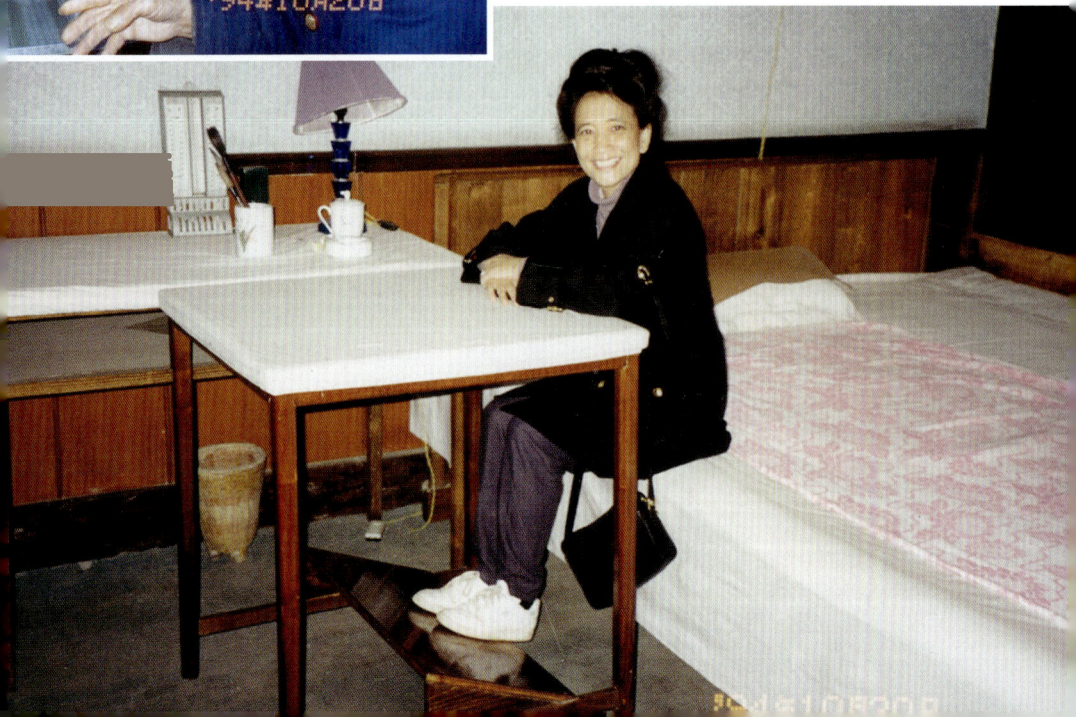

Making historical discoveries.
Top left: Finding the suppressed manuscripts of Mao's second wife Yang Kaihui. A guide pointing at where they had been hidden. **Middle:** Li Rui, China's most outspoken and renowned liberal senior official, gave me much help over the years. He was 100 when this picture was taken. **Bottom:** Interviewing Wang Guangmei, widow of former president Liu Shaoqi. On the table in front was the present I brought her: a bottle of Dior perfume from Harrods. **Top right:** With Grandma Deng, Deng Xiaoping's stepmother, before beginning our interview.

Revealing journeys. **Top left:** Jon and I visiting Albania, once China's only ally, where toppled giant statues of Stalin and Hoxha were, in 1998, being melted down for artists to make sculptures such as a curvaceous female figure. **Top right:** Jon and I interviewing Henry Kissinger, Mao's most prominent cheerleader in the West. **Below:** At the Luding Bridge, symbol of Red heroism created by another Mao propagandist, the American journalist Edgar Snow. Trying to hold on to a chain, I realised that the Reds could not have fought a battle crawling on chains like this, as the myth claims.

Jon. Top: With my mother at a market in my hometown Yibin, Sichuan. **Middle:** Jon introduced me to Rome, which we both adore. Having dinner at Piazza Navona. **Below:** In my study in London during the writing of our biography of Mao, which took us 12 years.

My mother. Top: Spreading flower petals on the tombs of my grandma (with white tombstone) and my father. On Father's tombstone is also Mother's name, covered by a piece of fabric, which will be peeled off when she dies and her ashes join his. **Middle left:** With me. **Middle right:** Aged 93 in 2024, talking to me via the mobile phone screen, as I am no longer able to visit her. **Below:** With all her five children at the celebration of her 70th birthday in Chengdu, 2001.

the post-Mao government started to right past wrongs, and he was given a pension of 49 yuan a month, somewhat higher than a labourer's wage. He was satisfied with this reward, even though it had come nearly half a century too late.

As a rare Red Army survivor, Niu was brought out to tell the stories of the Long March on official occasions, once even to some Canadian Maoists. I did not know whether he adapted his stories to his audiences, but to Teng and me he seemed frank. I had just read two memoirs by Long Marchers, and both mentioned that Mao and other leaders travelled in bamboo litters carried by labourers or soldiers, which had been a sore issue among the rank and file – and which had shocked me at first. One of the memoirs had been given to me by the author, the widow of the former Party number-one Zhang Wentian, when I saw her in Beijing. She had been an old friend of Mao, and wrote in her memoir how Mao had shown off his litter to her, telling her he had designed it himself, with an awning that could shield him from the sun and the rain.

When I brought up the issue of the litters, a sudden anger erupted in Niu's voice, and he said indignantly: the leaders 'talked about equality, but they lounged in litters, like landlords. We didn't dare to speak out loud, we talked in whispers . . .' The Party explained to the Red Army men that 'our leaders are having a much harder time. Although they don't walk or carry loads like we do, their brains never stop working and life for them is much tougher than for us. We only walk and eat, we don't have cares.' Niu was obviously unconvinced.

On this trip, my mother seldom joined me, and stayed for no more than a few minutes on each occasion. Most of the time she strolled with the wife of the manager who had arranged our car, or sat with her in small roadside teahouses. After we returned to Chengdu, I asked my mother, 'Why did you invite her in the first place? It would have been much more interesting to go around with Teng and me.' My mother said: 'She is a very nice lady, and I knew the trip would be a treat for her. But most importantly, you have been running around all over the place finding out all those things. They are dangerous things! My heart is always in my throat for you. I fear – well, at least with this lady coming with us, I could be sure that you would not have a "car accident" on this trip.'

My mother felt the danger of my work much more keenly than I did. But she never asked me to stop doing it or to pull my punches. She just tried to protect me at every turn.

13

Kidney Stones and Poison Plots

(the 1990s)

While I was researching in China, Jon was busy working in Moscow, delving into the voluminous archive material and interviewing people who had close relationships with Mao and the CCP. After its founding, the Chinese party was obliged to submit all its documents to the Kremlin, its boss, while it had no proper archive of its own. Those documents had been carried by messengers travelling thousands of miles from the Chinese interior to Moscow, before secret radio communications were established. After Stalin's death in 1953, the Soviet leader Nikita Khrushchev no longer sought to dominate Mao and gave most documents back to China as a friendly gesture. They formed the basis of the ultra-secretive Central Archives in Beijing, to which even official historians were not allowed easy access. I was told that if they wanted to read about a certain issue, and on the page were other issues, the document would be shown to them with the other items covered by blank sheets of paper. I would not be allowed in, and never tried.

But no matter, Jon was studying them in Moscow – thanks to Yeltsin opening the door and Jon's near-fluent Russian. After each trip, he came home weighed down with bags of invaluable papers, full of explosive revelations. When our biography of Mao was published in 2005, Beijing sent a delegation to Moscow with a list of the Russian archive sources we had quoted and photocopied all the documents, apparently spending, according to one Russian scholar involved, over $7,000 just on photocopying – which meant a lot of copies as photocopying was cheap and charged in roubles. Later, virtually all those files were closed or re-classified to make them less accessible.

For several years in the 1990s, I joined Jon and looked at some documents in Chinese in the Moscow archives. Jon knew Moscow well by now and took me to a good Georgian restaurant that had an unbeatable view of the Novodevichy Convent, where Russian leaders like Khrushchev (and in the years to come Yeltsin and Gorbachev) and great artists like Chekhov and Prokofiev were buried. One evening we invited Rishat Kudashev, the top Chinese-language interpreter for Soviet leaders, to dinner there. Kudashev, a very observant man with a superb memory, described to us the historic reception in the Kremlin in 1964 at which Russian defence minister Marshal Rodion Malinovsky said to Marshal Ho Lung, China's acting army chief at the time: 'We've got rid of our *Durak* [fool, referring to Khrushchev, who had just been deposed], now you get rid of yours, Mao.' Those fateful words thoroughly scared Mao and roused his worst suspicion – his Party opponents ganging up with Moscow to overthrow him. Purging all the suspects became one of his motives for the Cultural Revolution, in which Marshal Ho Lung, a host of army officers, and anyone who had dealt with Russia, would go through hell. Many would die appalling deaths, including Ho Lung.

During our meal, Jon was seized by a sudden pain in his abdomen and after great efforts to tough it out, he rushed to the bathroom. Kudashev said to me that judging by the sudden sharpness of Jon's pain, the problem was likely to be kidney stones. We hurried back to our hotel, and I called an ambulance, which rushed us to a hospital on the outskirts of the city. The roads were bumpy and inside the ambulance there was nothing for Jon to hold on to. All the time, he had to try not to fall off the bed. The hospital looked brand-new with few patients. From my experience in China, I guessed it had been built to serve the emerging rich and the influx of foreign tourists. Jon was put in a room with one other person, who had the television on at what sounded like full volume. Looking about the empty ward we asked for a single room. A babushka-looking nurse pooh-poohed our request and said to Jon, 'Why do you want to have a room of your own?!' She gave him one, nonetheless.

Kidney stones were diagnosed, and Jon was wheeled into an operating room, clutching his Russian–English dictionary. When he learned Russian as a child from the great-nephew of Tolstoy, he had only wanted to know about the palaces along the River Neva in St Petersburg and had had no interest in words to do with urological disorders.

I went to the next day's interview by myself. It was with the son of another political rival of Mao in the 1930s and 1940s, Wang Ming, who was to Mao as Trotsky was to Stalin. Wang Ming's prominence could be seen in the fact that when he died, in Moscow, where he had fled Mao's clutches, he was buried in the Novodevichy Cemetery. He and his family were the only Chinese interred in that prestigious burial ground in the Russian capital.

Wang junior, Danzhi, in his fifties and living in a flat in a featureless block that could be in Beijing or even Chengdu, was a historian working in Moscow's Institute of Far Eastern Studies. He had met Jon a couple of times before and was very fond of him. When I told him that Jon was in hospital with kidney stones, he exclaimed: 'I've got just the thing for him!' His father had survived three poisoning attempts by Mao, he told me, and as a result had developed dozens of kidney stones, which had only been cured by a particular herb. Danzhi climbed up a stepladder and from the top of a large heavy bookcase, piled with boxes and parcels, he fished out a dusty bundle containing herbs wrapped in yellowing newspapers. I took it to the hospital, and in the small kitchenette attached to Jon's room made a stew in a saucepan. Jon, who was sceptical about the magic of the herbs, took a sip and spluttered, saying he'd prefer to have kidney stones. (The herbs are still in a cupboard in our kitchen in London.)

While Jon was still in hospital, I went to see Danzhi again, listening to his childhood memories of the first time his father was poisoned in Yan'an in 1943. A doctor working for the leadership and particularly close to Mme Mao had prescribed a lethal combination of medicines which produced corrosive mercury chloride, and brought Wang Ming to death's door. Danzhi remembered that one day his mother, who nursed his father devotedly, came into his room, closed the door behind her and rolled on the floor, kicking and tearing at things around, tears streaming down her face and her sobs stifled by a rag she had stuffed in her own mouth. Then aged four, Danzhi was frightened and hid himself in a corner. After a long while, his mother stood up in exhaustion, wiped away the tears, straightened her clothes and smoothed her hair – and went back to his father's bedside.

His mother, Meng Qingshu, was a prominent feminist in

her own right. Danzhi showed me her unpublished memoir about his father, who died after years of agony living with severely damaged internal organs. Attached to the manuscript was a copy of the report of a medical inquiry into the poisoning, conducted at the time to report to Stalin. The document, signed by a fifteen-member medical panel, confirmed the poisoning attempt and named the guilty doctor – who would rise to a high position in Mao's regime. (I would interview the only surviving signatory, one of the most eminent physicians in China, on my next trip to Beijing. When I arrived at his apartment, he greeted me briefly but courteously before sitting down, quietly waiting for me to get my tape recorder ready, and he related the process of the medical inquiry. He had been sent to stay with Wang Ming and check his urine every day for a month, and the results established that Wang Ming had been poisoned. Judging by the wealth of detail in the eminent physician's narration, he had obviously prepared this testimony carefully. Neither he nor the inquiry in Yan'an mentioned Mao; they only stated the fact that a deliberate poisoning attempt had been made on Wang Ming. It was Moscow's representatives in Yan'an who pointed their fingers at Mao.)

As Danzhi's parents were buried in Novodevichy Cemetery, he took me there. In front of their tomb, we saw a couple of young Chinese posing for photos. Danzhi was pleased his father was still a name in China even if only as a villain. He knew many luminaries of the Communist world who were buried in the cemetery, and walking round with him was riveting. Then it started to rain and we rushed out. I invited Danzhi for dinner, and he suggested going to a McDonald's. I did not know that American fast food was in vogue in Moscow, and thinking that he was suggesting a cheap option, recommended strongly the smartest Chinese restaurant in town, Dynasty. And there we went. That night I had an attack of food poisoning, and lay in bed in misery – not so much because of the sickness but at the thought that Danzhi might also be suffering from food poisoning and might suspect my motives in taking him to that restaurant, which the Chinese embassy used for entertaining. He had told me that the third attempt by Mao to poison his father was after his family fled to Russia. Mao's secret police chief Kang Sheng had brought them some special food from China. His family were suspicious and fed it to their dog, Tek, who died on the carpet in front of them. (Khrushchev related this episode in his memoirs, only mistakenly referring to the pet as a cat.) I was on tenterhooks for days until a call came from Danzhi thanking me for the meal. He had been perfectly fine.

When it was time to fly back to London, Jon's right arm was badly swollen from impure painkiller drips. During the journey, he insisted on lifting our suitcases, heavy with our papers, as he felt embarrassed letting me deal with them. In the end I made him wear a sling so he would feel better when I moved the cases. The sling was a long white silk scarf – indeed a khata – given to us by the Dalai Lama with his blessings, from a research trip across the Indian continent, which Jon had organised.

In Beijing, Party rules about contact with foreigners made it impossible for Jon to see most of our interviewees. He met some historians; but the sessions were like committee meetings, and we ended up sitting through long, boring Party line spiels. Once, the children of a member of Mao's staff persuaded their father to come to dinner with us; but the old man tensed up when he set eyes on Jon, and his heavily built body seemed to be shaking when he saw Jon's name card from King's College, University of London, where Jon at the time was a senior research fellow at the Department of War Studies. As the old man pointed at the words 'war studies' with a trembling finger, it dawned on us that the term was dangerous as the regime was likely to regard anyone engaged in it as 'spies'. We asked the old man no more questions, only chatting about his health and children. On another occasion, an open-minded prosecutor of the Gang of Four in the post-Mao trials had agreed to talk to Jon, but when we arrived at the gate of his compound, having travelled a long way, we saw him pacing outside, and feared that he had changed his mind at the last minute. He apologised to Jon, explaining that he needed permission to see him, to apply for which was complicated, and even if it was granted he would have to be accompanied by others at the meeting.

Fear of contact with foreigners put off most people who would have loved to meet Jon. But one man defied the rules: Li Rui, the most fearless liberal senior official in China and possibly the best known internationally. He had been a government minister and worked briefly as a secretary to Mao. In 1959, during the Great Famine, he stood up against Mao's inhuman policies, along with several other brave souls, including the then defence minister, Marshal Peng Dehuai. The purge of these courageous men was a milestone in Chinese history. Peng later died while incarcerated by Mao, and the price Li Rui paid for his bravery was twenty years in and out of solitary confinement and forced labour camps. In a poem he later wrote for us, in graceful calligraphy, he referred to himself proudly as someone who 'dares to be the first to speak out'. Indeed he was exactly that person.

The man who opened the door to us bore lightly that horrific, and heroic, past – and his current moral renown. Facing us was a man with an exceptionally frank face and a total natural ease. In a certain way he reminded me of my father, who was of a similar age: they both had none of the 'official air' or inscrutability that were common with Chinese officials. And both exuded incorruptibility. While my father often appeared pensive as if in some internal conflict, Li Rui had a decisiveness about him. So he threw caution to the wind and spoke up during the famine, while my father wanted to but held back fearing disastrous consequences for his family. My father agonised for years and finally spoke up in the Cultural Revolution, for which he died a tragic early death, while Li Rui survived hell and lived to be 101 years old.

When Jon and I were travelling in the provinces, it was difficult for our interviewees to avoid meeting him, and so we all sat down together – to everyone's delight, as most people were curious about our relationship. Some became friends and went to a few places with us as we journeyed across parts of China tracing Mao's footsteps. If our friends had been told by the Party to keep an eye on us, which seemed to me to be highly likely, it did not matter, as nothing we did was clandestine, and we only felt great warmth from our new friends. I was often struck by how easily people took to Jon. He spoke only a little Chinese as I discouraged him from learning, telling him that memorising thousands of ideograms by rote would be a waste of his mental energy and talents, including his linguistic gifts (he knows eight languages). But our friends appreciated his qualities. They smiled seeing Jon carrying my coat or sweater which I had taken off when the weather got hot in the middle of the day, and laughed when I could not remember a date or a name at an interview and Jon supplied the answer instantly when I turned to consult him. At moments like these, I felt so proud of my husband.

One man who travelled with us for some days became very

affectionate towards Jon. He called Jon 'my brother', and teased him good-humouredly, with the little English he spoke. One day in a restaurant with an interviewee, Jon removed my beer glass, putting his in its place. The man asked with his facial expression and hand gesture: Why? Jon showed him that my glass had a chip on the rim and basically 'told' him that as I was concentrating on the interview, I might hurt myself. The man was so delighted that he slapped Jon on the back, laughing and crying out, in English: 'Jon, you are a good wife!'

14

Journeys on the Trail of Blood

(the 1990s)

Mao came alive bit by bit before our eyes as we travelled in the provinces. We went to Shaoshan, his birthplace in Hunan province, in autumn 1994. The year before, China had celebrated his centenary, and of the vast number of books that had been published, one was by the Shaoshan Mao Zedong Memorial Museum, which showed some of his possessions at the time of his death. Among them was a menu of Western cuisine, with scores of mouth-watering dishes under seven headings: seafood, chicken, duck, pork, lamb, beef and soup. It had been devised in 1961, in the depths of the Great Famine. To the public, Mao had famously announced that he was 'sharing weal and woe with the nation' and was giving up eating meat. Much of the Chinese population are still being moved to tears today by the declaration, as the crowds of pilgrims thronging Shaoshan daily testify.

When Jon and I were there, the village was clearly attracting few tourists. We visited Mao's family house, and afterwards passed by a cottage, where a man aged about sixty, in a padded jacket in boilersuit blue and a fake-fur hat, sat by an open door on a low chair enjoying the sun – just like the peasants in my village in Deyang on a sunny day. We paused and greeted the man, who invited us in; Jon being a foreigner did not seem to bother him. People here were used to seeing foreigners. Inside the door was a typical 'sitting room' for a peasant, including my own in Deyang: mud floor, mud-brick walls crudely painted, and a few battered farm tools leaning against the wall. At a bare square table there were a few benches. The man talked about life being better than in the past. I asked him 'in what way is it better than the past', as his room looked as shabby and as bare of possessions as all the ones I had seen before. At this, a younger man who had come in and had been, after a brief nod, sitting across the room fixing a farm tool, cut in, 'I have a full stomach today; in the past I didn't! There were a couple of years when I worked all the year round and ended up owing money to the commune, after they deducted this and that taxes and fees. Think about it: I worked from morning till night, and I had to pay them and go hungry myself!' I sensed his anger. There had been similar reactions during my interviews when the past was brought up. The younger man checked himself, and when I asked him which 'couple of years' he was referring to, simply answered: 'Nineteen seventy-four, seventy-five.'

Those were not the years of the Great Famine (1958–61), and I remembered seeing crowds of beggars in the mid-1970s – when the old Party rule forbidding peasants from leaving their villages to beg in the cities lapsed along with the weakening of Mao's grip on the country in the last couple of years of his life. In those years, peasants in many provinces were at their hungriest after the Great Famine. And the reason was that after Nixon visited China in 1972, world leaders came paying court to Mao, and the Great Leader suddenly found a lot of countries on which he could shower largesse. According to China's official foreign aid statistics, the number of countries receiving Chinese aid rose from thirty-one before Nixon's visit to sixty-six the year Mao died, in 1976. Mao's regime shockingly gave away an average of 5.88 per cent of China's annual expenditure, with 1973 the highest, at 6.92 per cent – immeasurably higher than any other, much richer, countries. On tiny and infinitely more prosperous Malta, Mao lavished US $25 million in one go, in exchange for its prime minister, Dom Mintoff, leaving China sporting a Mao badge. Such extravagant doling out of money and food at the expense of his own people, including those of his own home village, was stopped by Deng Xiaoping after Mao's death.

Leaving the house, Jon and I went to Mao's villa on the edge of the village, the Dripping Grotto. As we approached the grounds, I involuntarily let out a cry of amazement: in front of us was a wooded valley thick with spectacular trees and luxuriant bushes. The local guide told us that as many as eight hundred types of plants existed here, including dozens of rare species. I thought of my village in Deyang, which shared similar geographic features. But while here splendid woods flourished, the hills around my village were barren with virtually no trees and scarce shrubs. When I was living there in the early 1970s, every morning before breakfast I used to climb the hills with other women to gather firewood. We had to walk a long way, as plants were few and far between. Finding fuel was a daily struggle. Once when I expressed exasperation, the women told me the hills had been covered with pine, eucalyptus and cypress before – until 1958, when they had all been felled to feed the 'backyard furnaces' to produce steel for Mao's superpower dream.

That mad steel-making campaign deprived China of a large

part of its forestry. Bare mountains I had seen everywhere in my travels told the same story as my village. But here, I learned, the hills around the Dripping Grotto had been spared, because Mao's ancestral burial ground was in the woods.

I remembered the steel-making as, at the age of six, I had been involved. In my school, there was a crucible-like vat in the kitchen, and in the compound where my family lived, a furnace was erected in the car park. Government officials and schoolteachers alike were feeding those furnaces twenty-four hours a day, to ensure some (completely useless) molten steel came out. I recalled babysitting for our steel-making teachers and screwing up my eyes to search the ground for rusty old nails and other bits of metal to hand over as scrap iron, needed for the furnaces. I had a vague memory of my mother occasionally home, tired out from her round-the-clock duty tending the furnace of her office. But I could not bring up any image of my father by the furnace in the compound, for which his office was partially responsible. After the publication of *Wild Swans*, an acquaintance sent me a Cultural Revolution-era leaflet condemning my father for a number of 'crimes', one of which was that he had complained about the backyard furnaces, calling them 'a monumental waste', and had declined to take part by claiming illness and staying in bed.

The well-preserved landscape around the Dripping Grotto attracted Mao when he visited his home village in 1959. He said to the provincial chief, 'Mm, this place is rather quiet. Would you build a straw hut here for my retirement?' As this was the time the Great Famine was already raging, the provincial chief did nothing about what Mao euphemistically called 'a straw hut'. Soon the chief was purged – and would commit suicide at the start of the Cultural Revolution. A sycophant of Mao was appointed the next chief, and the first thing he did was to build the Dripping Grotto. The building plan was flown in from Beijing – the same plan for all Mao's at least fifty villas around China: gigantic in dimension, solid in material, and featureless in look with not a nod to beauty. Mao's priority was security. The villa had only one floor, as he did not want to be trapped upstairs. The driveway went virtually into the sitting room, and the huge steel gates would close tightly before Mao got out. The whole mountain range was sealed off, and the local peasants were relocated. There were wide escape tunnels inside the mountains and a big earthquake- and nuclear bomb-proof shelter.

Mao stayed at Dripping Grotto on the eve of the Cultural Revolution for just eleven days – the only time he used the villa. The visit was ultra-secretive even by his standards. On his way to the Grotto, a little girl, having noticed the unusual stream of cars, caught sight of Mao as he happened to wind down the car window, and she rushed home to tell her family with wild excitement. Police descended at once, and told her off: 'You didn't see Chairman Mao! Don't you dare to say that again!' Everyone in the village was warned not even to think that Mao was nearby.

Mao only went outdoors for the occasional stroll within the seamlessly enclosed grounds and spent most of his time in an enormous wooden bed, simple and hard, with no mattress, which he disliked. When he was in Moscow in 1949 and staying in the Kremlin, Mao had poked his fingers disapprovingly into the mattress and had it replaced with wooden planks. He liked books on his bed, so he could easily pick what he wanted to read while lying down. Staying in bed reading was Mao's favourite pastime – a pleasure he denied the Chinese population. It was at Dripping Grotto in June 1966, in that large wooden bed, half of which was piled a foot high with books, that Mao finalised his plans for the Cultural Revolution, and barely two months later, Red Guards would start raiding people's homes to seize their books to be burned or pulped – or, in the case of the books deemed valuable by the state, to go into state storage, from which Mao's staff would select what he wanted and put them up on the bookshelves of his sitting room. Meanwhile, the owners of the books were often beaten, some to death. China became devoid of books for a decade. I was one of the fortunate to lay my hands on books thanks to my entrepreneurial thirteen-year-old brother who bought them on the black market.

The next stop for us was Changsha, the capital of Hunan province. Mao had come here in 1911, aged seventeen, on the eve of the founding of the republic, and lived here for sixteen years. Those were the freest years in Chinese history, under a democratically elected Beijing government (a fact that had been suppressed by the subsequent regimes and remains generally unknown).* Mao enjoyed a liberal education from a teacher training college which charged no fee and offered free board and lodging. He could read whatever he liked, write whatever he wanted, travel to Europe if he so desired (he did not). International celebrities like the philosopher Bertrand Russell came and gave lectures, open to the public. In the auditorium a portrait of Marx had once hung. On the campus there was a little hill with a pavilion at the top where Mao and friends debated their blueprints for China. 'I am against the Great Republic of China,' he had written in a newspaper article in 1920. He called on his thirty million fellow Hunanese to 'smash

* Jung Chang, *Big Sister, Little Sister, Red Sister: Three Women at the Heart of Twentieth-Century China*, Chapter 4.

the misguided dream for a big, centralised country' and 'build Hunan into a separate state'.*

I thought of my own youth under Mao decades later. Anyone who spoke or wrote those words would have landed in prison – or worse. They still will, today.

Because Mao's early articles were written with freedom of thought and expression, they were later suppressed by him. Book-burning did not spare his own works, and during his rule he only permitted four slim volumes of strictly selected and heavily edited writings to be published, in addition to the Little Red Book, which contained only dictums. In the post-Mao era, some of his suppressed writings were collected to be published. I had already bought one of the collections of his articles written in Changsha and was looking for the rest. And I heard that there was indeed another volume – but before publication, Beijing had ordered all the copies to be pulped.

One evening in Changsha, having dinner with a former local official, I lamented not being able to get that volume. He smiled, and said, 'Heaven always rewards a dedicated pursuer. Look what I have brought you!' And out from a much-used plastic bag came the book.† It turned out that he had been one of the officials in charge of its compilation, and his personal copy had escaped the liquidation machine. As he handed me this unique copy that contained vital information about Mao's life, unavailable anywhere else, I was overcome with joy, a sensation I had never felt at the thought of reading Mao.

*

* See https://www.marxists.org/chinese/maozedong/1968/1-023.htm
† Mao, *Jiandang he dageming shiqi Mao Zedong zhuzuoji* (Mao Zedong Writings during the Period of the Formation of the Party and the Great Revolution), Dec. 1920–July 1927, CCP Archive Study Office & CCP Hunan Committee, comp., unpublished.

On the outskirts of Changsha was the family home of Yang Kaihui, Mao's second wife whom he regarded as the love of his life. Born in 1901 into the family of a university professor, she had been educated in a missionary school. Her family house was large, with yellow brick walls and black roof tiles over black timber beams. Clusters of bamboo screened it from behind. It was picturesque but unexceptional – except for her tomb. For Kaihui died at the age of twenty-nine, executed by a Kuomintang general, Ho Chien, in 1930, because she was Mao's wife, and Mao, then living as a 'bandit chief' spending his days 'burning houses and killing people', was attacking Changsha, the general's base. Kaihui was asked to renounce her relationship with him. She refused – even though she knew that Mao had abandoned her and their three young sons. On a cold winter day, she was taken to the execution ground wearing only a thin blouse, her outer garment, a dark-blue long gown, having been peeled off by the executioners as spoils. As she walked through the streets, tied up with ropes, normal treatment for someone about to be executed, an officer, perhaps taking pity on her, hailed a rickshaw for her, while soldiers of the firing squad ran along on both sides. After they shot her, they took off her shoes and threw them as far as they could: otherwise, legend went, they would be followed home and haunted by the ghost of the dead. While they were having lunch afterwards at their barracks, news came that Kaihui was not dead, so several of them went back and finished her off. They found that in her pain her fingers had dug deep into the frozen earth.

Between Mao leaving her in 1927 to begin a life as a Communist outlaw, and her arrest and execution three years later, Kaihui wrote many pieces of reminiscences, a diary in poetry, and (unsent) letters, expressing her love for Mao and her heartbreak at being abandoned by him. She also ruminated on violence, cruelty, her loss of belief in the ideology to which Mao had introduced her, and her yearning for a new faith:

'Perhaps one day I will cry out: my ideas in the past were wrong! . . . Ah! Kill, kill, kill! All I hear is this sound in my ears! Why are human beings so evil? Why so cruel? Why?! . . . I must have a faith! I must have a faith! Let me have a faith!!'

It was the museum staff who alerted us to Kaihui's writings. We were the only visitors, and they had time to chat. They told us that she had wrapped her works in wax paper against dampness and hid them inside the house when she was about to be taken away to be executed. And they showed us the two places where she had hidden them: between two bricks in the wall and tucked in a corner under a beam outside her bedroom. Kaihui had wanted to show them to Mao one day, to make him understand her and reflect on his own life. But they never met again, and Mao was long dead when the papers came to light during renovation work in 1982 and 1990.

Because her writings did not fit in with the personality cult of Mao, most were not made public. I searched hard for them until one day, a distinguished old Hunanese historian heard about my search and gave me his copy. Jon and I gained invaluable insights into Mao from the writings. We saw a stone-hearted man with attractive qualities, capable of rousing the passionate love of someone as exceptional as Kaihui, so that she would rather die, and orphan three little sons, than renounce him. He undoubtedly loved her – although he repeatedly hurt her through unfaithfulness and ultimately deserted her. But the biggest finding from the relationship was how totally Mao had, by the time of Kaihui's death, become addicted to *power*, an addiction that had replaced any loving emotions to be his only and true love. It was this only and true love that cost Kaihui her life.

General Ho Chien, who executed her, had left her alone for

years after Mao was gone. But in 1930, he narrowly escaped death at the hands of a separate Red Army branch under Peng Dehuai, who attacked Changsha unsuccessfully. Then Mao came to assault Changsha again, besieging it for weeks. Mao would undoubtedly have been aware that the general would be furious and could well take revenge on his wife, who lived on the outskirts of the city, and that her life was in danger. Mao could at least have warned her to stay away with their children. That would have been extremely easy to arrange, as her house was right on his route to Changsha, and he was there for weeks. Yet Mao did nothing – not a note to her, not a word. His action – or inaction – could only have been because he was totally focused on his goal and could not spare a thought for his family. Mao's goal was not to seize the city, which was impossible and which he did not seriously try; he wanted to take over Peng Dehuai's branch of the Red Army, which had not been put under Mao's command by the Kremlin, the boss of China's Red Army. Mao was using the siege of Changsha as an excuse (that it needed unified command) to take over Peng's forces. (Moscow was far away and the CCP centre was in Shanghai.) Continuously scheming to take over other Red forces was how Mao expanded his power in the CCP. 'Power grows out of the barrel of the gun,' he said at this time, and his career rose and rose by grabbing more and more Red forces, along with their guns. In this pursuit, there was no room for any love except lust after ever-increasing power.

Thanks to a succession of take-overs of different Red forces, Mao built up the largest Red Army branch in China by the end of 1931, when the Kremlin decided to set up a Communist state. Not surprisingly, it crowned Mao the 'Chairman', although it did not make him the number one. Moscow gave that post, the Party Secretary, to the loyal super administrator, Zhou Enlai. Mao had too often defied Moscow's orders in his take-overs, and so was not completely trusted by the Kremlin. Still, Stalin appreciated his unmatched hunger for power, regarding it as essential for the small CCP to conquer China one day. Stalin was indeed smart.

The capital of the red state proclaimed that year was the town of Ruijin, in Jiangxi province, southeast China. In 1994, Jon and I travelled there, to the place that had given birth to the later world-famous title: 'Chairman Mao'.

At the local Red Museum, we talked to a Party historian who had come from a village in the region. At the mention of the red state, his voice betrayed bitter emotions. 'In Ruijin, basically, all the [able-bodied] men were killed. The presentable young lads were taken to be the bosses' body-guards or orderlies; others were sent to the front to fight; and a lot were killed as "AB".' 'AB', standing for 'Anti-Bolshevik', was the name of a long-defunct Kuomintang organisation, which Mao resuscitated to condemn Red Army men who had resisted his take-overs. He also used it to suppress opposition to his leadership or disobedience to his orders. Starting with the arrest, torture and execution of officers and soldiers in Peng Dehuai's army who had defied Mao's take-over in 1930 outside Changsha, this first large-scale purge by Mao slaughtered tens of thousands of the Reds and locals, often involving ghastly torture, as the many volumes of documents I found in the various Red Museums, publishing houses and bookshops revealed. In one intra-Party report: 'There were so many kinds ... with strange names like ... "sitting in a pleasure chair", "toads drink-ing", "monkeys holding a rope". Some had a red-hot gun-rod rammed into the anus ... In Victory County alone, there were 120 kinds of torture.' In one county the victims were paraded through the streets to their execution with rusty wires through their testicles.

One of the victims was the father of a man we met in Yudu, a nearby riverside town where the Reds had departed for their Long March to northwest China after being driven out by Chiang Kai-shek in autumn 1934. On the bank where the Reds had crossed the river on a pontoon bridge, the man, now seventy-four years old, had been strolling but courteously stopped to chat when we approached. He lived by the crossing point in a corner house, which, he told us, had been a small store owned by his father. I asked about his father, and he gave me a hand gesture with his thumb and index finger to form the figure of 'eight' in Chinese, telling me that he was eight years old when his father died. I asked whether the death was due to illness or on the battlefield; he shook his head: 'No, no. Neither. But I can't say, I can't say . . .' He kept repeating those words, yet did not walk away, his eyes engaged with mine, seeming to want to tell me things that he really wished he could say but could not. I did not press him. Judging from the time of his father's death, 1930 or 1931, it was at the height of the slaughtering of the 'AB', and I had a strong feeling that his father might have been killed in the purge. Afterwards a local historian who specialised in that purge confirmed my hunch. Still later, a multi-volume collection of documents about the Ruijin state made it unambiguous that the AB accusation had been used routinely to squeeze money out of locals, of whom shop owners, who had more cash than others, had borne the brunt.

The seventy-four-year-old had been twelve when the Reds left on the pontoon bridge. He had peeped through a crack in the door, holding his breath, watching them passing in front of his home, the store. By then it had been stripped of its possessions, and was 'as bare as having been washed by floods,' he said.

When the CCP came to power, it marked the crossing point

with a large stone slab, on which, below a red star with a hammer and sickle at the centre, these words were vertically engraved: 'The Worker-Peasant Red Army Crossed Here to Begin the Long March'. Now the red colour of the star had all but gone, and the slab lay in the muddy ground, surrounded by vegetables laid out to dry on basket lids and chickens and sparrows fighting for bits of grain or insects among the rubbish. Its edges served as a stand to dry wet shoes. The red state seemed far away, a terrifying episode of history that was fading into the mist over the Yudu River, and then gone with the waves.

In our hotel in Ruijin, the past felt even more unreal. It had been built for Mao after he seized power in China, in anticipation of his return to the place where he had been installed 'the Chairman'. But he never came, and after decades of being left empty, it had just opened to the public. Jon and I were probably two of the first clients and were given the 'No. 1 Villa', which had been intended for Mao to sleep in. The building looked nondescript like all Mao's other villas, conforming to the same blueprint delivered by his guards from Beijing. But the interior decoration followed the post-Mao trend, including a comfortable mattress – and the use of marble everywhere. Any hotel that aspired to be 'smart' in the 1990s had to be decked out with this un-Chinese material. The humidity in the area was high, and without the traditional timber to absorb moisture, surfaces were perpetually covered with water. When we walked in, I thought they had just washed the floor. It was impossible to put a book on the bedside table without it getting soaked, and I could not see my face in the mirror as it was behind a watery veil. Still, all the problems paled into insignificance as soon as we took a stroll in the grounds which, like those of all Mao's other villas, were vast and spectacularly beautiful. Here the most unusual feature was the large number of giant old trees, including osmanthuses that flowered at all seasons and perfumed the air. I could not have enough of the trees and the scent and, reluctant to return to the room, walked on and on deep into the night, listening to frogs croaking in a pond, and catching sight of bats flying about. In complete seclusion, as there were few people staying (and Jon had gone to bed), I whispered into my little tape recorder what I had learned during the day, including the gruesome types of torture and execution. Finally, before going inside, I stepped through the cascading roots that had dropped into the earth from the branches of a huge tree and, leaning on its mighty trunk, gazed out at the silhouette of the grounds in moonlight. The perfume of the osmanthuses wafted around me. It was sublime. Yet it was at this very place that unspeakable things had happened. I had just glimpsed the predecessor of the Cultural Revolution, and I wished with all my heart that there would never be a successor.

15

Around the Globe in Pursuit of Mao

(the 1990s)

To research our biography of Mao, Jon and I travelled to many parts of the world in addition to China and Russia, working in some thirty archives and talking to hundreds of historical witnesses. Jon made an exhaustive list of Mao's overseas acquaintances, and we contacted them one by one. They agreed to see us largely thanks to *Wild Swans*.

We interviewed Henry Kissinger, who as national security adviser to Richard Nixon helped bring about the rapprochement between the US government and Mao's regime – *not* to be confused with opening the door of China, which he did not do. Nixon's visit to Beijing in 1972 brought Mao, hands dripping with the fresh blood of the victims of the Cultural Revolution, to centre stage as a benign wise leader and a star with incomparable allure – so much so that even spittoons, into one of which Mao had constantly spat at their meeting, became a fashion item. Once I was invited to lunch by an Australian friend and to my horror the salad was served in a Chinese spittoon.

When we met Kissinger, in his office in New York, he was rather laid-back at first and gave us his official spiel about his meetings with Mao. At one point I contradicted him as politely as I could, 'But that is not what the transcripts say . . .' Kissinger lurched forward in his chair, and with alarm in his voice said: 'Transcripts! Where did you get those? Did the Chinese give those to you? Very bad! Privileged conversations with a foreign head of state.' In fact, the transcripts had come from an archive in Washington, which Jon had dug out.

Kissinger asked me about one thing which was in the transcripts: Mao talking to him about women. Mao: 'There were some rumours that said that you were about to collapse. (laughter) And women folk seated here were all dissatisfied with that. (laughter, especially pronounced among the women) They said if the Doctor [Kissinger] is going to collapse, we would be out of work.' 'Do you want our Chinese women? We can give you ten million. (laughter, particularly among the women).'* Kissinger asked what I thought about those remarks. I said Mao was teasing him, using coarse sexual allusions, which was Mao's way to show intimacy. Mao knew Kissinger's reputation for being a womaniser and expected him to feel flattered. (Mao acted even more crudely complimenting Kissinger on his love-making with Nancy, his wife, on account of the fact that she was much taller than him.) Kissinger said he agreed with me, but the State Department had insisted on attributing some political significance to the remarks, claiming they revealed Mao's displeasure with his wife Jiang Qing.

Creating a mood of intimacy and massaging Kissinger's vanity was, of course, politics. Mao was softening him up to

* Burr, William (ed.), *The Kissinger Transcripts: The Top-secret Talks with Beijing and Moscow* (Free Press, New York, 1999), pp. 92–5

get what he wanted. His major goal was to persuade America to lift its embargos so China could lay its hands on 'advanced technology', as he told the North Korean dictator Kim Il Sung. Kissinger obliged, once telling Mao's envoy, 'In particular, you have asked for some Rolls-Royce [engine] technology. Under existing regulations we have to oppose this, but we have worked out a procedure with the British where they will go ahead anyway. We will take a formal position in opposition, but only that. Don't be confused by what we do publicly . . .'* (To make the British more cooperative, Mao set out to seduce Prime Minister Edward Heath with a charm offensive. Heath 'felt like a king in China', he told us in our interview.)

The greatest service Kissinger did Mao was promoting him in the mainstream West. He became the most prominent cheerleader for Mao, extolling the Great Leader and his henchmen as 'a group of monks' who had 'kept their revolutionary purity', and who would 'challenge us in a moral way'. One of his compliments about Mao was that Mao's sitting room looked like 'the retreat of a scholar', lined as it was wall-to-wall with bookshelves. A large number of the books had in fact been looted by Red Guards in violent 'house raids' during the Cultural Revolution. Mao had given long lists of titles he wanted to his staff, who revealed that they went to the storage place to find the books, and after cleaning them up, having them sterilised by ultraviolet rays, put them on Mao's shelves. Those raids were notorious for the way the Red Guards beat up the owners of the books: with the brass buckles of their leather belts. Of course, Kissinger would not have known this when he made the remark. But after the atrocities were well

---

* Burr (ed.), *The Kissinger Transcripts*, p. 144 (Kissinger to envoy Huang Zhen, 6 July 1973).

known, as recently as 2011, Kissinger flew thousands of miles to China to attend a rally of a hundred thousand Chinese singing propaganda songs lauding Mao and the CCP, in celebration of the Party's ninetieth anniversary. He stuck to his characterisation of Mao as a 'philosopher'. (Kissinger used another bizarre one-word description about Hitler, as the transcripts show. When Mao observed that it was an 'error in policy' that Hitler 'didn't cross the sea after Dunkirk' and seize Britain, Kissinger replied, 'Hitler was a romantic. He had a strange liking for England.'*)

The succeeding Chinese governments, who all claim to be Mao's heirs, have never forgotten their 'old friend'. Our interview was conducted at Kissinger Associates in New York, his consulting firm for some of the world's largest corporations, which paid him enormous fees to have the best access and best treatment in China. Kissinger had built up an extremely mutually beneficial relationship with Beijing.

While Kissinger, along with Nixon, shaped the view of the mainstream West in Mao's favour, the man who first created an attractive aura for Mao was the American journalist Edgar Snow, whose book *Red Star Over China* influenced generations of the left from the 1930s. Even China's own left-wing youth like my mother, and possibly my father, fell under its influence. Snow died in 1972, the year Nixon went to Beijing. We interviewed Snow's widow, Lois Wheeler Snow, at her home near Lausanne in Switzerland in 1996. By then she had changed her views on Beijing, speaking up in particular for the women who had lost their children when the tanks rolled into Tiananmen Square in 1989. Her disenchantment

* See https://history.state.gov/historicaldocuments/frus1969-76v18/d12

had started in 1973, when she was invited to China to bury half of her husband's ashes in the grounds of Peking University, where he had taught. After a lavish ceremony, she was hosted to a dinner by Premier Zhou Enlai, who had always treated her and Edgar Snow with maximum attentiveness. This time she was seated between Zhou and Mme Mao but Zhou said hardly a word to her. For the entire evening, he talked across her with Mme Mao as if Lois did not exist. Gone were the attention and the courtesy. The change was so abrupt and so striking that she could not help thinking that now that her husband was gone, she was no longer useful, and Zhou did not bother to switch on his charm for her. It was her first taste of the cynicism of the regime.

Some Western enthusiasts for Mao had their illusions shattered earlier. By chance at a dinner, I met one of them, a Chinese-speaking Belgian, who had been such an ardent Maoist that he had gone to Beijing in 1968, hoping to make China his home. Upon arrival he found himself being put with other Western Maoists and trucked into the Western Hills outside the capital. There, to his astonishment, they were made to learn how to use explosives and arms, in addition to studying 'Mao Thought'. They were cut off from Chinese society and only permitted out on a few tightly organised outings, during which he saw the gloominess of the city, devoid of the exciting and festival atmosphere he had imagined. He could hear hand grenades exploding in nearby hills, but was told it was a camp for Africans, with whom his group was strictly forbidden to socialise. Before long all his illusions about China vanished and he only wanted to escape. It was there that he learned the skills of disguising his true feelings, and was eventually judged ready to be sent back to Europe as an agent. As soon as he was back in Belgium, he went to the authorities.

*

Many heads of state helped us in our research on Mao, and one memorable encounter was with former president George Bush Sr in 1995, in his office in Houston which had a stunning view over the city skyline. He and Barbara Bush oozed easy-going charm. They had lived in Beijing for a year when George Bush was chief of the American Liaison Office in 1974–75, and had witnessed life in the Cultural Revolution. Their appreciation and sympathy for Deng Xiaoping and his post-Mao reforms were immense and played a decisive role in the West swiftly lifting the sanctions against Beijing imposed after the Tiananmen suppression in 1989. Bush's decision enabled China to enjoy fast economic growth and considerable personal freedoms in the 1990s. It was thanks to that decade's liberalisation that I was able to run round China researching Mao.

As Bush had been the head of the CIA in 1976, the last year of Mao's life, we asked him about the agency's knowledge about China then. He said, 'The CIA knew little about what was really happening. If we did, *Wild Swans* would not have been such a surprise to us.' He was, of course, being charming, but it also seemed to be the case that America knew astonishingly little about Mao's regime.

When we saw former president Gerald Ford, in his house on the edge of a golf course at Rancho Mirage in California, he confirmed this ignorance, describing Nixon's reaction after his visit thus: 'No question he was impressed.' Impressed by Mao and China in the Cultural Revolution! This was incredible to me, as there had at least been refugees, who had risked their lives swimming through shark-infested waters to Hong Kong. But their stories were ignored. People either did not believe them or did not want to believe them, or, even, did not want to hear what they had to say.

Ford's own meeting with Mao left him with a more personal

observation. He saw Mao's eyes flash when his tall, blond daughter Susan was introduced. Mao, who would die in nine months, was 'very obviously' attracted, Ford told us.

In 1994 in Hong Kong, we interviewed Mobutu Sese Seko, the president of Zaire (today's Congo), infamous for being a brutal and kleptocratic dictator. I had bumped into him in the hotel hair salon, while he was sitting under a hooded drier, with towels around his neck and wads of cotton wool along his hairline. As I was led to have my hair rinsed, I paused in front of him and requested an interview. The next morning, his doctor-cum-assistant rang and said, 'This morning it's no good for the interview. The president is having a manicure and a pedicure.' He offered seven o'clock that evening in Mobutu's presidential suite. During our opening small talk, I asked Mobutu how he liked the hotel's beauty salon. He said, 'Not bad, not bad', whereupon he stuck out his hands – the hands that were said to have strangled a political opponent during dinner. That opponent had apparently been one of the people Mao was backing to try to topple him. The attempt failed, and Mao had a rapprochement with Mobutu, inviting him to China in 1973. Mao received him sitting up in bed in the middle of the night, and, beckoning for him to come over to the bedside, said, 'Mobutu, Mobutu, is that really you? You know I've spent a lot of money trying to have you overthrown – and even killed. But here you are.' (This exchange was confirmed by Chinese records.)

Jon, who conducted the interview in French, asked Mobutu, 'How did you feel talking to a man who had just told you he had tried to have you killed?' Mobutu smiled and answered, 'I felt good. Once Mao said this, I knew everything would be all right.' With this Godfather-style reconciliation came generous funding from Mao, who let Mobutu defer loans indefinitely, or repay China in worthless Zairian currency, which China printed. Mao also provided Mobutu with a masseur. China's march to Africa had started a long time before the present day, under Mao.

The former first lady of the Philippines Imelda Marcos gave us an interview in her apartment in Manila in 1993. Notorious for owning three thousand pairs of shoes, she had been no stranger to me while I was still in China, when she met Mao in 1974. In those years, newsreels in cinemas of Mao receiving foreign dignitaries were virtually the only entertainment for the population, and when Marcos appeared on the screen in her glorious national costume, the audience audibly gasped. Chinese women had only shapeless jackets and trousers – the Mao suits – to wear, ever since the Red Guards, following Mao's order to 'smash' anything 'bourgeois', cut up skirts and dresses in the street in summer 1966. But on the screen, Mao picked up Marcos's hand amorously and put it to his lips – a gesture that had been condemned as 'unspeakably decadent'. The audience was stunned. Mao's photographer told me he had been too shocked and too afraid to take a photo. Luckily, the newsreel camera was rolling and recorded the moment – and Jon and I had a unique illustration for our biography.

At that meeting Mme Mao donned her unbecoming army uniform and cap next to the former Filipina beauty queen. Her envy was unmistakable to the photographer and Marcos, who told us that Mme Mao was scrutinising her out of the corners of her eyes. 'She [Mme Mao] was really eager to please her man,' sighed Marcos. Indeed, after that encounter, Jiang Qing designed a 'national costume' for Chinese women. But it was a collarless top plus a three-quarter-length pleated skirt, both highly unflattering. When pictures emerged of China's female athletes wearing the ensemble abroad, it was met with universal derision. Nobody missed it when the Politburo vetoed it – for its own economic reason: long pleated skirts would use a lot more material than the Mao suit, the most fabric-saving and utilitarian outfit possible, which was its point. Mao's policy was to cut to the minimum consumer spending in order to fund military industries. Still, after Jiang Qing wore the costume herself, skirts and dresses stopped being taboo, and I was able to wear a skirt as an adult in 1975, when I was twenty-three.

In a gold-coloured dress, her fingernails painted in three shades of gold along the contours of the nails, Marcos talked without pause for five hours, during which she claimed that Mao had started coughing during their meeting, and she had taken a pill from her handbag and handed it to him. According to Marcos, her son Bongbong (later president of the Philippines) gave her a kick, trying to stop her, but Mao had already popped the pill into his mouth, such was his total trust in her. I checked this story with Mao's staff. They all laughed and said it was nonsense as Mao was extremely careful about security and would never have put anything in his mouth without it having been tested. Mao's food was cooked with the housekeeper watching over the whole process and tasting it before serving it to him.

On our interview list were many major figures in the disintegrating Communist world. I was very struck by the fact that while Mao had fascinated Westerners, he had few admirers among the Communists. Albania was China's only ally in the Cultural Revolution, and the Chinese had been told that its leader, Enver Hoxha, worshipped Mao. This turned out to be completely untrue, as Jon and I learned on a trip to Albania in 1998, when the country was casting off its totalitarian past. We visited a foundry, where toppled giant statues of Stalin and Hoxha were waiting to be melted down for artists to make modern sculptures, including a flamboyantly curvaceous female figure. Mao was nowhere to be seen. When I asked our Albanian friends whether there had ever been any statue or portrait of Mao in their country, they were surprised by the question as they had never been told to look up to Mao – even though he had lavished such largesse on Albania that its population never experienced rationing, not even while the Chinese were dying of starvation in the tens of millions. Albania's chief trade negotiator with Beijing, Pupo Shyti, told us that in China 'you could see the famine'; but 'the Chinese gave us everything', and 'I felt ashamed . . .' When Mao's officials flinched, Mao waved his hand and told them to oblige the Albanians. He bought no gratitude from Hoxha.

We worked in the Albanian Archives – the first foreigners to do so – and read about Beijing's insults of Cuban leaders such as Che Guevara. Mao had tried to put him and Fidel Castro under his wing but had failed.

Many years after the Albanian trip, in 2013 in Cuba, I met Castro's eldest son, known by the diminutive Fidelito, 'Little Fidel'. He had read *Wild Swans* and the biography of Mao, and we talked about China. When he was a teenager, his father had dispatched him to Beijing as his representative, and he had been entertained by President Liu Shaoqi and Premier Zhou Enlai. Fidelito reminded me of Li Na, Mao's daughter, whom I had met, and Stalin's daughter Svetlana, whom I had read about. The dictator fathers of all three seemed to have had high hopes when they were children that they would one day be of assistance politically. Fidelito had been sent to study nuclear science in the Soviet Union, after which he was put in charge of Cuba's nuclear programme – something obviously close to Castro's heart. Like Li Na, he disappointed his father, who relieved him of the job. Indeed, Fidelito did not strike me as dictator material. Like the other two daughters, he seemed to have had a lot of mental anguish, and would take his own life in 2018, at the age of sixty-eight.

As with Castro and Guevara, many other Communist Party chiefs incurred Mao's wrath, and one particularly badly, Kenji Miyamoto, then leader of the Japanese Communist Party, a major party in Japan. When I was a child during the Cultural Revolution, I had seen his name in Chinese characters written upside down on huge wall posters, covered by giant ink crosses that signalled a death sentence. Mao, who had regarded the Japanese party as his subordinate, had repeatedly told Miyamoto to 'launch armed uprisings' in Japan, but Miyamoto always refused, telling Mao he had renounced violent revolution. When Jon and I were in Japan, Miyamoto invited us to tea at his home, an exceptional gesture of goodwill as the Japanese seldom invited people to their homes. At his recommendation, his party opened its highly revealing archives to us.

The man who took us to see Miyamoto and translated for us was the London correspondent of the Japanese Communist newspaper *Shimbun Akahata* (*Red Flag*), which at the time, the early 1990s, had more than three million daily subscribers, and had serialised *Wild Swans* prominently for weeks. After the visit the journalist said with relief that he was very pleased that Miyamoto lived simply and was transparently incorrupt. It seemed the young man had been drawn to communism for its puritan image, which reminded me of my father in his youth.

Well aware of the attraction of the leader having a simple lifestyle, Beijing has been cultivating this image for Mao. A bathrobe of his, with apparently seventy-three patches, has been – and is still being – much trumpeted as evidence of his puritanism. But the population are not told as I was by Mao's staff just how extravagant the patching was: the bathrobe was flown specially to Shanghai and mended by the country's best craftsman, costing immeasurably more than a new one. Mao's other quirks included not brushing his teeth nor having a bath or a shower for twenty-seven years – during his entire rule. But he liked having his girlfriends or servants rub him with hot towels.

'Simple living' was so much associated with communism that a young Spanish scholar who introduced us to the former Spanish Communist leader Santiago Carrillo, nearly turned down a lunch at the Ritz in Madrid on Carrillo's behalf. We were discussing which restaurant to invite Carrillo to for our interview, and I suggested the Ritz, where Jon and I had been put up by our publisher. The scholar said, 'Oh no, that won't work. He won't want to come as he is an old Communist.' By then I had met a lot of old Communists and knew that few remained immune to luxury, and I insisted. Indeed, not only did Carrillo accept our suggestion with no hesitation, it turned out he was a frequent visitor to the Ritz. When he walked into the lobby, we saw the doorman bowing and saluting him – 'Good afternoon, Don Santiago!' – and the Spanish foreign minister leaning forward to shake his hand. Carrillo had played a key role in Spain's peaceful transition to democracy after General Francisco Franco's death, for which he was widely respected. Inside the restaurant, the head waiter led us straight to a corner table that had a view of the whole room, and referred to it, to Carrillo, as 'your table'. Among the interesting vignettes Carrillo recounted during our lunch was that the then North Korean dictator Kim Il Sung had confided in him that he, Kim, had started the Korean War – and that Mao had been a far keener supporter of launching it than Stalin.

Most of the dozens of old Communists Jon and I interviewed, like Carrillo and Miyamoto, had effectively turned their backs on the brutal ideology. But one old Soviet spy from 1930s China, Ruth Werner, latterly known as 'Agent Sonya' in Britain when she acted as the courier for Moscow's atomic spy Klaus Fuchs – thus contributing significantly to the development of Russia's nuclear weapons – insisted she still believed in it. She claimed she had no regrets even though many of her spy friends had perished in Stalin's purges. Jon showed her a photo of Karl Rimm, a fellow spy in Shanghai with whom she allegedly had an affair, and who was arrested and shot when he was called back to Moscow. It was at that moment that a look of sorrow appeared, and she said wistfully, 'I was also recalled but I didn't go. If I had gone, I would have been shot, too.' She survived the purges, no mean feat in the Stalinist world, but was treated far from kindly. When we visited her in Berlin, where she had been born and where she had settled, I was taken aback by how meagre her home was, even though I was familiar with old Communists' often skimpy accommodations. After all, she was the most highly decorated GRU (Soviet military intelligence) female officer ever, and was known as 'Stalin's best female spy'.

Other major spies fared much better. The East German spymaster, Markus Wolf, seemed to have done well right into the post-Communist era. The former head of the foreign intelligence service of the Stasi (the Ministry for State Security of East Germany) had once been the object of intense curiosity and featured in renowned Cold War thrillers, known as 'the man without a face': Western agencies reportedly did not know what he looked like for years. We interviewed him in 1999 in a colourless restaurant that he chose in former East Berlin. It was a freezing November day, and he arrived with his coat collar turned up and his face half hidden, apt for his sobriquet.

In 1950, in his mid-twenties, Wolf had been the East German chargé d'affaires in Russia and had witnessed a historic moment in the Stalin–Mao rivalry, during Mao's first visit to Moscow to celebrate the Soviet leader's seventieth birthday. He had just triumphed in China, but Stalin, who knew Mao had ambitions beyond the Chinese borders, made a point of humiliating him and showing that he, Stalin, was the Big Boss. When Mao planned to give a farewell reception at the Metropol Hotel, Stalin at first declined to attend, claiming that he never went to parties outside the Kremlin. Mao had to beg, and Stalin finally consented. On the day, Wolf saw the Big Boss arriving, carrying his own bottle, and the crowd erupted into a frenzy of cheering, looking as if they were about to break the big glass partition separating them. No one was interested in what Mao was doing. Wolf noted the frosty mood between the two Communist giants. Stalin used his toast to deliver a veiled warning to Mao, that the Chinese leader must never contemplate rivalling him. Stalin's words were heeded, and Mao only started trying to seize the leadership of the Communist camp after Stalin's death in 1953.

The restaurant where we met Wolf did not have any other clients. It seemed that Wolf had chosen it for a reason. Halfway through our lunch, his daughter dropped by, accompanied by an armed bodyguard. She had married one of the richest men in the former East Germany, newly wealthy after the fall of communism. When the interview was over, Wolf walked out with us, saying, 'Look, I can walk perfectly safely down the street.' True, I watched his disappearing back, his coat collar turned up, and nobody seemed to be paying him the slightest attention. It was his daughter who now needed guarding. I pondered on the intricate connections of the old world and the new.

16

Mao Exposed

(2001–06)

For my mother's seventieth birthday on 4 May 2001, Jon and I and my siblings gathered in Chengdu to celebrate with her. The day before, we went to pay our respects to the tombs of Grandma and Father – to 'sweep the tomb', as the Chinese say. This was my first visit: public cemeteries had only recently been permitted, and my family had bought two lots outside Chengdu in the foothills of the Himalayas. Xiaofang, my youngest brother, who had arranged for the graves to be built, drove us there.

My brother loved driving, and for two hours on mud roads, he smoothly took us increasingly deeper into the cloud-shrouded mountains. I gazed at the terraced rice paddies and bamboo groves on both sides, and thought of another visit to a cemetery more than thirty years before. I had passed Yibin on my way to Chengdu from Ningnan, the mountainous village where I had been sent to work as a peasant, and had gone to visit the tomb of Dr Xia, who had died days after I was born in

Yibin and had been buried on a hill overlooking the Yangtze. Aunt Junying, my father's Buddhist sister, whom I adored, had taken me there, carrying some rare 'silver money' to burn at the tomb – a traditional ritual that had been banned. We searched up and down the hill, but could not find the grave. The whole cemetery was gone, levelled by the Red Guards, and all we could see were pieces of smashed tombstones, none of which was Dr Xia's. When I got home in Chengdu, I mentioned the trip to Grandma, as I had heard her expressing sadness at not being able to visit his tomb. A sudden intense flame lit up her eyes when I started talking; but the next minute, the flame extinguished, when I said the tomb was gone. I shall never forget her heartbreaking look of disappointment, and regret not telling a white lie.

My grandma, as most Chinese of her time, believed with religious conviction in burials. Aunt Junying's only luxury in life was a good-quality coffin, which stood in the place of honour in her sitting room, giving me quite a shock when I first saw it. To her generation, a dead soul would only rest in peace when it entered the earth, otherwise it would be doomed to wander perpetually without a home. When Dr Xia died in 1952, burials were still allowed by the new Communist government, and he was given a decent funeral. But as the Communists condemned religion as 'superstition' and religious rituals as 'feudal', my father had vetoed a Buddhist ceremony with monks chanting the sutras for Dr Xia and musicians playing the *suona*, a woodwind instrument that sang out to bid him farewell. My grandma was so upset that she fainted during a row with my father.

Father expressed remorse to me for those past wrongs when I stayed with him in his camp. He said how much he regretted being so harsh about his family's religious feelings. He told me his disapproval caused Aunt Junying to hide her statue of the Buddha and pray in secret when she was staying with our family. When his mother died, after he had moved to Chengdu, his family did not inform him in case he refused to allow the burial, which the Communists had by then banned. I could see how sad Father was that because of his intransigence he had not been with his mother when she died.

Xiaofang drove us to the gate of the cemetery. Having been destroyed everywhere in China, cemeteries, for the burial of ashes alone, were allowed at last just before the twenty-first century. We got out in front of a little store that looked smaller still being squeezed by precipitous mountains. Rows of small tombs rose all the way up to the peak that was hidden by thick mist. The store sold items for the traditional tomb-sweeping ritual: bunches of firecrackers to scare away evil spirits, papier-mâché houses (which looked like fantasy castles in foreign films) and cars and mobile phones, the latest status symbols – all to be burned at the tomb for the dead to enjoy in the other world. The old silver money which Aunt Junying had carried when we went to visit Dr Xia's tomb had been replaced by replica paper money. As Chinese banknotes all show Mao's face, they cannot be burned, and so the shop sold fake outsized US dollars, in astronomical denominations. Xiaofang, who had been here many times, knew the owner of the store and bought several bundles of the imitation green bills along with a few other things. Back at home, my siblings and I had debated about what we should burn as offerings to our father, as we knew he would have frowned on being offered worldly possessions as if those were what he craved. But we could not think of any alternative, short of Father's favourite cigarettes and liquor, which we brought along. Jinming had wanted to burn his doctoral thesis, which was something that would please Father, and I had thought of burning a copy of *Wild Swans*. But the burning of books and academic theses had such bad associations that we rejected the idea. In the end, we brought a large basket of flowers and spread their petals all around the tombs.

Our plot of land was tiny, and the marble tombstones were simple. The one dedicated to Father had Mother's name carved next to his but covered with a piece of fabric, which would be peeled off when she died and her ashes joined his. With a bucket of water and some rugs borrowed from the store, we cleaned the tombstones, and laid flowers. We sprinkled the ground with Father's favourite liquor – a part of the ritual – and then took turns to bow and murmur silently what we wanted to say to them. My mother was the last to perform this, and she broke down in sobs. After we supported her down the slope, she sat quietly on a stool, gazing up the hill for a long time.

On our way home, we stopped at a roadside restaurant. That evening I had food poisoning. I was taken to hospital and put on an antibiotic drip. My sister stayed with me overnight and alerted the nurses when the drip was about to run out. I told her not to tell Mother, who had gone to bed wiped out by the trip, especially the emotional turmoil. In the morning, my sister went home to change for a celebration lunch for family and some close friends, and I felt well enough to join them. I sat through the banquet not daring to eat anything, apart from a few mouthfuls of plain rice.

Food poisoning, and bad stomach trouble, plagued me on virtually every trip to China throughout the 1990s, as I mostly ate in restaurants. I got quite experienced at going to hospitals, in the provinces as well as in Beijing where, with a foreign passport, I was entitled to go to less crowded sections for 'foreigners and high officials', the two groups of people often sharing the same preferential treatment. Large quantities of medicines were always prescribed, some useful and others unnecessary. Drips were put on for the smallest of things, with antibiotics pumped in. Once in Changsha, I was on a drip in a room with a broken window and a cold wind was blowing in. Our local companions seemed blasé, taking food poisoning as a part of everyday life. After chatting cheerfully for some time by my bedside, they got up to go for lunch, and tried to persuade Jon to go with them. He declined indignantly, pointing to the drip, which in Britain would have indicated that the case was serious. They said that in China one would get a drip for a cold, and left. As it happened, Jon may well have saved my life. When impure penicillin dripped into my veins, I reacted badly and had a convulsion. Jon rushed to call the nurse, who pulled the needle out and I gradually recovered.

The year 2001 was the last time that I had bad food poisoning during my research trips in China – when I returned in the years after, it no longer pestered me. I found this miraculous, and only learned later that this was due to China becoming a member of the WTO (World Trade Organization) in December 2001, and being obliged to abide by its food safety regulations.

It is impossible to exaggerate the importance of joining the WTO for China – 'to enter the world' (ru-shi). It was thanks to this that the Chinese economy was linked up with that of the West, and became the second largest in the world. It was because of this that hundreds of millions of Chinese were lifted out of poverty, and the country grew rich. Professionals like my sister and my friends began to travel abroad as tourists.

In anticipation of the boom in commercial activities after joining the WTO and the influx of Western businessmen, smart hotels and venues were built across the country. In Chengdu, a conference centre had just been completed and stood empty, and my family was able to hire a hall not very expensively for a large party that included many people who had worked with my mother. The room surprised me with its grandeur with glass walls and an enormous chandelier that cost millions of Chinese yuan. Looking around at the extravagant interior of the cavernous building, I wondered how they were going to fill it, not knowing that before long the pivotal impact of joining the WTO would render it inadequate and it would be bulldozed to make way for an even bigger and smarter conference and exhibition centre.

After the birthday celebration I went to Beijing to continue my research, staying in the former state guest house, the Diaoyutai, Imperial Fishing Villas, which had been the headquarters of the Cultural Revolution. Mme Mao and her team had operated from here, and Mao had come to give orders every now and then. This place had just been opened to the public and was offering a discount rate to attract clients. The guest villas were featureless, even ugly, with equally unremarkable interiors. Having stayed in one in the 1980s, Margaret Thatcher later told me, 'It was a place where you wished you had a bucket of water and gave it a good scrub!'

Few people seemed to know that this guest house with the highest political connection was available, and I appeared to be the only non-state guest. I was given a room in the villa where Henry Kissinger had stayed. After checking in, I dialled room service as the estate was far from any restaurants. I was told that the kitchen was normally closed when there were no state events, and the only thing the chef could make was a bowl of plain noodle soup. It was the most expensive noodle soup I had ever had (costing 200 yuan, when an average one would cost at most a few), but it tasted sublime – a comment on the culinary standards for its usual clientele.

The next day, when I was going out, the young soldier who with the greatest solemnity stood upright on a stand in the middle of a square facing the front gate spotted me and, abandoning his guard-of-honour posture, called out sternly, asking who I was. I told him I was a hotel guest and showed him the pass I had been issued, which he scrutinised suspiciously. He came down from the pedestal to take me to the concierge by the gate, where he argued disapprovingly with the administrators who had clearly been behind the decision to turn the guest house into a money-making hotel. Later, a friend who came to see me and only got in after some hassle said, 'You've got to move out of this place. No one would dare to come and see you here!'

Before I left, I lingered outside Mao's villa, which was the only one under lock and key. Like the other Mao villas, it resembled an aeroplane hangar, two storeys high from the outside but one storey inside: no stairs so Mao would not be trapped on the upper floor. The grey monstrosity looked depressing, a reminder of decisions made here which had devastated countless lives. I was so glad that this place could open its door to the public, even if the door to Mao's villa remained shut.

Soon after I moved into a normal hotel, my sister called to tell me that Mother had broken her back after falling into a ditch on a street that was virtually a building site. She had not been able to see the road surface clearly. I berated myself again for the delayed treatment of her detached retina which had left her with this incurable eye defect. But when I spoke to my mother, she was cheerful, jokingly saying that it was fate that she should take some knocks as she had been too happy having all her children and many relatives and old friends around her. I wanted to return to Chengdu to see her, just three hours by plane. She urged me not to, saying that breaking a back was no big deal, all she had to do was to lie still for a few months. My time was valuable, she said, and must be used to write a good book.

*

After researching Mao for nearly ten years, Jon and I now focused on writing the biography. Back home in London, we worked throughout the day. When we went out in the evenings, sometimes at a crowded party we would find ourselves talking to each other, trying to solve some puzzles to do with Mao. We wrote in our separate studies and emerged at lunchtime in the kitchen to talk. We were together day in day out, year in year out, never tired of each other's company. There were so many things we wanted to say to each other, we never had enough time to say them.

My desk was and is still a long plank of wood sitting on two sets of wooden filing cabinets, made by a carpenter friend many years ago. The top is piled high with books and files, with colourful stickers poking out: my notes and memory aids. I sit in the middle, between two floor-length sash windows. Outside the window to my right, a huge plane tree with massive branches dominates the sky. Under the tree is a typical London street scene: red double-decker buses swaying past well- or not-so-well-tended front gardens, pedestrians walking in sunshine or under umbrellas, and a black lamppost coming to life at dusk. This is the view I gaze at whenever I pause from writing, and it never fails to enchant me. Sometimes a full moon rises from under the plane tree over the roofs of the houses across the street, enormous when it first appears, silver or golden. I am compelled to take my eyes off the desk, switch off the lights, leave the curtain open, to watch it rise, until it is high in the sky and becomes small. Such moments give me a profound sense of peace, with surges of gratitude – grateful for being a writer, grateful for being able to call London home, grateful to have Jon with me, close, and Mother at the other end of the telephone.

The sense of peace was especially precious during the writing of the biography of Mao, as I was conscious that I was writing about true evil. Although I had known that Mao was bad before I started the book, I had had no idea he was this bad. One of the things that really shocked me was the discovery of the cause of the Great Famine of 1958–61. I had thought that it was largely the result of incompetence, and had not expected it to be deliberate. Now I found out that Mao had known his people would be starved to death *before* it happened, as he was planning to export the food they depended on for survival to the Soviet bloc to pay for the military industries he was buying. China had historically been unable to produce enough food to feed its population, and the last de facto royal ruler, Empress Dowager Cixi, had started importing huge quantities of food from 1867, a policy that had continued into the Republic of China – until Mao, who banned food imports a few years after he seized power and was now exporting food on an unimaginable scale. Mao even said: 'With all these projects, half of China may well have to die.' Jon and I painstakingly calculated on the basis of yearly death rates that close to thirty-eight million people had died of starvation and abuse in the four years of the Great Famine. (A leading Party historian subsequently revealed an official death figure: 37.558 million, which is virtually identical to our estimate: 37.67 million.) When I stared at this figure and Mao's words, I felt the hair standing up on the back of my neck. It was with a similar sensation that I came to the conclusion with Jon that during his twenty-seven-year rule, Mao was responsible for the deaths of well over seventy million of his own people in peacetime.

Discoveries like these made me conscious of the subversive nature of our book and the risks we were taking. As the twenty-first century was arriving, Beijing had made a decision to redouble its promotion of Mao. It put his face, and only his, on every Chinese banknote, to replace the previous design of having the heads of other CCP leaders as well. This highly symbolic gesture demonstrated to the Chinese – and to the world – that no matter how 'capitalist' China was becoming, the regime would never turn its back on Mao.

It became clear to me that my life would change after the publication of the biography, that Beijing would view me as a kind of enemy, and I had to be prepared for the worst. But I decided to push all concerns to the back of my mind, resolving to deal with whatever would come when it came.

My stomach churned though, when I thought of my mother and what might happen to her and my siblings living in China. I longed to talk to her face to face – and to prepare her for the revelations in the book. I worked flat out to produce a Chinese draft after handing the English manuscript to the publishers, and invited her to Hong Kong to read it before publication in 2005.

My mother sensed that I needed her and went through a lot of trouble to get her exit visa to come to Hong Kong. There, in her hotel room, she spent two full days reading the draft. Afterwards she told me that a great number of things in the book were new to her, and so they would be to others; I must make absolutely sure that all the facts were checked and double-checked, and all the conclusions solidly backed up. The one specific point she made was that since we maintained that Mao was not a founding member of the CCP, we should name all the founding members, as well as providing credible sources. I said I would add the names of the eight founders of the CCP in the Chinese edition, and gave her the sources for the information: a Moscow repre-sentative's report from the Russian archives, and the recollections of the surviving founders, recorded by Party historians. It seemed that my mother was hoping, as I was, that the fact Mao was not the founder of the CCP might help the Party draw a line between itself and Mao and turn a new page, claiming legitimacy, perhaps, from its own post-Mao achievements. But this was only a wish: no achievements would guarantee that the Party would rule forever – which was what the Party wanted.

I asked my mother for more comments. She declined, saying that this was my book, and she was certain I would say what I believed to be the truth – and that her principle regarding her children was always not to interfere with what we did and not to tell us what to do. Suddenly I had a feeling that my mother seemed to be rehearsing her response to potential interrogators. It occurred to me that this was what she would say to protect herself – and through her own safety protect my siblings in China. For a moment I was terrified, thinking that I had made a big mistake by making my mother read the manuscript. If she had not read it, she could quite truthfully say she had had no idea what was in the book. Now I had deprived her of that line of defence. Seeing my anxiety, my mother gave me a comforting smile and an optimistic sketch of China at the time. The Chinese economy was taking off at an extraordinary speed thanks to the country being linked to the West and becoming 'the factory of the world'. To keep the West's goodwill was important to Beijing, and its way of governing was becoming more humane as a result. She did not think the government would punish my family for my book – certainly not as horribly as under Mao.

But my mother was not untroubled. She was worried about me. She had previously told me that what Jon and I were doing amounted to 'Digging Up [the Party's] Ancestral Tomb', which in Chinese culture means an act that inflicts the deadliest damage. There would be unforeseen hazards lying in wait. She was pensive while we strolled after our last dinner in Hong Kong on the walkway along Kowloon harbour, the lights across the water dazzling and us in relative shadow. The next day, we went to the airport together, and I sat with her outside her departure gate before she flew to Chengdu. For a long time, we sat silently, my mother's arm around my shoulders. We had sat together like this before. On the last night of August 1966, the then fourteen-year-old me was sitting with her at Chengdu railway station, waiting for her train to leave for Beijing at dawn. My father had just been taken away from home into detention because he had written to Mao to oppose the Cultural Revolution. My mother was going to Beijing to try to get him out – and I had come to the station with her to keep her company and to bear witness in case something happened to her. That night I had lain down on the bench and put my head in her lap. She spread her raincoat over me, still hugging me over the coat. At some point I was woken up by a twitching movement of her body. I opened my eyes and saw a couple of official-looking people standing in front of us. In a low but severe voice, they told my mother to abandon her trip and go back. She said no to the order firmly. They threatened to drag her forcefully into a car that was waiting, and she said that if they did so, 'I will shout for the Red Guards.' They whispered to each other and walked away.

When I recalled the event some years later, I asked my mother how she could be sure the Red Guards would help her rather than the officials. 'Suppose they denounced you to the Red Guards as a class enemy who was trying to escape?' Mother replied, 'I calculated that they would not take the risk. But I was prepared to gamble everything.' That trip of my mother's secured my father's release, even though it was for only a short time.

With such a brave and resourceful mother next to me, I felt

I could face anything. I put my head on her shoulder, and she enfolded me in both her arms, a pair of reassuring wings.

Finally, after twelve years, *Mao: The Unknown Story* was published in 2005 in English. On its eve, I was given an all-clear about my cancer, after twelve years of monitoring. With this piece of good news, I was doubly elated by the book's mainly fantastic reception. Reviewers used words like 'magnificent', 'stupendous' and 'a triumph'. *Time* magazine called it 'An atom bomb of a book'. It went on to be translated into some thirty languages. Jon and I savoured our achievement together, knowing that our book would play a significant role in the world's understanding of Mao, one of the most important figures of the twentieth century, and that we would help change the rose-tinted image of Mao that had been created by Edgar Snow on the left, promoted by Henry Kissinger on the right, and perpetuated by the many Mao apologists who had largely dominated academia in the West.

The Mao apologists naturally did not like our biography. Interviewed by the German newspaper *Die Welt* soon after publication, Kissinger said it was 'a great pity' and 'grotesque'* – with a bitterness usually reserved for personal spats. (Later, he seemed to have had a rethink and in his 2011 book *On China* described our biography as 'one-sided but often thought-provoking'.)

We had a rather eventful book tour in America. In New York, going into the Asia Society to give a talk, I was accosted by a man waving leaflets. He said, 'Are you going to the lecture? This is what you really should know', whereupon he handed me a leaflet, whose headline described Mao as a Great and Glorious Leader. I took the piece of paper and said to the youngish man,

* Kissinger interview, *Die Welt*, 27 December 2005.

'I am actually giving the lecture.' He was rather taken aback. At Washington University in Seattle, a small angry bunch charged towards us screaming slogans, so ferociously that they had to be carried out of the hall by security guards. I was accused of writing the biography to avenge the deaths of my family members, insinuating that the book was therefore unreliable. To this assertion my answer was: 'There is nothing wrong in Mao's victims wanting to get even. But in this case, I can honestly say that I was not motivated by revenge, which to me was a negative feeling that would have made me miserable. I love life too much.' Indeed, I enjoyed my time writing about Mao, as Jon and I were like a pair of detectives solving endless mysteries about Mao's seemingly mad policies and figuring out what went on in his head. I felt tremendous rage when we uncovered yet more of Mao's atrocious deeds, but I tried to control my emotions and be fair to him. And Jon, ever the historian, was always there to make sure that we never overstated the case.

One American journalist was a friend of one of our interviewees, Zhang Hanzhi, Mao's English-language teacher and interpreter; and the journalist, as he wrote, 'checked' with her. 'Zhang Hanzhi said that she had indeed met informally with Chang two or three times but had declined to be interviewed and never said anything substantial.' Our accusers often used this quote to claim that we had misrepresented our interviewees. Friends who were angry at the slur urged me to put in the public domain a photo of me with Zhang, in which a tape recorder was clearly visible on the table. But I declined. I regarded Zhang's reply as entirely understandable, as she was living in China and had to protect herself. In fact, Jon and I had written our book in such a way that our interviewees could deny association with us if their safety was in jeopardy. It is only now, when twenty years have passed and Zhang Hanzhi has died and cannot be hurt, that I am putting the record straight.

As a matter of fact, we only quoted Zhang for one thing, which the Notes of the book make perfectly clear. It is something that could well be described as 'insubstantial': she told us that Mao had professed love for her and she had turned him down.

In the past two decades since the publication of our Mao biography, Zhang Hanzhi was the only person who produced a half-denial, but she was put on the spot. Otherwise, not one interviewee has accused us of misquoting them or getting the facts wrong. I believe that our interviewees could tell that we were responsible and cared about protecting their safety as well as finding out the truth. This was why they trusted us and told us what they knew, mostly on tape. All the tapes, transcripts and notes are in safe storage today, waiting for the day when they can be made public without causing harm to anyone involved.

As for our accusers, Western apologists for Mao, we felt it was a waste of time to argue with them. Before our book was published, I had hoped that there might be scholarly debates over our many new discoveries. But it turned out that the apologists only wanted to insist that Mao was good – as was clear from the title of a collection of their writings criticising our book: *Was Mao Really a Monster? The Academic Response to Chang and Halliday's 'Mao: The Unknown Story'*. When so many facts about Mao's misrule were already well known through so many memoirs of people who lived through it (*Wild Swans* had been out for fourteen years), I did not know what more we could say to argue over this point. It would also hurt too much to hear those heartless defenders of Mao discount the deaths of my father and my grandma, the sufferings of my mother, the deaths and sufferings of my teachers, my fellow pupils, factory workers and commune peasants, and the countless I knew and heard of and read about. I decided to ignore them and get on with my life.

I felt – and I feel – saddened by the choice of those Western-ers to stick with Mao. Because they were supposed to be 'China experts', their standing by Mao has meant that even in the West, Mao has not been put firmly and squarely in the place he belongs: in the company of Hitler and Stalin. As a result, the Chinese regime has had too easy a job dismissing the atrocities documented by us and others, denying Mao's responsibility, and brainwashing China's younger generations who have not lived under Mao and do not know what life was like then. His portrait remains on Tiananmen Gate, its status more secure today than at any time since his death, as his true successor, Chairman Xi Jinping, is engaged in an unprecedented revival of Mao, with whom he identifies. It is with the Western apolo-gists' helping hand that Xi has dragged China back onto the road towards a Maoist hell – even if it is unlikely he will get there.

After *Mao* was published in English, I worked on the Chinese-language edition, which was ready for publication the following year, 2006. Obviously the book could not be pub-lished in China; we signed a contract with a publisher in Taiwan. Just before publication, our Taiwanese publisher wrote to ask me to delete the passages about a well-known top gen-eral under Chiang Kai-shek, General Hu Tsung-nan, now dead. Our research had convinced us that General Hu had been a Red 'sleeper'. His son, Hu Jr, demanded the deletion, and our publisher asked me to oblige him. Our publisher felt unable to resist the pressure, not because Hu Jr had threatened legal action, which he did not, but because Hu Jr was the ex-deputy chief of the State Security Bureau, that is, the intelligence agency of the Kuomintang government in Taiwan. That agency was notorious for bumping off people who incurred its ire.

One of its most famous victims had been the biographer of Ching-kuo, pen-named Jiang Nan, assassinated in 1984 in California, in the United States.

I sympathised with our publisher, but refused his request, as any writer with integrity would. He dissolved our contract, later telling the press how much he regretted losing what would surely be a big bestseller. Publication in Taiwan became impossible. A number of well-known Taiwanese and American Chinese historians and journalists were also approached to write denunciations of our book and of me, and they duly did as told, some rather nastily. One person declined to oblige: Wei Jingsheng, the first person in post-Mao China to call for democratic reforms, for which he had been imprisoned for eighteen years, before being exiled to America. In prison his warders used to say to him when they tried to make him recant, 'Look, you say you are fighting for freedom for the Chinese, but all other Chinese are free to enjoy themselves except you.' Those words held a grain of truth and could have destroyed many a resolve – but not Wei, a man with the courage and principle to stand alone.

It went without saying that I was threatened. A 'historian' tried to enlighten me about the Kuomintang intelligence: 'You know what the State Security Bureau is? You should know!' I stuck to my guns, only adding more details about General Hu in the Chinese edition. My brother Xiaohei gave me all his support by writing about what was happening on the internet and in a Taiwanese newspaper – after all, the place was now a democracy, albeit a young and timid one. Several commentators spoke up. Many Chinese readers sent their good wishes, telling me to watch out and not to become 'the Second Jiang Nan'.

Talk of the threats to me spread from Taiwan across the sea to Chengdu, and my friends and family heard about them. It was at this moment that my mother made her only telephone call to me about my books. She asked whether I was afraid. I said, no, I am ready to deal with whatever comes. My mother responded, 'Good. Don't let them scare you. Their days of scaring people into obedience are gone.'

I knew from the stories my mother had told me which I had included in *Wild Swans* that she had loathed the Kuomintang intelligence service whose agents had murdered her friends, and that the loathing had made her defiant and helped drive her to join the Communists. When she rang me up, my mother sounded as outraged as she must have been all those years before, but she also calmly analysed the situation for me: 'The times have changed. Taiwan is a democracy now. I don't believe the Kuomintang today would endorse violence against writers. Your book in English and other languages has been out for nearly a year; the story is widely known. What goal can they achieve by harming you? It would only trigger investigations which could expose more unpalatable truths. Their threats have already given your book plenty of publicity among the Chinese. Imagine what more attention an "incident" would bring. Those who are making threats would not want to do something so stupid as to start a fire only to burn themselves' (*yin-huo-shao-shen*).

My mother's words fortified me, and during those unpleasant months, I was unafraid and unanxious. In the end, Jon and I found a Hong Kong publisher who brought out our biography of Mao with meticulous care in autumn 2006, giving its publication in the Chinese language a resolute happy ending.

17

'Renounce Your Book or Else . . .'

(2007–08)

When the Chinese language edition of our Mao biography was finally published in Hong Kong in late 2006, copies of the book were carried by travellers into mainland China, where Mao remained sacrosanct. Not surprisingly, the book created waves. Many readers agreed with *Time* magazine that 'it was indeed "an atom bomb of a book".' Instantly, pirated copies appeared for sale on the street. (I collected a dozen editions.) Some enthusiasts took the trouble to convert the text from traditional characters used in Hong Kong and Taiwan, into simplified characters used on the mainland to help the younger generations who had little exposure to traditional ideograms unlike the older generations. In the name of research, the Chinese Social Science Academy made two hundred photocopies for its staff.

Beijing quickly clamped down on the book, and finally decided to do something about me. So far, compared to other offenders of the regime, I had been given kid-glove treatment, partly thanks to *Wild Swans'* fame. That I was not an activist in the dissident movements abroad helped. The biography of Mao changed the equation of Beijing's calculation. A warning shot was fired at me. One morning, when I went into my upstairs study, I was struck by an eerie sensation that the place was empty. I looked at my bookshelves and the papers around, and they seemed to be untouched. Then I realised what was missing: on the balcony outside, separated from the room by glass doors, all my plants were gone, including a mature Japanese acer shaped like an umbrella and a large jasmine bush whose massive shoots had twined the trellises. They had all been cut by someone with a serrated knife just an inch from the soil. The intruders had brought bags and taken away every leaf and branch of the desiccated plants. It would have taken several sacks to hold them. Someone would also have had to untangle the numerous shoots that had become attached to the house without making any noise. Jon and I were sleeping just above the balcony when all this took place, and we were both light sleepers.

The police came, so did Special Branch, the counter-terrorism unit of the Metropolitan Police. They found the area – the balcony, the garden and the fences – undisturbed, and the doors and windows not tampered with. They concluded that the 'criminal damage' done to our house was not the work of vandals, but highly skilled professionals, who got onto our balcony (something that the police officers said they would not have been able to do themselves) without leaving any marks. I thought of the film *The Godfather*, in which the mafia sent a message to an uncooperative man by putting the severed head of his favourite horse in his bed while he was asleep. It was obvious to me that the intrusion into my house was also a coded message saying 'we can get you'. I did not know what precise things they wanted of me, but decided I would carry on with my life as normal. I believed that the post-Mao regimes had on the whole been sensible and would not do things too rashly. I think my sanguineness was not misplaced – even though I was shaken enough never to have told my mother about the episode.

Special Branch gave us advice and protection. They suggested that we grow a type of especially thorny climbing rose so that any future intruders would inescapably leave traces of their identity. As a result, gorgeous ramblers have wrapped themselves around our house, their blade-sharp thorns guarding our home, while their clusters of pale pink blossoms delight our eyes.

In October 2007, when I applied for a visa to go to Chengdu and see my mother I was turned down.

This was what I had dreaded most. Now aged seventy-six, my mother had recently suffered a stroke and had also developed aneurysms in her intestines causing frequent haemorrhages. Doctors warned that she should not travel by plane, certainly not fly long-distance, to avoid triggering life-threatening bleeding. Following medical advice, she had cancelled her plan to visit my brother Jinming in Canada. It was impossible now for her to come to me in London. I told myself that I simply must get the visa rejection revoked, otherwise I might never see my mother again.

I asked the Foreign Office for help, telling them that if the Mao book was the issue, I could promise Beijing that I would not talk about it in China. British diplomats pressed my case repeatedly with the Chinese ambassadress. Several grandees wrote and pleaded for me. The ambassadress, a seasoned diplomat, expressed sympathy for my mother's illnesses and for our desire to see each other. But she said the decision had been made in Beijing, and, after consulting Beijing, she delivered the reply: I could only go to China if I stopped talking about Mao, not only inside China, but also outside, anywhere in the world. Moreover, Beijing made clear that I 'would not be welcome in China' unless I 'issue a statement apologising for writing that book on Mao'. When the ambassadress relayed those words to Lord (Geoffrey) Howe, the normally extremely mild-mannered former foreign secretary was so angry that he burst out: 'Immediately stop that line of argument!'

I wrote to the foreign secretary, David Miliband, and he replied with encouraging words: 'I am most concerned about what has happened . . . We have already made representations to the Chinese Ambassador in London, and I have asked Sir William Ehrman [British ambassador in China] to take similar action with the Chinese Foreign Ministry . . . we will continue to raise your case with the Chinese authorities, and I am willing to do so personally when I have that opportunity.' Sir William requested an urgent meeting with the assistant foreign minister in Beijing, during which, I was told, the Chinese diplomat took notes and did not say a word when normally he would have said something. I was also told that the Chinese foreign minister, Yang Jiechi, was about to visit London, and Miliband would raise the issue with him.

Words could not adequately convey my gratitude to my adopted country and to my friends for all their efforts to help. But I could not be sure whether we would succeed. What if Beijing dug in and ignored all the approaches? I decided to prepare for the other option: to appeal to my readers, hoping they would put pressure on Beijing to allow me to see my mother. At the time, *Wild Swans* was an international bestseller, and millions of readers around the world felt they knew my mother and identified with her. To hold her, now elderly and ill, at ransom, to force me to renounce my book, was shocking and unacceptable to most people, and I felt there was a chance that Beijing might change its mind. Western public opinion mattered in those days, before China had grown rich and powerful as today. And, very importantly, China was about to host the 2008 Olympics, something Beijing wanted desperately. I had seen huge slogans hanging over Chang'an Avenue on both sides of Tiananmen Square, entreating: 'Give us the Olympics and we will return the world a miracle!', which had surprised me somewhat as the tone verged on begging and would normally have been regarded as losing face. Beijing needed goodwill from the West, and that gave me hope.

I had not told my mother about the visa rejection as I had hoped that some private channels would work, in which case I did not need to distress her unnecessarily. Now I felt I had to put her in the picture. I called her; and she urged me not to go public. Knowing the Party, she thought it unlikely it would give in. There were many Chinese exiles who had offended the regime far less and who were not allowed to visit their parents, and the Party always rode out the storm. Publicly fighting the Party would make it resent me more, and make future applications impossible, and if I spoiled the Party's Olympics in any way, it would hate me with venom. But I felt that if I allowed the visa 'rejection' to be lodged in my record, it would create a 'precedent', and nobody would repeal it in the future. And I had a feeling that the success of *Wild Swans* might give me a unique opportunity, which my mother, living in China and speaking no English, did not fully appreciate. I decided not to take my mother's advice this time and went ahead with preparations to go public.

My English publisher fully supported me and hired a public relations agency, which devised a 'strategy'. All the major media outlets contacted showed great interest. My foreign publishers were gearing up to engage the media in their own countries. I drafted a letter of personal appeal to my readers, and made a list of influential people who had expressed admiration for *Wild Swans* and to whom I planned to write. By temperament I did not relish campaigns and appeals, and dreaded the thought of having to write those letters. But never to see my mother again was too unthinkable a prospect. I felt I must try everything possible. The campaign was to kick off on 13 December 2007, after I had returned from a Singapore writers festival.

I did not discuss any of the plans with my mother, cautious that her phone might be bugged. Before I flew to Singapore, I called her on 2 December and told her briefly what I was about to do. On this call, I stressed that I was forced to make the move by the Party's 'condition' for me to see her – that I had to disown my book. At the mention of this, defiance rose in my mother's voice. She said, 'Oh, I hadn't quite registered that. It changes everything. Their "condition" amounts to blackmail and is totally unacceptable.' Perhaps with a surreptitious listener in mind, my mother called the people who made the demand 'stupid': their objective was to suppress my book, and yet by forcing me to go public they would only give the book the biggest possible promotion. My mother said emphatically to me: 'I entirely support what you are planning to do.' The next day when I rang again, she told me not to talk to my siblings living in China: 'If they know nothing, they can't be blamed.' As for herself, she said she had thought it through and would give me whatever help I needed. She only cautioned me: 'Not to hold out hope for a win.'

As I jotted down what she was saying on the phone, I was so proud of my mother. I found my thoughts wandering back to the time of the Cultural Revolution when she had been blackmailed with the threat of never seeing her children again. She had been detained in a cinema, under pressure to denounce my father and to admit to being 'a Kuomintang spy' (which would mean naming fellow 'spies'). She refused the demands. One day I went to the cinema taking by the hand my six-year-old brother Xiaofang, to deliver a package of food and clothing which Grandma had packed for her. The ad-hoc prison refused to take it, giving us the impression that Mother was dead. In panic, Xiaofang and I stood outside the walls of the cinema and screamed towards the rows of windows we could see, 'Mama! Mama!', hoping desperately that she would appear. She heard us, as she told me later; her guard even opened a window wider so that our voices would come through louder. The guard told her that she could see us straight away if she agreed to the demands; but if not, she might never see us again. My mother said no to the demands – just as she was now encouraging me to say no to renouncing my book.

Beijing relented at the last minute. A few hours before I left home to fly to Singapore, a call came from the Foreign Office. The Chinese embassy had rung and asked me to go and collect my visa. From now on, I would be given a visa for ten to fifteen days a year for many years, although those visas were not guaranteed and each time I had to make a fresh request and wait for it to be granted, a process that was extremely time consuming and emotionally draining.

Behind the visa counter a row of rather stylishly dressed, giggling young women greeted me with frank and not unfriendly curiosity, one or two calling out to the rooms behind, 'She's here. She's here', and out came more girls to steal glances at me. Jon, who was with me, observed, 'The girls were riveted at seeing you.' I smiled back, feeling brightened up by the fact that the Chinese embassy was staffed by such spontaneous and cheerful young people.

In Singapore, my optimism was somewhat dampened. There was a group of Chinese writers from Beijing's official Writers Association, and I bumped into a writer-cum-official at some event. Instinctively, I said a friendly hello, as I would do to any stranger. She returned a look of such stagey coldness that I was instantly transported back to the days of the Cultural Revolution, when I had been on the receiving end of many a similar obnoxious face for being my father's daughter. I could never get used to it, and each encounter had sent a shiver up my spine. For a moment I was frozen in my tracks, and was reminded painfully how many people were still stuck in the Maoist mode.

Still, no one could prevent me from seeing my mother (not at that time anyway). When I arrived in Chengdu from Singapore, she greeted me with a joyous 'We won', and we embraced each other. It sank in finally just how much this 'victory' meant for me.

As we caught up, my mother told me that Auntie Deng, our former neighbour and half-sister of Deng Xiaoping (who had died in 1997), had paid her a visit recently, for the first time in years. The last time they met had been in spring 1989, when my mother, Jon and I had been invited to dinner in her flat. After that, with what happened on Tiananmen Square, the darkening of the liberal mood, and the ban on *Wild Swans*, she had stopped visiting my mother. This time they had a long conversation, and Auntie Deng praised me in superlative terms. Although my book on Mao never crossed their lips, there seemed little doubt that she was there to convey her appreciation. She was a truly brave woman, as her half-brother would not have endorsed the book if he were alive.

In Chengdu, my mother and I were together the whole time,

as we had not been for over a decade, when research had taken up most of my time in China. Now the book was finished – and the scare of the visa rejection had made me doubly treasure our time together. My mother, never a shopper for clothes, even went to a few shops with me. My sister took me to little silk stores, which were selling their stock of exquisitely soft scarves. In this ancient silk centre, silk factories were sadly closing down, defeated by easy-to-produce artificial fabrics. An old tailor made several beautiful silk jackets for Jon, in which he really cut a dash in London.

My brother Xiaohei came home too, and my family went sightseeing like a group of excitable tourists. One day we visited an old town hundreds of miles to the southwest. It was a World Cultural Heritage Site, because it was supposed to be ancient and show the cultures of different ethnic groups. I was utterly disappointed to see a place which to my eye had plainly been rebuilt with the help of bulldozers, and looked like a garish stage set. The local men and women serving the tourists dressed in theatrical costumes, but when I asked them to which ethnic group they belonged, all answered they were Han Chinese, who dominated the population.

The saddest thing on that trip was to realise how much my mother's health had deteriorated. In the old town, which is at an altitude of 2,500 metres, she was unable to walk, her lips purple for lack of oxygen. Even at home, she had to take oxygen every day. Her body seemed to have become small all of a sudden. My mother had always been considered 'big', which was not exactly a compliment, as the standard of beauty was to be 'slim'. But when I was a child embracing her ample body and putting my head against her stomach, I had often thought how lucky I was that my mother was not skinny. If she were, how could I feel her strong presence, how could I be assured that everything would be all right? Now she was slim, and frail – she was only human and was losing her energy and dynamism with age, even though she was still mentally strong. Hugging her goodbye, I wished my arms were large wings that could fold round her body and press some of the strength it had given me over the years back into it.

I spent a few days in Beijing meeting friends and some interviewees. Among them was Li Rui, China's most courageous and eminent liberal senior official who, having spent two decades in solitary confinement or China's Gulag, continued to speak up in the post-Mao years. He took me to a gathering of old Party liberals, who gave me a wonderful welcome on account of the Mao biography. A few of them had reacted with shock when they first read the biography in the previous year. It was as if their mental furniture had been drastically rearranged, leaving them momentarily disorientated and uncomfortable. Now, a year later, most seemed to have come around to our approach, finding it making sense and convincing. Li Rui could not be more appreciative.

From our interviewees came high praise, which touched me, making me feel that all the hard work and potential dangers were worth it. One quoted a classic expression 'to spend ten years sharpening a sword', meaning that great efforts produce something outstanding. Kuai Dafu, the former Red Guard leader who had been a major actor in the Cultural Revolution as Mao's instrument in persecuting President Liu Shaoqi and his wife, thanked me for treating that episode 'accurately' and 'fairly'. Mme Liu, Guangmei, had by now died, but when I was in Beijing in 2006, I had been able to take her a copy of the book in hospital.

Thanks to the Mao biography, new friends came into my life. Among them was Z.D., one of China's new multimillionaires.

His mother had been executed in the Cultural Revolution when he was a child, which scarred him for life. After Mao died, his mother's name was cleared, and with the compensation of 500 yuan, more than a year's salary, he started his business. Now he bought hundreds of copies of the Mao biography to give to friends, employees, and anyone he thought would like it. He threw a banquet for me and invited a group of businessmen and women, who had similarly become rich recently. With their new wealth they embraced leisure and had begun to play tennis and golf and travel overseas. One man mentioned his first ever holiday abroad, telling us that his wife had tried to book the cheapest air tickets, which involved being at the airport in the middle of the night, and that he had stopped her: 'We have money now and we must adjust our lifestyle.'

Most of the people who became rich from the bottom of society had had miserable childhoods, and had seized the post-Mao opportunities to flourish. A distributor who was selling our Mao book in pirated editions told me on the phone that they were the main buyers, along with Communist officials and intellectuals. The buyers, he informed me, often purchased more than a hundred copies at a time to give to others. I had spotted the distributor in an internet advertisement and had rung him to buy a copy for my own collection, without telling him I was one of the authors. He apologised for the book being 'expensive' at 40 yuan a copy, plus 10 yuan for express delivery, 'but you know, we are running a risk selling it'. He was sorry for the poor quality of the paper and some wrong characters, but assured me that 'They would not affect reading.' After I received the book and saw that it was decently produced and the channel of purchase was working, I rang again to buy more copies. But his phone had been disconnected.

I told Z.D. that I was concerned that the clandestine

publishers might get into trouble. He reassured me that they all had ways to protect themselves, with the police often looking the other way. The same was true with his businessmen friends, who had come to his dinner for me knowing it was risky. Z.D. himself had been warned by several people against entertaining me, one working in the security apparatus telling him that I was 'under full surveillance throughout the journey'. He had shrugged off the warnings, telling me: 'You are not afraid of writing the book, and so I am not afraid of entertaining you.' He was admirably daring; but it was also true that in the first decade of the twenty-first century, under Hu Jintao, the general atmosphere in China remained relatively relaxed, as it had been in the 1990s under Jiang Zemin. The people I met seemed to think the government was largely doing the right thing, with the economy racing ahead and other reforms 'going forward in mincing steps' (*sui-bu-qian-jin*). There seemed to be hope.

Nevertheless, fear was still embedded in people's hearts. One day I went to meet a poet friend in a teahouse. He had written me some excellent poems (one after reading the Mao biography) and as I loved Chinese poetry, I had looked forward to having a good chat. When I arrived, I saw him waiting in a private room, with someone who turned out to be neither a fellow poet nor a reader of my books. After we greeted each other and sat down, the poet shot up, walked to the door that had been closed, and pulled it wide open. He looked nonchalant but I could see he was fearful, and careful not to give anyone grounds to suspect a secret meeting. The other person was clearly there as his alibi. I lost my enthusiasm to talk and the conversation went cheerlessly.

An old friend who had given me interviews for the Mao biography immediately and excitedly agreed to lunch when he heard my voice on the phone. After I put the phone down, on second thought, I felt I should have reminded him of my changed status having written the Mao biography. I called him the next morning, and his relief at my offer to cancel our lunch was palpable. 'It's impossible they are not following you closely,' he said, and admitted he had spent the night tossing and turning, nervous about the meeting. Days later, he called again, sounding very sorry about the way our friendship had ended. He said he had been searching the internet and found that things to do with me had been thoroughly deleted – whereas a short while before there had been hundreds of thousands of entries, including blogs. Indeed in London I had had the surreal experience of seeing a blog about me vanishing in front of my eyes. I was reading it when the screen went milky except for a notice: 'This item is being examined. Please wait.' A second later the blog was gone, dramatically swept off the screen by a whoosh of digital wind. My friend was trying to explain that he was only forced to avoid me, which I of course understood only too well.

I stopped contacting most friends I had had, and saw only a handful of people who assured me that they were not afraid, or that they were on the surveillance list of the State Security anyway. The bravery of these friends moved me deeply, especially so as when I returned the following year, 2008, they immediately started helping me with the research of my next book – a biography of Empress Dowager Cixi, the imperial concubine who launched modern China.

18

Up Close with the State Security

(2008–11)

It was *Wild Swans* that kindled my interest in Empress Dowager Cixi, the last titanic ruler of monarchical China. Because my grandma had suffered from crushed, bound feet, I looked into the history of foot-binding. And I found out that the thousand-year-old practice that had tortured my beloved grandma all her life was first banned by the Empress Dowager in 1902. Yet in history books she was – and still is – a villain, a die-hard reactionary and a cruel despot. Getting rid of foot-binding has been credited to others, including Mao. As recently as 2006, London mayor Ken Livingstone remarked publicly: 'One thing that Chairman Mao did was to end the appalling foot-binding of women. That alone justifies the Mao Zedong era.' This ignorance is shared by many.

Then, when I was researching the Mao biography, I was again struck by the fact that China had embarked on the transformation from the medieval to the modern in 1861 – the year Cixi launched a palace coup and made herself the power behind the throne of her five-year-old son, Emperor Tongzhi. She was the one who opened the door of China and left a legacy that enabled the young Mao, a peasant lad, to enjoy freedom and opportunities I could not dream of when I was growing up under Mao decades later.

The Cixi I had glimpsed was so different from the established image that I saw another 'unknown story' like that of Mao beckoning and decided on her as my next subject.

I was in luck, as I discovered. In Beijing, the First Historical Archives of China, which hold the documents of her dynasty, the Great Qing, were open, and scholars had been working on them, sorting, publishing, even digitalising them – so there was a colossal documentary pool for me to dive into. I was impatient to get into China and begin my research.

As I was planning the trip in 2008, an earthquake of 8.0 magnitude shattered western Sichuan, with Chengdu only fifty miles from the epicentre. My mother was at home on the tenth floor when the quake struck and the whole building shook. She managed to walk downstairs into an open space, and soon Xiaofang arrived with his car, which had been gyrating 'like dancing in a disco' when he got into it. He had driven like a racing car driver to get to her, and with Mother, his wife and our sister all in, parked the car in a street away from the high rises. My Chengdu family stayed the night in the car, while outside, unprecedented thunder and lightning raged throughout the night. In London I watched the earthquake on television, wishing I could help in some way. I put in my visa application at the first opportunity, immediately after the 2008 Olympics, and was issued a visa for ten days.

At the smart new Beijing airport terminal, the passport control official scrutinised my visa and took me to a side

room to 'wait while we ask for instructions from the authorities'. A couple of hours later, when I was finally let through, a
young man, who had greeted me at the door of the plane and
escorted me all the way, waiting patiently outside the side
room, now conducted me to the hotel car. I had asked him
whether he was from the hotel, and he had given me an enig-
matic smile, which suggested a yes. On the way he led me to a
counter to change money and buy a local SIM card. I thanked
him for his helpfulness; he smiled indecipherably again.

I started seeing historians of the Qing dynasty at once
through the introduction of my few brave friends, and was
thrilled by their willingness to help me. I was even invited to a
conference straightaway on a major historical issue (the death
of Emperor Guangxu, Cixi's adopted son whom she was
accused of poisoning), where I met many scholars. I had worried the Mao biography might scare them off, but it turned out
to be the very reason why they were so welcoming. One scholar
referred to it as 'the book that Got the Chief' (*san-jun-duo-
shuai*). By the end of a mere few days, I had, in addition to
meeting scholars, been directed to specialist bookstores selling
collections of documents and scholarly works, where I bought
everything relevant and had them shipped back to London. I
had been given access to the main institutions of Qing studies,
one located in a grand European-style building constructed
under the Empress Dowager at the beginning of the twentieth
century, to house the headquarters of her newly founded Ministry of the Army; later, after she died and her dynasty gave way
to a republic, it served as the first presidential palace. Most
exciting of all was to wander around the closed private quarters
of the Forbidden City, which in the old days had been inhabited by palace staff and were now the offices, including a palace
library. One evening, I followed a scholar out of the labyrinth
of courtyards to the main palaces after the visitors had all left.

The vast, completely empty palace grounds took my breath away. In the gathering dusk, along alleyways inside high red walls, people working there rode bicycles to the gate to go home, many turning to say hello to my friend as they passed us.

This wonderful reception was even more amazing as the scholars knew I had seriously offended the regime and was under the surveillance of the State Security. One or two of them jokingly hinted at it. It did not deter them from seeing me, though we cautiously stuck to the Qing history in our conversations. With the same mixture of caution and daring, a great-grand-nephew of Cixi came to see me and told me stories in their family lore. He showed me round the Summer Palace on the outskirts of Beijing, an architectural jewel which she had created, and in which he was now an administrator. Roughly the same age as me the man, who would have been a prince had the Qing dynasty not fallen, had only recently been promoted to that managerial post. Most of his life, he had lived as an outcast for being related to Cixi. His parents had warned him never to mention his great-grand-aunt. During the Cultural Revolution, when the Red Guards were raiding people's homes, his family had panicked and destroyed most of her gifts, including priceless porcelain pieces, which today would have made them a fortune. He invited me to his flat. I was shocked to see bare concrete floors and old newspapers serving as tablecloths. There was nothing that suggested a royal past. When he came to have dinner in the Palace Hotel, which was an imitation of his ancestral home, he was ill at ease and nervously spat into the luxury carpet before hurrying to rub away the phlegm with his shoes.

He was timid: Cixi was (and is still) the national villain, blamed for the 'hundred-year humiliation by the West'. The Qing historians knew this was not true, but they could not dispute it. When a scholar-filled board in charge of compiling the history of the Qing Dynasty invited eminent historians to write a series of biographies on all its major figures, nobody was approached to write on Cixi. She was the only person without an official biographer. I was amazed and asked some board members why. They replied vaguely that Cixi was 'too big': her life was the history of China in the first half-century of the country's modernisation. They did not spell out that there was a Party line on Cixi, and no scholar in China was able to write a truthful biography of her. I said, thrilled and only half in jest: Are you keeping Cixi for me?

On the last working day of the week, I buried myself in the First Historical Archives inside the Forbidden City. A new friend had taken me from a side gate to the archives, which were housed in an early twentieth-century building with palace-style red pillars and sweeping yellow roofs. I registered at the reception with my passport and started working like in any other archives around the world. This was beyond my wildest dreams.

I had barely dumped my bag of notes from the archives onto the bed in my hotel room when the desk phone rang. On the other end of the line a man said, 'I am—,' he gave a surname, then, 'from the State Security Ministry. Can we come up to your room to talk to you?' Flashing across my mind's eye were thugs barging in and putting a pillow over my face. I said into the phone, 'Please don't come up. I am changing and I will come down to meet you in the lobby when I am ready.' The other side agreed without hesitation, and I asked: 'How do I recognise you? Would you be carrying an umbrella?' My mother had told me that when she was doing underground work for the Communists, they often carried an umbrella as identification. This tongue-in-cheek joke came out involuntarily as I suddenly felt a frisson. The man on the other end of the line seemed to have taken it well, and said, 'We'll recognise you.'

I was composed as I rode the elevator down to the foyer. Two pleasant-looking men, one in his early thirties and the other younger, were outside the elevator and greeted me. So began my dealings with the officers of the Chinese State Security, the *guo-an*, for a decade, each time I went to China.

At this first meeting, we sat down, and the thirtysomething gave me his surname again and that of his colleague, offering no more specific information. I did not ask, wishing to have as little to do with them as possible. He was immediately recognisable as the boss of the two, because of his air of confidence and the fact that he did most of the talking. I later heard his team referring to him respectfully as *'wo-men-ling-dao'* – 'our leader', which rather surprised me as I usually associated the term with someone older. The Young Leader informed me of the purpose of their visit, in a polite manner. I had just accepted an invitation to lunch the next day, and they would like me to back out of it. An old friend, Liu Jiaju, one of those who had said they were not afraid to see me as they were already on the surveillance list, had rung with the invitation when I was in a taxi en route to the hotel from the archives. Obviously either his phone was bugged or mine was – I thought of the young man with a Mona Lisa smile at the airport who had waited for hours to escort me to the car and had led me to the counter to buy the SIM card.

Jiaju had been the founding deputy editor-in-chief of the leading liberal history journal, the *Yan-huang-chun-qiu (China Through the Ages)*, a magazine that had had the endorsement of a host of liberal Party elders, including Xi Zhongxun, father of today's Chairman Xi Jinping, and had published many of their memoirs. It had been a must-read in the 1990s for those who were interested in historical truth. A thin man with boundless energy, highly connected partly because of his job, Jiaju had introduced me to many interviewees during my research on Mao. On the phone he said that some readers of the Mao biography were keen to meet me, including several influential bloggers, and he would really like me to see them. My dilemma was that I had promised not to talk about the Mao book in public in China. But I hated to turn down my friend, who had done so much for me. I reasoned with myself that it could be argued that a few friends chatting over lunch might not count as speeches 'in public', and said yes reluctantly. Jiaju would come to the hotel the next morning to take me to meet the bloggers at ten, and then on to lunch.

The Young Leader asked me to ring Jiaju and decline the invitation, reminding me of my promise. I put up a sort of resistance ('It is only a lunch') and accepted his argument ('You can't be having lunch at ten'). I was actually relieved as I knew I must not break my promise. But when the Young Leader asked me to give a false reason for the cancellation and not to mention the intervention of the State Security, I refused, saying, 'I will not lie.' I told them I hated the practice of telling lies at the drop of a hat. They suggested I say, 'You understand' (*ni-dong-de*), adding: 'Everyone here knows what this means.' I retorted, 'Then what's the point of using this "euphemism"?' They did not insist, probably because I had already agreed on not going. I said I would like to invite Jiaju and his friends to a 'pure supper' to compensate for letting them down, and the Young Leader said fine. I dialled Jiaju, and he understood at once without me having to say a word of explanation. But when the dinner time came the next day, I could tell that the bloggers had been warned off as only two non-bloggers came with Jiaju, with excuses for the others that were transparently lies. Even those two spent the whole meal avoiding my eyes (for fear of starting a conversation, I guessed) and talking exclusively to each other, leaving Jiaju alone to talk to me, the host. I would have been annoyed had I not understood that they were only protecting themselves.

And so the State Security stepped out of the shadows into the open. In future, when I applied for a visa in London, I was obliged to contact them first by telephone or email, and send them my schedule for the trip, and they would tell the embassy to issue the visa. When I arrived in Beijing, they would come to my hotel to 'have a chat', which boiled down to them making demands. One was that I promise 'not to see sensitive people' – to which I answered, truthfully, that I did not know who these people were, and please could they show me the list. They never did, but asked me to give them the names of the people I planned to see. I refused, saying, 'You cannot possibly expect me to do this.' They said, 'Nothing would happen to those people. We only want to know who you are seeing in order to tell you whom you mustn't see, because there are some people whom once you have seen you would never be able to step into China again.' I replied, 'Even if this was your real reason, I could not give any names.'

Another demand was that I not disclose my conversations with them, which, they claimed, was in accordance with Chinese law; everyone who met with the State Security must sign a piece of paper promising to keep their talks confidential. I expressed incredulity about the 'law', and, having said no several times, eventually said, 'In that case, please give me the piece of paper you said everyone had to sign, and I will show it to the British embassy. They can advise me whether it is appropriate for a British citizen to sign such a document with a foreign State Security.' They dropped the demand after that.

In fact, I kept the British embassy informed about all my meetings.

Yet another demand was repeated with more insistence: they wanted me to write and sing Beijing's praises. One day the Young Leader invited me to lunch, in an elegant old villa, a jewel in a sea of indifferent high rises. He expressed amazement at the fact that my books had sold some fifteen million copies outside China, and asked me to write an article saying nice things about the country, 'such as the economic achievements'. 'If you do that, you will have no problem coming back to see your mother any time and staying as long as you want.' I said I never wrote articles, which required different skills from writing books, skills that I did not possess. This was true, and I had declined many invitations to write in the Western media. Still, they kept trying to persuade me over the years, and finally I said, 'What about you taking Mao's portrait down from Tiananmen Gate? That way, I will be so inspired that I will write the most wonderful things about China.' This generated a suitably furious response.

To my relief, they never demanded that I stop researching my biography of Cixi. I guessed that for them, it was better if I wrote about a historical figure rather than current politics. The Empress Dowager had nothing to do with the Communists, or so they thought. Still, I noticed that the First Historical Archives closed their doors to me after my visit. In the following years, every time I was in Beijing and tried to go there, they were always 'temporarily closed for internal reasons'. But I was able to hire a researcher to find the documents I named.

At least two minders were designated to go around with me – initially 'when you are outside Beijing', which suggested to me that the capital was tightly covered by surveillance (so it was unnecessary for them to follow me). This actually suited me as some places I planned to visit were out of the way, even 'in the wilderness'. One such place was the Royal Hunting Lodge in Chengde (not to be confused with Chengd*u*, where I grew up), on the edge of the Mongolian steppes, some one hundred and twenty miles northeast of Beijing beyond the Great Wall. It was where the Empress Dowager began China's modernisation in 1861. When the Young Leader at our first meeting asked me where I planned to visit, I answered with alacrity that I wanted to go there the very next day, and he assigned two minders to go with me, one of whom was a young woman: 'It would be better to travel with a woman comrade,' he said. My mother was delighted that I would now go with two 'bodyguards', as she had heard about crimes in that region. The minders bought the train tickets and dealt with other chores; not wishing to owe them anything, I paid for the taxi fare back to Beijing, as we missed the last return train.

I enjoyed the trip – and I believe so did my minders who had never been to the lodge. On the train, which took over an hour, I talked to them about the history associated with the place: how Cixi had fled there with her husband, Emperor Xianfeng, after the Old Summer Palace, the magnificent Yuanmingyuan, had been burned down by the English and the French, how he had died in Chengde in self-imposed exile because he could not bear returning to Beijing and 'living under the same sky' with foreigners, and how Cixi had carried out her coup, which led to the opening up of China. I also talked about Mao, reckoning that my promise not to talk about him 'in public' did not apply to the State Security officers. And they did not stop me – or try to argue with me. I supposed that their orders were to just listen. And they listened intently, with as much interest as they could show, to the stories that were not in their history books.

The minders were virtually the only people in China with

whom I could express my views frankly, without inhibition. With most other people, especially friends, I was always anxious about what I said, in case it caused them trouble. Caution killed the fun of many a conversation, and I was permanently tense. But my minders were licensed to listen. Being able to speak freely in some ways compensated for my loss of freedom.

The female minder, a bright young woman in her early twenties, in a trendy top just like an average fashion-conscious girl in Beijing, was designated to escort me to Chengdu – presumably to brief the local State Security people how exactly to deal with me. As we moved to our separate lines to board the plane, she told me that after the plane landed she would just go her own way without saying goodbye. I gave her a copy of *Wild Swans*, which I later noticed in the cabin that she seemed to be absorbed in. She said that she and her colleagues would like me to enjoy the company of my mother and so the local agents would not be bothering me; but could I give them a ring every day to tell them how things were? This reminded me of Mao's days when 'class enemies' had to check in with the police regularly to report their whereabouts. Angrily, I told her I could not possibly do this, and that if anyone wanted to know anything, they could telephone me. She left it at that. And no one called me when I was in Chengdu.

The following year, 2009, with the Olympics over, whatever openness there had been was ebbing. Before the Chinese embassy issued my visa, the counsellor in charge asked me to sign a pledge that while in China I would 'not engage in sensitive activities'. As the word 'sensitive' could cover anything, including researching Cixi, I changed it to a one-line statement: 'I undertake that in China, I will not take part in activities to do with politics.' I was not a political activist and meant the promise sincerely. The counsellor watched as I wrote this line in Chinese and after taking that piece of paper stamped my passport with the visa, adding that she would be held responsible if I broke my promise in the period the visa covered.

In Beijing, when the Young Leader and his team came to the hotel, they demanded that I write a similar 'undertaking' to the State Security. I did not wish to write anything to them, and said that I was only obliged to give an 'undertaking' *for my visa*. The subject was dropped, although it would be picked up again in the following years. In 2011, they said that the 'undertaking' had been written in 2009, and that the Chinese government needed one for 2011. So I wrote on a copy of the old one: 'This undertaking is applicable to other journeys inside China.' And I signed and dated it. I was cautious not to promise anything I could not stick to, so Beijing would have no excuse to ban me from visiting my mother.

In 2009, my successful businessman friend Z.D. gave another dinner for me, at which one guest turned out to be under surveillance, and another was an informer for the State Security, so the authorities knew that I had met 'sensitive people', which the Young Leader and his team were supposed to prevent. They were severely reprimanded, one of them told me. The Young Leader said to me angrily that from then on I would be followed in Beijing as well as outside. A car and officers would take me wherever I went. 'But I can't bring the State Security to people's doorsteps,' I said, and was then told that I had to choose between this awful scenario and telling him whom I was going to visit. I decided on the only alternative: seeing no one. I knew most people would not want the attention of the State Security, and stopped seeing virtually all my remaining friends. Z.D.'s dinner became our last.

There was an exception: the Qing scholars, whom the Young Leader agreed that I could continue to see without telling my minders. 'They haven't been disturbed so far, have they?' said he. Indeed, none of the Qing scholars showed any sign of having been harassed. Cixi was no immediate threat to the regime. And the informer's report about Z.D.'s last dinner also showed the authorities that I had said nothing about Mao, voiced no political views and remained mostly reticent. I had kept my 'undertaking'. The authorities decided that I had 'no political aspirations', and seemed to be relieved. I was allowed to carry on with my work on Cixi; still, I was careful and only saw a couple of scholars who had become friends and were keen to meet up.

Two fearless friends, Li Rui, the country's most outspoken liberal, and Jiaju, the former magazine editor, told me I was welcome to give their names to the State Security. And so I did, and went ahead to have a happy dinner at Li Rui's home, followed by a memorable trip to the mausoleum of Cixi with Jiaju.

In October 2010, I was in the Maldives for a literary festival and planned to go from there to Beijing on the sixteenth. That day, when I got to the airport, a bizarre thing happened. I was checking in when a porter appeared and removed my suitcase from the conveyor belt; he took it out of the departure hall to somewhere I was not allowed to enter. I followed and asked him what he was doing, but he refused to answer, signalling to me that he spoke no English. I rushed round to try to get some help, and told the festival organisers. But nobody could give me an explanation. So I missed the once-a-week flight to Beijing – and only then spotted my suitcase, in a corner outside. This mystery remained unresolved in my head until I was researching this book and put two and two together. On 13 October that year, Li Rui, then ninety-three years old and having just had his second pacemaker fitted, had been the lead signatory of an open letter calling for press freedom in China, which was published under the headline 'China Must Abandon Censorship' in the *Guardian* in Britain. The open letter reflected a widespread yearning, a rising aspiration from the thinking people in China at that stage. The regime did all it could to prevent follow-ups, and isolated the signatories in their homes. Police officers were stationed outside Li Rui's apartment and physically pushed away his visitors.

I did not know about any of this at the time, as the island I was staying on had no newspapers or internet. If I had gone to Beijing according to my schedule on the sixteenth, it would have been right in the wake of the open letter, possibly creating a situation the regime did not want to see. So, it seems, my minders, who had my schedule, arranged for me to miss the flight, which as it happened seems to have been extremely easy to organise. I only arrived in Beijing when the reverberations of the open letter had passed.

Unaware of all those events, isolated in the Chinese capital as much as I had been on the Maldive islands, I told the Young Leader that as per our agreement I was going to see Li Rui, whom I had called and who had invited me to dinner. He said sharply, almost shouting, that it was out of the question; if I saw Li Rui, I would be deemed to have been involved in political activities, and would never be allowed into China to see my mother again. He repeated those words several times to drive home the point that he meant business. I thought of defying the 'ban' but was worried about being barred from seeing my mother in the future, and walked for a long time to force down my fury before telephoning Li Rui to let him know that I was unable to come. He sensed my complete ignorance about the open letter and was beginning to tell me, before he seemed suddenly overcome with exhaustion and stopped. His voice, permeated with anger and sadness, still rings in my ears.

Similarly, I was absolutely forbidden to see Jiaju, even though he had not been involved in Li Rui's letter-writing. The reason given by the Young Leader was that Jiaju was under the surveillance of another branch of agents and that branch was bound to report his meeting with me, which would bring the Young Leader and his team another reprimand. When I telephoned Jiaju about the prohibition, he listened, and said nothing. Silently, we put the phone down. He rang again almost immediately and asked me for a photo of us at the mausoleum of Cixi from our last meeting a year before. The photo would be a souvenir of our friendship. His voice was tinged with resignation that China was unlikely to become freer in our lifetime, and we might never meet again. We never did.

That the authorities went back on their word alarmed me: they might ban me from going to Chengdu for my mother's eightieth birthday the following year, 2011. So I made a point of telling the Young Leader and his team: 'I have kept my word, and you have no excuse to prevent me from seeing my mother. You have cut me off from all my friends. I feel like a prisoner in China. But if you stop me from seeing my mother, you will be making a sworn enemy out of me. I will – maybe there is not a great deal I can do, but I will at least give you headaches. Perhaps your bosses can weigh the pros and cons.' They said nothing, and the next year they gave me an extra five days on my visa.

My mother's birthday celebration was very moving, with even more friends and relatives coming than a decade before for her seventieth birthday. Some had travelled a long way, like from Yibin, my father's birthplace, as many older people feared this might be their last time to see each other.

Her birthday party reflected the rising prosperity of the country. There were event organisers now, and the one Xiao-fang hired did a job that wowed everyone. The gigantic cake featured a swan at the top, and each guest received with their piece a silver-plated spoon which they could take home as a souvenir. The handle of the spoon was beautifully crafted like a swan stretching out its neck about to spread its wings. A young photographer snapped away. His hair was dyed in multiple colours, a shapely blond lock constantly dropping to cover half his face, which he flipped back with a languid hand movement. His get-up and mannerisms looked very Western, and in the not-too-distant past people would have frowned on him. Now no one batted an eye. The society had really become more tolerant and non-judgemental, which comforted me. The photos he took had many laughing faces, including those of my childhood friends. Judging by the number of strangers present (some of them could have been distant relatives or Mother's old colleagues whom I did not know, or just gatecrashers), I was fairly certain that the occasion was monitored – discreetly.

A dark shadow hung over the party, as my brother Xiaohei was banned from being there. Living in London, he wrote essays in the Chinese-language media and social media, and had recently penned an article supporting a fellow writer from Sichuan, Tan Zuoren, who had been sentenced in 2010 to five years in prison for trying to organise independent investigations into shoddy buildings that had collapsed during the 2008 earthquake and buried large numbers of schoolchildren. Xiaohei did not have my good fortune of being protected by the fame of *Wild Swans*, and so was unable to fight for a visa. Mother had a catch in her throat when she took his phone call but said not a word to dissuade him from the path in life he had chosen.

Jon came with me and spoke a few words in Chinese at the party, with some imperfect tones that everybody found endearing. Travelling with me in China over the years, he had accumulated a wealth of anecdotes of the Chinese approach to foreigners. On this trip, a novel incident was added to the collection. After we settled into our hotel in Beijing, I had to go to the lobby for an appointment with the Young Leader and his team. Jon offered to come with me. Just before we reached the lift to go down, my phone rang: it was the Young Leader, who said, 'Your husband does not have to come.' I had always been told that top hotels were thoroughly equipped with bugs and spies. Now, hearing the surveillance being so unambiguously revealed to us, Jon and I had a laugh. Even the State Security, whose job description surely included dealing with foreigners, seemed to have problems meeting this foreigner.

After my mother's birthday, Jon and I travelled to a beauty spot in western Sichuan, the Jiuzhai Valley, a Tibetan-inhabited area. Along the way, the landscape of grey mountains and green fields was dotted with eye-catching bright red spots: Chinese national flags above doorways, a sight I had not seen anywhere else in China. Flag-hanging was obligatory in this region, to remind the local Tibetans that they were part of the Chinese nation. On our way back we stayed a night on the road. The hotel, a large sprawling building with some Tibetan features, stood against a wild landscape some distance away from the dusty, empty road, a stretch of which was lined with rows of low dwellings like something out of a Wild West movie. As we entered the enormous hotel lobby, I was struck dumb by a brand-new giant statue of Mao, brightly gilded and dwarfing everything around. The receptionists told us that when the hotel was first built in the 1980s, a deer had stood there, to symbolise Buddhism. Only recently had the deer been replaced by Mao, under whose reign the mass settling of Han Chinese in Tibetan regions had begun. For the first time in the post-Mao years, I was aware of a strong vested interest in holding on to Mao's legacy. The Han settlers here, as in other comparable regions, felt the need to assert their right to call this their land.

　　Over my ten years of going to China under explicit surveillance, I met as many minders. Much though I loathed the idea of having to deal with them, I have to say that on a personal level the individuals I dealt with were no brutes. They were doing an obnoxious job, and they did it without additional personal nastiness. I even spotted some play-acting. I noticed that whenever there was a new minder, he or she always looked aggressive on the first day, and thereafter perceptibly amicable. Once when a young new female minder slapped a piece of paper on the coffee table in front of me and barked, albeit in a low voice, 'Write!', I, while saying an emphatic no, looked her in the eye and said mockingly, 'So it's your turn today to play the bad cop?' The next time I saw her, her behaviour could not have been more different.

　　Apart from the Young Leader, the other minders changed every two years – perhaps in order that they would not develop any empathy with me, or become receptive to my ideas, which those intelligent young men and women were quite likely to do. Once, two of them followed me to a bookshop. My specialist books were on the first floor, and they browsed on the ground floor among books of general interest. Afterwards on our way to the car one of them said animatedly, 'In the Era of Spring and Autumn (770–476 BC), China produced so many thinkers! I am sure now with the country doing so well, it will produce great thinkers again.' I could not help snapping, 'Thinkers? You must be joking. I wrote a book and I am now cut off from all my friends and followed by you lot. How can anyone dare to think up original ideas in this environment? How can a country like this produce thinkers?' They fell silent – looking like they were mulling over my argument.

One man, referring to Western protests about China's human rights abuse, remarked to me in exasperation, 'Why do Westerners like to mind other people's business?' I replied, 'If they didn't, [the bright young woman in her twenties who was present] and I would still be having bound feet!' Then I told them how it was Westerners' passionate lobbying that had prompted Empress Dowager Cixi to ban foot-binding. Again, they seemed to be taking in a new thought.

On yet another occasion, a minder asked me, 'In Britain, is there an organisation like the "Chinese Writers Association"?' I said, 'No, there is no such official set-up, but there is something called PEN, which fights for freedom of expression and helps protect writers. Anyone who writes books and believes in those ideas can be a member, and I am a member.' After a brief pause, I added, 'PEN particularly helps writers in prison. If one day you put me in prison, PEN will fight for me.' He and his fellow minder made pained faces and muttered words to the effect that 'you mustn't think such bleak thoughts' – which touched me.

My minders knew that my problem with the regime was because of my books, especially the biography of Mao which I had written with my husband. But most of them had no access to it. Their curiosity was not surprisingly intense: the book was considered so dangerous that their job was to ensure that I was isolated from the locals, and yet they had no idea what was in it. Many asked me for copies – to which I had to say that I did not have it as I could not bring any into China. Eventually, after much badgering by a pair of minders, I gave them the only copy I had – and was very happy to watch their excitement as they could not wait to tear the book open.

I could tell that my mother approved of the way I handled things with the State Security. She was impressed that I had secured our yearly reunion, which she had not thought possible, and that I had even achieved something more: to research in China for my next book, which she could see would also rewrite history. Indeed, when it was published (in 2013), entitled *Empress Dowager Cixi: The Concubine Who Launched Modern China*, in his review for the *BBC History Magazine* the historian Simon Sebag Montefiore wrote: 'Filled with new revelations, it's a gripping and surprising story of an extraordinary woman in power. Using Chinese sources, totally untapped by western books, this reappraises one of the great monstresses of modern history . . .' My mother was proud that I had managed those goals without compromising our principles. When Jon and I were leaving Chengdu after her birthday, she stroked me on the back and said to Jon that she felt she could really put her feet up now and trust everything to me.

But my mother knew that any goodwill from individual State Security officers ultimately meant little in the face of Party orders. She never stopped fearing for me when I was in China. My sister told me that every time I landed in the country, Mother became preoccupied and tense. Once I did not call her for two or three days – I usually called her every day – and she was thrown into such a state of anxiety that my sister was worried about her health. She would only relax when I boarded a plane and flew out of China.

19

The Return of Mao's Ghost

(2012–13)

Chairman Xi Jinping's rise to power in 2012 had a direct impact on me. That year I could not visit my mother in Chengdu, even though she had twice been rushed into the A&E at a hospital with intestinal haemorrhages. I rang and emailed the Young Leader many times, urgently asking for a visa. He was sympathetic and promised to present positive recommendations to his superiors. But when the reply eventually came, it was for me to wait till after the Party's 18th Congress, the date of which was a state secret. The congress would produce a new leader for China. Although this seemed to have nothing to do with me, I had to be kept out of the country.

The two previous leaders, Jiang Zemin and Hu Jintao, had each been number one for ten years, the maximum term stipulated by the post-Mao Party. Those two had grown up and been educated before the Cultural Revolution and had been technocrats. Candidates for the coming new leader, however, had to have a novel qualification: they had to be children of top old Party officials – the so-called 'Princelings'. Apparently, this stipulation had been dictated by some Party elders who had said, 'Our children must one day inherit our power.'

The Party elders judged that it was time to install the Princelings after more than three decades of reforms. The country had made spectacular progress towards prosperity, and the population had begun to entertain strong aspirations for further reforms and more freedoms. In particular, some of the newly rich and superrich wanted a voice in the country's political process. The CCP was facing the prospect of its absolute power being eroded. This was the juncture at which many in the West had assumed that China would go for democracy. But the Party had its own plans. Its bottom line had always been, as an interviewee from the very top circle of the CCP had spelled out to me way back: 'We will let you [the population] have all sorts of things, but we will never let you have our throne!'

The Princelings and other members of the red aristocracy of their generation, called the 'children of high officials' (*gao-gan-zi-di*, with 'high officials' defined as being 'above Grade 13'), had the most incentive to keep the Party's monopoly of power. As the post-Mao reforms were conducted by the Party, the smart members of this elite acquired cushy positions in state enterprises, or made fortunes by linking up with private businessmen, who invariably sought connections with them.

Apart from the financial interest, this elite had been indoctrinated with a sense of 'mission': that one day they would take over the 'red state' (*hong-se-jiang-shan*) created by their fathers and make sure that it would go on forever. The indoctrination was at its most intensive in the 1960s, when most of them were teenagers, especially at the time when Mao was about to launch the Cultural Revolution and earmarked them to be his first Red Guards.

I myself supposedly belonged to the elite, as my father, at Grade 10, was a 'high official'. But when I was growing up, my father always made a point of ridiculing the existence of a red aristocracy to my siblings and me, telling us never, ever, to think of ourselves in terms of belonging to such a group. But I knew many people who subscribed to that sense of belonging. In 1982, when I decided to live in Britain, one of such 'children', who had risen quite high in the Party hierarchy, tried to persuade me to do as told by the Party by reminding me that I belonged to this group and must not let the side down. Not even an acquaintance of mine, he nonetheless wrote and claimed he felt like my 'older brother', and told me that we must not forget our mission: to perpetuate the 'red state' our fathers had founded. He said that even if our fathers had suffered in the Cultural Revolution, we must put the tragedy in perspective, and must not let it interfere with our mission. 'Errors were inevitable,' he wrote, referring not only to the Cultural Revolution but also to the other bloody purges in the history of the CCP. I was disgusted and did not reply.

In another case, in spring 1993, when it briefly seemed possible for *Wild Swans* to be published in China, I met in Beijing the head of a major publisher, daughter of a high official who had been a well-known victim of the Cultural Revolution. Her publishing house had expressed interest in *Wild Swans*, but after reading the book, she not only said no, but also came to my hotel to give me a personal lecture, telling me that I was bad to have let the tragedy of my family blind me to my identity as a daughter of the Party. I was dismayed by her warped way of thinking.

Even some of my own friends, who, if they had tolerated *Wild Swans*, reacted indignantly to my biography of Mao, regarding it almost as a betrayal of our shared background.

Chairman Xi Jinping, the current leader of China, was a member of the elite and the product of the indoctrination. Born in 1953, he is a year younger than me and lived through similar experiences. From my observation, he seems to be one of those in the elite who fell under the spell of the 'mission' and remained fanatically devoted to Mao, and unlike many others who had grown out of the indoctrination he kept the mind-set. His father, Xi Zhongxun, had been an old Communist on the receiving end of endless purges from the age of twenty-two, in 1935, when he had nearly been buried alive by his own comrades. In the Cultural Revolution, he had been subjected to brutal denunciation meetings and thrown into prison. But Xi senior remained loyal to the Party and Mao. It was not surprising to me that his son, who did not even suffer what the father had suffered, should be stuck in the same mental rut – like some other 'high officials' children'.

Xi Jinping vied to be the leader of China with other Princelings, all of whom had vowed to be loyal Maoists and devoted perpetuators of the 'red state' before they had entered the competition. Xi came out on top, perhaps because he had learned the most from Mao on how to gain power and keep power. He had successfully terrorised his colleagues to an amazing degree, as shown graphically in the extraordinary video footage of the closing ceremony of the CCP's 20th Congress (in 2022). When on Xi's order his predecessor, Hu Jintao, was forcefully taken from the stage and passed by all the top officials, not a single one of them moved a muscle to express any feelings to their old boss and China's former number one, not 'How are you?', not 'Goodbye' – not even a glance. They did not dare. When I watched that scene on the internet, I saw Mao's shadow filling the congress hall.

*

As soon as the Party's 18th Congress was over and Xi was confirmed China's number one in November 2012, I contacted the Young Leader and submitted my application to the Chinese embassy for a visa. There was a long wait, and on New Year's Eve I received a 'Notice of Visa Rejection'. My heart sank, and I tried frantically to think how to get the decision reversed. The person who might be able to help, I decided, was the Young Leader. It was seven o'clock in the evening in Beijing when the Chinese capital was getting ready to celebrate the new year, and I did not hold out hope that he would even pick up the phone. To my indescribable relief he did, telling me that he had not wanted to but had decided to as he thought how distressed I and possibly my mother would be during the long New Year holiday.

He sounded apologetic, saying that the rejection had not been his recommendation, and that he would do his very best to help on 4 January 2013 when the offices reopened. He was as good as his word. On the 4th, a man from the Chinese embassy rang and told me to go and collect my visa. The man was clearly annoyed with this change and informed me in a curt voice, putting the phone down before I finished saying 'Thank you'.

Still, I got my visa, and was filled with gratitude to the man who had been in charge of my surveillance, for the humanity he had shown – and his sense of fairness as I had scrupulously kept my 'undertaking' and China had no grounds to deny me a visa, according to its agreement with Britain. But I was unable to thank him: when I arrived in Beijing, his colleagues informed me that he had been removed from his position and transferred to another department. From the way they mentioned him this and other times, I got the distinct impression that the Young Leader had lost his job because he was considered to have fought too hard for me.

A successor had been appointed to keep in touch with me. But he no longer had the authority to make any decisions, unlike the Young Leader in the past. The successor would act only as a messenger between me and a newly formed five-ministry Outfit that was responsible for my case. Apart from the State Security, four other ministries were represented in the Outfit: the Foreign Ministry, the Propaganda Ministry, the Entry-Exit Bureau of the Public Security Ministry, and another ministry whose name I did not catch. It was this Outfit that had decided to tear up China's agreement with Britain and deny me a visa. Looking back, I think mine might have been one of the first cases that marked the shift to the later famous 'wolf diplomacy', featuring thuggish foreign policies and aggressive diplomats. It foretold the end of the fundamental post-Mao policy that China must make friends with the West.

A Mao-era atmosphere was palpable at the Beijing airport. Queuing to go through passport control, I saw large overhead screens warning in harsh language that it was strictly forbidden to bring in books and magazines not published in China, and anyone violating the rule would face dire consequences. Any friendliness I had encountered was gone. Before, one year while I was waiting for the airport officers to contact my minders, their boss had come to have a chat. Very amicably, he had expressed curiosity about my books, asking for a copy, telling me he had no access to the books his officers confiscated, which were all sealed in storage. That was bad; but at least we had sighed together. And as far as I know, the owners of the confiscated books had not been punished. But they began to be now, judging by the public announcements of Party officials being sacked, and subjected to worse, for 'carrying, keeping and reading unauthorised publications from Hong Kong and Taiwan'.

The airport staff seemed to have been told to behave mercilessly towards people who had displeased the regime. After I was led into the side room to wait, a man with stagey sternness on his face, rare in post-Mao years, came in with a rather large camera to take a photograph of me. Instead of doing so in the room, where the walls were blank and white, he signalled for me to follow him to the empty place immediately beyond passport control, where he made me stand against a wall facing the crowds queuing to come through. As he was positioning me, his stony face and disdainful body language shouting out that this was no photoshoot of a celebrity but something of a mugshot of a criminal, the old Mao-era scenes rushed back to me, and I realised that he was trying to humiliate me by doing a mock *shizhong* – 'display to the crowds', an age-old Chinese punishment used widely in the Cultural Revolution. My mother being paraded through the streets and my father tied up on a slow-moving open truck in Chengdu, not to mention the countless denunciation rallies – they had all involved the insult of being put on public display. Although the throng of people I was made to face cast glances at me without hostility, my heart nevertheless jumped to my throat, and an inexplicable sense of humiliation and fear momentarily took hold of me. I felt the ghost of Mao hovering.

The visa which the Outfit had given me came with a restriction: that I had to enter and exit China through Beijing. It was such a bizarre and unheard-of specification that when I was going through passport control, the female official let out a cry of amazement and called out to her colleagues to come and look, before they all stared at me. None of them seemed to have seen such a restriction on a visa.

The Outfit wanted me in Beijing not because they wanted to see me, as might have been the reason. There was no meeting with anyone. At first I thought they just wanted to give me the run-around in China's air space to make me suffer. My travel programme, which they had seen, made clear that after staying with my mother in Chengdu, my next destination was Yangon, Myanmar (for the first Irrawaddy Literary Festival at whose opening ceremony I was to deliver a speech). From Chengdu to Yangon, to the south, the flight distance was just over a thousand miles. But if I flew from Chengdu in the other direction to Beijing in order to exit China, then turned round and flew south all the way to Yangon, I would be flying three thousand miles, nearly two thousand miles more.

A more sinister design by the authorities dawned on me only later. After I flew from Chengdu to Beijing and spent a few hours of the night sleepless in an airport hotel, just after five o'clock in the morning when Beijing was still asleep in a black wintry fog, I was queuing for the Beijing–Yangon flight. When the check-in was completed and with the boarding pass in my hand, I was about to turn away from the counter and casually asked the lady behind it where passport control was. Her answer horrified me: Beijing was not the exit point for the flight; passport control was in the city of Kunming, near the border with Myanmar, where the plane would touch down. So, if I took this flight, I would not be 'exiting from Beijing', as stamped in my visa. I jumped away and hurriedly dragged my suitcase off the conveyor belt, which was just about to disappear behind the flapping black rubber barrier. I rushed to the information desk to confirm that my visa did not permit me to exit from Kunming. In other words, I would not be allowed to leave China. Worse: my visa expired that day, and if I remained in China, I would be deemed 'overstaying', and 'violating Chinese law', for which I could be 'legitimately' barred from entering the country to see my mother ever again. A thought went through me like a shot: this was what the Outfit intended.

I called the Young Leader's successor and complained bitterly. I said that the Entry-Exit Bureau of the Public Security Ministry on the five-ministry Outfit would surely have known that the

Beijing–Yangon flight in my programme did not 'exit from Beijing'. Did they make me come to Beijing deliberately so that after flying round China I ended up not being able to leave the country? Were they trying to make me overstay my visa, so they could have an excuse to bar me from seeing my mother again? The successor, who remained genial despite being woken up by my phone call before dawn, acknowledged that the whole thing was unfathomable, and offered words of sympathy. But he was unable to do anything. For a while I was lost about what to do, and wandered listlessly in the airport hall with my luggage, obsessively thinking the scary thought that I could easily have walked sleepily onto the flight and never seen my mother again. Outside the airport hall, it was already daylight in Beijing, and suddenly my mind was alert. I told myself that what I needed to do most urgently was to find a flight to get out of China, hopefully to a place not too far away from Yangon. I enquired at the information desk, and luckily there was a flight to Bangkok.

Sunny Yangon, with its temples, coconut trees, and the tremendous buzz about the festival, a major event in the new democracy (the general election had been held in 2010), lifted my spirits. Surrounded by warm Burmese writers, I felt that the last couple of days had been no more than a bad dream, already vanishing in the sunshine. I was told that *Wild Swans* had been translated into Burmese and would be discussed at a session by local writers who would also talk about their own lives under Myanmar's dictatorship. Many writers here had been imprisoned and tortured for what they had written. Compared to their plight, what I had been through was mere inconvenience. I thought no more of the episode and never talked about it. I especially did not tell my mother as I did not want to distress her. As I carried on with my normal life, at the back of my head lingered the thought that there were devious minds out there scheming to harm me. I had had another taste of the coming era.

20

Why I Can't Go to
My Mother's Deathbed

(2014–24)

The nasty trap in 2013 to make me break Chinese law so I could be punished set alarm bells ringing about future tricks, and in 2014, after I had made the request to visit my mother to the Young Leader's successor and heard nothing back for nearly a month, in a sudden panic I withdrew my application. As a result, I did not see my mother that year.

I felt able to make the decision because my brother Xiaohei, in London and banned from entering China for the past few years, was finally going to Chengdu. Xiaohei had missed seeing our mother badly and appealed to some friends who had connections with the Chinese government for help. The regime knew the yearnings of emigrants to visit their families in China, especially elderly parents, and so dangled the granting of a visa to get them to toe the Party line, even to serve the regime. Xiaohei wrote well and his sharp and lively articles were popular among Chinese overseas. Beijing saw an opportunity to get him to shut up, and gave him a visa for two weeks, with the restrictions of not going out of Chengdu and not seeing any 'sensitive people'. A couple of days after he arrived, a telephone call came from the Sichuan Bureau of the State Security, inviting him to tea in a teahouse. There, in a private room, seven or eight men were waiting, one of whom complimented him for looking much younger than they had expected. Indeed, my brother, then aged sixty, was handsome and youthful. As he sat down, the head of the posse produced some notes and started talking, while others took pictures and made a video recording. After this meeting came another invitation, to dinner with a higher official. Both times, their focus was to persuade Xiaohei to stop writing articles critical of the Party, and instead to write nice things about 'China's economic achievements'. On the occasion of the dinner, before they were seated, the higher official pointed at an unremarkable-looking man sitting inconspicuously across the room and said to Xiaohei: 'Look at him, he is a billionaire. If you accept our advice, you can work with him at once and in a few years' time, you will be a billionaire too.' Xiaohei listened, and committed only to writing 'objectively', 'in the best interest of the people of Sichuan'.

When Xiaohei returned to Mother's apartment after his first meeting in the teahouse, as he was opening the door, he saw Mother shoot up from her chair, with worry written all over her face. She had been waiting for him, fearing he might have been detained – something that had happened to other people. Unlike me, Xiaohei was not protected by 'fame', and was more vulnerable. Mother told him that she had been so worried that 'I thought I was going to have a heart attack.' Then she said, clearly having thought it out and made up her mind, 'Don't come back to Chengdu again. If you love me and want me to live longer, don't come back to see me.' Xiaohei understood that Mother saw he could only be safe staying away from China. And, in order to spare him the agony of being the one to stop trying to visit her, she made the decision hers. It was typical of our mother, and Xiaohei was greatly moved. He accepted that this would be his last visit.

Before he was barred from China, Xiaohei had been going to Chengdu every year. Even then, Mother, knowing some of his views, had feared for his safety. Once, he had not come home when it was very late (he had lost his way among the many identical high rises), and she became so anxious that she did the most unusual thing of standing on her tenth-floor balcony shouting his name to the blocks of flats around. People thought Mother had lost her dog. (Xiaohei, literally meaning 'Little Black', was a common name for a pet. My brother had been given the name when he was a baby as an endearment, and the family continued to use it even though as a grown-up his proper name is Pu.)

Xiaohei was gregarious, and in Chengdu he had been going out every day with friends, coming home often when Mother had gone to bed. She had complained one day, 'I thought you were coming back to see me. But I hardly set eyes on you; you are gallivanting all over every day.' After he had made up his mind not to return, he stayed at home every day with Mother – until she said, 'We've done enough talking. You have another week left. Go out and enjoy yourself with your friends.' At the end of the two weeks, they said goodbye, with no more than their usual show of feelings.

In this way, Mother set Xiaohei free from his emotional ties that could inhibit his writing. She might not agree with some things he wrote or the views he held, just like her not agreeing with some things I wrote or the views I held, but she knew we were trying to do the right thing, and left us alone to lead our lives. She would only try to protect us the best she could. My brother and I often talk about her, feeling immensely privileged to have her as our mother.

Xiaohei continued to write what he wanted and soon produced a novel, *A Tibetan Girl Called Ata*, which was published in Taiwan. The regime was infuriated. In 2017, at a gathering of some Chinese in London, the consul overseeing the affairs of overseas Chinese (even though they may be British or other nationals) told those present to break from Xiaohei, using language which when I first heard it I thought belonged to school playgrounds: 'If you hang out with him, you can't hang out with us!'

My brother loves antiques and helped found a Chinese Antique Collectors' Association in Britain. The embassy consul told the board to get rid of Xiaohei, warning in particular the chief who owned restaurants in London that if Xiaohei remained, he would tell people from China not to eat in his restaurants. The board members wanted to do business with China and so tried to persuade Xiaohei to stop writing: 'Why write those things that displease the Chinese government? Wouldn't it be better just to enjoy antiques?' After an emotional confrontation, Xiaohei was forced to resign.

I could see that my brother was hurt, and was dispirited for some time. But he was resourceful, and soon bounced back with his own Chinese Antique Collectors Club UK, which today has over five hundred members. Some of them have also been warned to keep a distance from him; they simply ignored the 'advice'.

In April 2015, my mother had another fall, breaking her hip, and had to have an operation, at the age of eighty-four. Operations were dangerous for her, as she was prone to haemorrhage and the medication that stops bleeding ran the risk of bringing on strokes, from which she had suffered. I wanted to be with her for the operation, and the moment I heard the news, I rang the Young Leader's successor and requested an urgent visa. It was a Saturday, but he took my call, said he was happy to help, and promised to report to his superiors on Monday – adding that he might be able to give me an answer on Tuesday. This incredible helpfulness came as a total surprise. Only now when I am looking into those years do I realise that my request had come at a moment when preparations were underway for Xi Jinping's visit to Britain in autumn that year, and the regime did not want the issue of my visa to mar his trip. China was then seeking a good relationship with Britain mostly because of the high-tech Britain possessed – top advanced technology was, and is, what Beijing really wanted when it pursued good relations with the West. As the then British government seemed obliging, Beijing entertained high hopes, and I got my visa with no problem. The ease lasted several years, when Beijing was supposedly in a 'golden era' in its relationship with Britain. In 2016, when I told a minder in Beijing that I wished to visit Li Rui, to congratulate him on his hundredth birthday, the minder, instead of saying no as a few years before, said an instant yes, and I had a very moving time with Li Rui and his wife, recalling our friendship over nearly a quarter of a century.

But the control was getting much tighter overall. I was no longer able to do any research for my next book, *Big Sister, Little Sister, Red Sister: Three Women at the Heart of Twentieth-century China*, about the Soong sisters who were at the top of two antagonistic political camps: Ching-ling, the honorary president of Communist China; May-ling, Chiang Kai-shek's wife and chief diplomat; and Ei-ling, one of the richest women in the country under Chiang. My research was extensive as before, but none of the work was done in China in this period.

It was mostly carried out in America, to whose institutions the papers of the sisters, Chiang Kai-shek and most other eyewitnesses had been donated; and in Taiwan, where democracy had brought undreamed-of ease in accessing archives. Research in China was now out of the question – unlike the relaxed 1990s or even a few years before, when I was studying Empress Dowager Cixi with the State Security watching me. This time when I contacted a historian who had helped me while I was researching Cixi, offering to give him a copy of the biography as a thank-you present, he replied in a polite and formal tone, asking me to post the book to his work unit, a response I had never encountered in all my years of research. Another friend who had introduced me to members of Ching-ling's staff sounded evasive and scared when I expressed a wish to see them again, in stark contrast to his previous enthusiasm. It was clear that the authorities only let me in to see my mother extremely reluctantly, and once in China I was to be kept in a strictly isolated bubble, sealed more tightly than ever before. The general atmosphere outside the bubble was dismal. In the bookstores, few books straying from the Party line were visible and scholarly papers had all but disappeared from the internet, unlike all the previous post-Mao years. China was once again an arid land for the study of the humanities; 'a hundred flowers' were withering, leaving a few dwarfed stems.

The same thing was happening in Hong Kong. Its thriving publishing industry was being smothered. My books could no longer be published and had to find a new home – which meant Taiwan. Fifteen years before, in 2006, Hong Kong had been able to publish the biography of Mao while Taiwan could not; now it was the other way round. When I asked our new publishers of the biography whether they felt any pressures and worries, they laughed and said, 'Today the place is entirely different.' Democracy truly does wonders.

Xi made a point of stressing that 'hostile forces' were using the writing of history to destroy the CCP's legitimacy, asserting that it was the rewriting of the history of the Soviet Communist Party that had led to the fall of the Soviet Union. He was determined not to allow in China what had happened in Russia. Jon and I were condemned in Party journals as 'historical nihilists', who 'blindly seek truth', although, not wishing to give us publicity – public denunciation would inevitably rouse people's interest – the condemnation did not go beyond the Party websites (which had few visitors). We were totally blocked on the internet, and were non-persons. In this environment, I just stayed at home with Mother and saw only family members.

Mother was getting increasingly frail, and on one trip I found her using a Zimmer frame to stand up and walk. Her mind was still sharp and when I told her I was writing about the Soong sisters and their husbands, including Chiang Kai-shek, whose regime she had risked her life fighting, she asked if I would let her read the Chinese text when it was ready. Her request was put tentatively, suggesting that she did not want me to think she was trying to influence my portrayal of Chiang. This was the only time she asked to read the manuscript of any of my books. She said she was intrigued to know what I made of Chiang. It struck me that she wanted to know more about him in order to look at her own youth, to understand whether she had made a mistake fighting Chiang and joining the Communists. That my mother, in her late eighties, was reflecting on her life, touched me, and I worked as hard as possible hoping to produce a Chinese translation shortly after the English publication scheduled for 2019.

I was never able to show my mother the book; 2018 became the last year I visited her. That March a crucial event took place in Beijing: the National People's Congress made Chairman Xi the supreme leader for life by changing China's constitution and removing the two-term limit. Because of this, I was blocked from taking part in the Macau Literary Festival, which coincided with the congress. The regime did not want any unfavourable remarks in the foreign media, especially as Macau was just across the border.

On my trip to Chengdu that year, in May 2018, I learned some ominous news that promised to affect my life dramatically. As soon as he became the permanent supreme leader, Chairman Xi issued an order on 1 May, decreeing that 'any insult or slander of the honour and reputation of heroes and martyrs' was a crime punishable by imprisonment. As Mao was regarded as the primary hero of the nation, it began to sink in that as a biographer of Mao who had documented his misrule, I faced incarceration when I was in China.

Another piece of bad news was that Beijing was reasserting its Communist identity, emphasising that it was a Communist state with only some capitalist features. It was definitively changing its fundamental policy to be friends with the West, a policy that had underpinned the post-Mao reforms. The West was now a foe. In particular, Chairman Xi wanted to dislodge America to be the world's number one, to reign supreme. Having studied Mao, I knew this had been Mao's dream. Mao had died a melancholy man feeling he had failed to realise his dream. Xi made it his mission to succeed. And he seemed to be confident of his success as he was ruling a China that had become rich and powerful. Moreover, for this goal, Beijing was prepared to have a showdown with America. It gave tremendous credit to the so-called 'Thucydides Trap', which asserted that when one great power threatens to displace another, war is almost always the result. Some in Beijing were saying that 'there is bound to be a war between China and America'.

Beijing believed it would win, perhaps not so much in terms of traditional warfare, but by other means such as cyber warfare, which Beijing was good at. At the time much hope was placed in the Chinese telecommunication giant Huawei, which had strategically and deeply embedded itself in the vital telecommunication systems of many Western countries.

Having realised this, I felt fear for the first time in four decades. I feared that the Party might indeed dominate the world one day, when there would be no place for me to flee. For a while the long-vanished nightmares, filled with horrible scenes from the Cultural Revolution, returned to haunt me. But my immediate dread was that I might not be able to continue visiting my mother – especially as I saw how Xi dealt with Hong Kong in 2019. When millions of people took to the streets to voice opposition to Beijing's decision to impose on them a repressive law, instead of finding some compromise as his predecessors had done, Xi refused to budge one inch and simply took over Hong Kong completely, tearing up agreements with Britain without so much as a diplomatic word.

I had naively assumed that Beijing would make some conciliatory gesture as Hong Kong was still economically and financially important to China, even if not as critical as before. The stark reality gave me a better understanding of Chairman Xi: his priority was that the Party's grip on absolute power must not loosen one iota, beside which China's economic loss, or its international image, mattered little. And he had shrewdly judged that no matter how much the Chinese economy deteriorated, it was unlikely to be so bad that the Communist rule might be threatened. This conviction gave him immeasurable advantage.

Britain was unable to protect Hong Kong. How could I expect it to protect me? So instead of fearing not being let into

China to see my mother, I began to fear being let in but not let out.

When I started to think about not trying to see my mother, I was in agony. This self-imposed ban could last as long as I lived, as Chairman Xi was my contemporary. Sometimes I was very tempted to take a risk and go. Maybe nothing would happen. But then the stakes could be life and death. 'To go or not to go?' – this was the dilemma burning inside me in 2019. I was in its grip when Jon and I travelled to Rome. One day we were in the church of San Luigi dei Francesi and, after admiring the paintings by Caravaggio, I sat and stared vacantly at the magnificent ceiling, taking in nothing, and then walked out without my mobile, which I had left on the seat. Halfway to the Pantheon, Jon's phone rang and a woman's voice said she had picked up my phone on the seat. We rushed back and gratefully took it from her hand. I was in a daze and did not even ask her how she got Jon's number. Or perhaps we did ask but I failed to register her answer.

I did not apply for a visa that year and so did not see my mother. Then came Covid-19, and as China went into draconian lockdown and practically closed its borders for three years, my dilemma was suspended. My mother spent those years mostly in a hospital, after she had been taken in for another emergency just before the pandemic, and where she was 'locked in'. Most of the time she could not even see her children living in Chengdu – my sister and my brother Xiaofang – as the hospital did not allow visitors. But at least she was well looked after: the medical staff were kind people and exemplary professionals. Whenever the lockdown rules were briefly relaxed, my brother and sister would come outside her window and deliver daily necessities and her favourite foods. They even brought her home and celebrated her ninetieth birthday – to my indescribable joy when I saw the photos of her little birthday party. I rang my mother on my mobile, and just as she was losing her hearing video calls came into our life. That we could see each other on the screen made a world of difference to me.

We used WeChat to communicate. I had been introduced to this app by a minder who had urged me to install it for communications with people in China. His strong recommendation left me in no doubt that WeChat was under the thorough control of the regime. But there was little choice, as Western apps were mostly banned. Mother did not have a mobile, so I rang her carer, or my siblings when they were with her.

At the end of 2022, Beijing abandoned its stringent lockdown policy with the snap of a finger and left people like my mother, who had not been vaccinated, to fend for themselves. (In China, only Chinese-made vaccines were permitted, and many people, including medical staff, distrusted them. So the elderly, instead of being given priority access to vaccination, tended to be exempt from it.) My mother was infected with Covid, like countless others, including the mother of her long-term domestic and carer, Lin, who had to leave to look after her own mother. For days my mother drifted in and out of delirium.

While her life was hanging by a thread, I was unable to see her even on the screen. My siblings could not visit her because of hospital rules, and her new carer, who had recently come out of a village, was terrified of receiving calls from abroad. After my first call to her, she told me that as soon as she had answered, a recorded message warned her that the caller was in a foreign country and she must watch out. She refused to take my calls after that, and I was out of contact with my mother. It was only when my siblings were permitted to resume their visits that I saw her again on the phone. And the carer, seeing that they talked to me without danger, accepted my calls. In the end, my mother pulled through.

From late 2023, I noticed a change in Mother, now ninety-two. She was physically demonstrative as she had never been. Whenever I rang her, she kissed me on the mobile screen and blew me kisses, again and again. We used to hug a lot, but I don't remember her kissing me as an adult, even while I kissed her on the cheek. She also told me in so many words that she missed me terribly, which was most unusual. One day she said, 'I miss you. I miss you so much these days! I don't know why – perhaps I am about to die.' I said, 'Mama, but you are looking at me right now.' She said, 'It's not the same thing. It's not the same! I want to touch you and to hold you in my arms. I can't do that with the screen.' Her voice sounded anguished. I was startled, as she had never been so emotionally forthcoming. Again, I asked her whether she would like to move to London, but I knew, as she knew and said to me, it was now more impossible than ever: she was too old and too ill.

I found her pain unbearable, and said, 'Mother, I will try to come and see you.' She seemed to want to say something, but conflicting thoughts stopped her, and in the end she said tentatively, 'But you can't get in. There are problems.' Her carer thought Mother was referring to the lockdown and interjected, 'People can come into China now. [So-and-so's] children have come from abroad and seen their mother.' I could not explain to the carer what my problems were, for fear that she might be frightened and leave Mother, or even mistreat her. I said to Mother, 'I will try to come. I will try.' Mother did not immediately respond. After a while, out of the blue, she said with appreciation in her voice, 'You are indeed fearless' (*bu-xin-xie*).

She had never made this comment, or praise, about me, and I felt surprised and touched.

I had not talked to Mother about my fear of returning, as I did not want to distress her. I was also wary of talking about it in front of the carer. My mother had stopped following the news for some time. But I felt sure that she knew the gravity of my problems, if only from the fact that I had not been back to see her for more than five years, whereas in the past I had been visiting her almost every year. As it happened, after the outburst, the next day I rang, she said apologetically that she had let herself be taken over by a 'complaining mood' the day before, and I was not to pay attention to what she had said. She was clearly afraid that her words might put pressure on me, and I might take dangerous risks. From that day on, my mother never said anything about missing me. But the carer told me that at night, when she could not fall asleep fully, which was often, my mother would talk to herself, and she would say, 'Er-hong, where are you? I miss you' and, 'I want to see you before I die.'

As far as I knew, my mother had only said similar words once in the past, decades before in 1969, when she was in her quasi-labour camp in the mountainous Xichang County. She had to labour fifteen hours a day with no days off, as well as enduring other forms of mistreatment. The bleeding from her womb worsened, and then she was struck down with hepatitis, her whole body swollen like a barrel. As her hepatitis was infectious, she was moved to a pigsty to sleep alone. The upper wall on one side of the enclosure was open, and during many a sleepless night, my mother, lying on straw on the mud ground and listening to the grunting of the pigs and the howling of the wolves in the nearby mountains, looked out to the vast sky lit up by massive stars, with the occasional meteors shooting across. Xichang, later China's satellite launch base, was famed for the clearness of its sky, the numerousness of brilliant stars, and the fullest possible moon. As the roundness of the moon symbolises family union in Chinese culture, my mother found herself missing her children with an unbearable pain. It was on some of those nights that she called out to me in whispers, 'Er-hong, where are you? I miss you' and, 'Will I ever see you again?'

Ten days before the Chinese New Year 1970, my mother and the other inmates were lined up in front of their camp waiting for the inspection of the big boss, an army commander – when they spotted a tiny solitary figure climbing up along the dirt track leading from the distant road, bent double under a large bamboo basket. They felt it could not be the boss as he would have come by car with an entourage, and he would certainly not be carrying a basket on his back. As the figure moved closer, and was clearly a woman as her head was wrapped in a big scarf, my mother felt it looked like me. She told me afterwards how her heart had started pounding as she thought, How wonderful it would be if it was Er-hong!, and then with what rapture she finally decided it was me and she was not imagining it. She told me how much my visit had meant to her and made her bleak life bearable.

Now she could die at any time, and though she did not say so, I knew my mother longed for me to be with her at her deathbed. I yearned to be at her bedside, too, to hold her hands and hug her to my bosom. I continued to explore the possibilities of going to Chengdu. One friend told me she knew people who had got their elderly parents to Japan, which was the nearest safe place from China, to meet and say goodbye. But my mother was too frail to travel. In fact her physical condition ruled out any meeting outside the hospital. I sounded out more people who had recently been to China to get a feel of the place, and everyone reacted in horror to my contemplating going and urged me not to think about it. Indeed, a prominent artist named Gao Zhen, who had made irreverent sculptures of Mao in the 1980s, was arrested because of them when he, now living in America, returned to China to visit his family. Several journalists and writers, who had Western nationalities, were publicly condemned for allegedly being 'spies', and one was even given a suspended death sentence. These and the continuous hounding of private businessmen scared people so much that they were fleeing the country in droves, leading to the coinage of a Chinese word: '*run*'. The number of Chinese abroad who dared not return to visit their families shot up.

Mother always said to Xiaohei when he rang, 'Don't come back. Don't come back.' That he would be in danger once in China was at the front of her mind. With me she had never said it. She was leaving the decision to my judgement. She was hoping against hope things might change. My mother never abandoned hope. When I gazed at her enfeebled but still strong face, a thousand memories surged in my head, of this extraordinary woman, my mother, and of how much I owed her in my life: my freedom, my happiness, my career as a writer, and being the person I was – and I am. It was on one of those occasions that this book *Fly, Wild Swans* took shape.

In March 2024, my mother had another haemorrhage, and a doctor called and told my sister to be prepared for her death. This would be the time for her children to gather at her bedside. But I had to decide not to go. When I called her, I saw Mother lying in bed looking very weak, her eyes closed. When she heard me, she opened her eyes with an effort and fixed them on my face for some moments. Then she said, slowly, gently but forcefully, in a whisper that was clearer than for a long time: 'I am over ninety. Life will naturally move on to death. It's not a big thing, and don't think too much of it. Do your own things well and be happy, and I am happy.' And, as if she felt she might not have been explicit enough, she added, with more force, 'Don't come back for this.' There was no doubt that by 'this', Mother meant her death. She could see from me appearing on the phone screen the gravity of the problems that prevented me from flying to her. She now specifically asked me not to come, to make sure I would not take any risks. She was telling me this was her wish, so I would not feel bad for not trying to come to her deathbed. With these what might be her last words, my mother took the agony out of the most unbearable decision of my life. Unburdened as I had always been after talking to her, I pressed my lips on the mobile screen and kissed her beautiful face.

EPILOGUE

The fear that returned to haunt me in 2018, when I realised that Chairman Xi Jinping had ambitions to build a neo-Maoist state and dominate the world, has subsided. Increasingly, I feel sure that those ambitions will ultimately be doomed. In China, repeated efforts to recreate a Mao-style society have produced only limited results. And in the wider world, people have woken up to the existence of those ambitions and their tyrannical nature. Many are trying to thwart them. Democracy will not be beaten by Maoism, in whatever form. I believe this with my whole heart.

I tend to be optimistic. It is in my nature, ingrained in me when I emerged from my mother's womb after a perilous birth that had threatened to be disastrous but ended in joy. Optimism is at the core of my mother's character. She never abandons hope however despairing the situation. Rooted in reasoning, her hope drives her to fight against all odds, and to achieve the seemingly unachievable. I want my optimism to be like my mother's.

Jung Chang
July 2025

ACKNOWLEDGEMENTS

I would like to thank all the people who have supported me in my life's journey covered by this book: the people who helped me gain freedom, who made it possible for me to become a writer, and who assisted my investigations in my writing about historical figures. My gratitude also goes to those who appreciated my books and gave me wonderful encouragement – my publishers, reviewers and above all readers.

I am grateful to everyone who has worked on *Fly, Wild Swans*. In the making of the book, I have benefited enormously from the comments of my editors, agents and friends: Arabella Pike, Iain Hunt, Clare Alexander, Lesley Thorne, Eric Abraham, Lizzie Spender, and my brother Pu Zhang.

My friend Geordie Greig has given me invaluable and detailed advice on the manuscript, not least contributing many of the chapter headings. I cannot thank him enough.

As always, I have relied on the judgement of my husband Jon Halliday. He and my mother, the two dearest people in my life, are both a part of the book and the original enablers of my writing. I owe them my fulfilment.

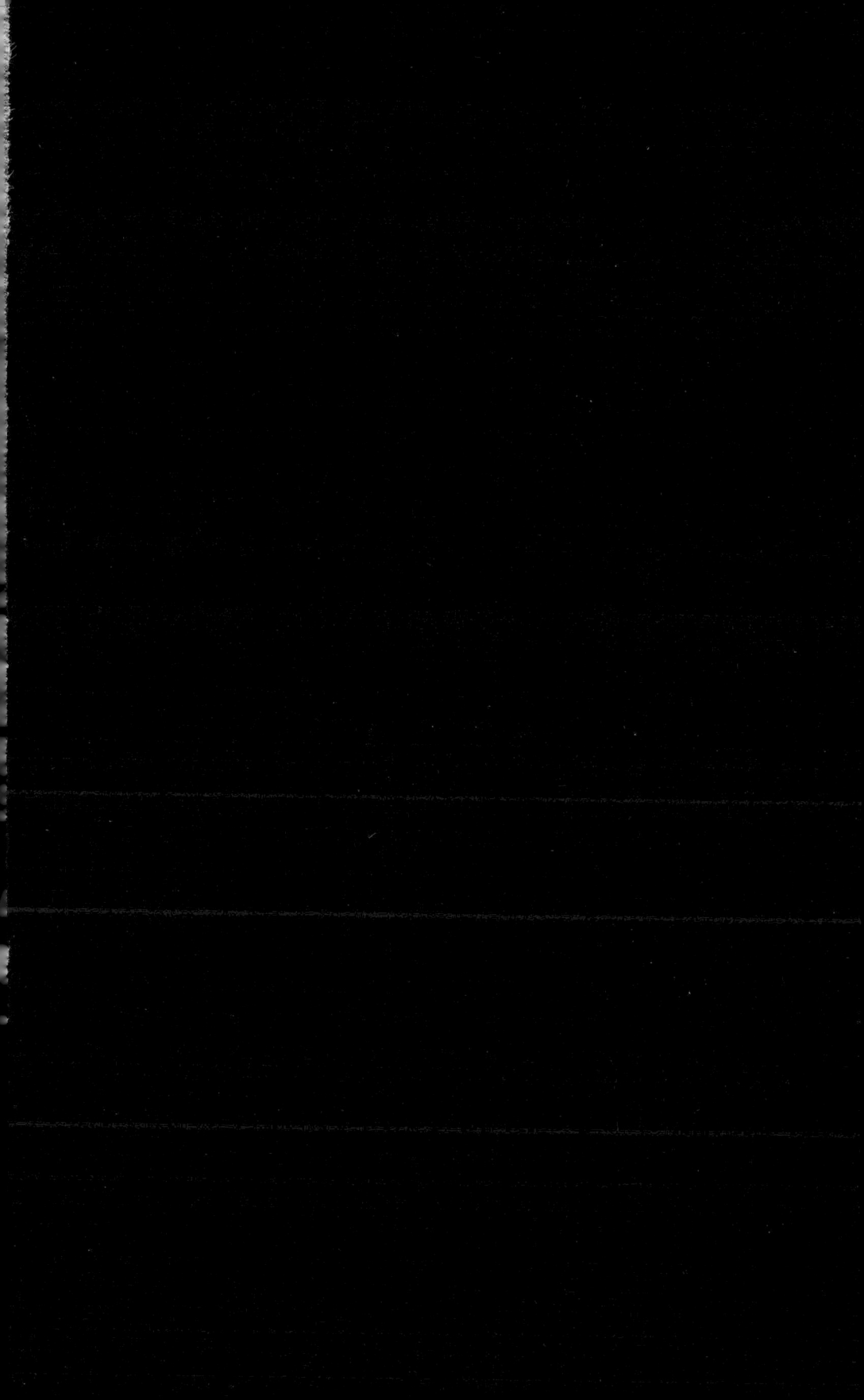